SimplySatisfying

THE EXPERIMENT

BECAUSE EVERY BOOK IS A TEST OF NEW IDEAS

Also by Jeanne Lemlin:

Quick Vegetarian Pleasures: More Than 175 Fast, Delicious, and Healthy Meatless Recipes
Main-Course Vegetarian Pleasures
Simple Vegetarian Pleasures
Vegetarian Classics: 300 Easy and Essential Recipes for Every Meal

SimplySatisfying

OVER 200 VEGETARIAN RECIPES YOU'LL WANT TO MAKE AGAIN AND AGAIN

Jeanne Lemlin

THE EXPERIMENT
NEW YORK

Simply Satisfying: *Over 200 Vegetarian Recipes You'll Want to Make Again and Again*
Copyright © Jeanne Lemlin, 2012
Photographs copyright © Cara Howe, 2012

The Experiment, LLC
260 Fifth Avenue
New York, NY 10001–6408
www.theexperimentpublishing.com

Simply Satisfying was previously published by Alfred A. Knopf in 1986 in significantly different form as *Vegetarian Pleasures: A Menu Cookbook.*

The Experiment's books are available at special discounts when purchased in bulk for premiums and sales promotions as well as for fundraising or educational use. For details, contact us at info@theexperimentpublishing.com.

Many of the designations used by manufacturers and sellers to distinguish their products are claimed as trademarks. Where those designations appear in this book and The Experiment was aware of a trademark claim, the designations have been capitalized.

Library of Congress Cataloging-in-Publication Data

Lemlin, Jeanne.
  Simply satisfying : over 200 vegetarian recipes you'll want to make again and again / Jeanne Lemlin.
      p. cm.
  Includes bibliographical references and index.
  ISBN 978-1-61519-062-1 (pbk. : alk. paper) -- ISBN 978-1-61519-160-4 (ebook) 1. Vegetarian cooking. I. Title.
  TX837.L4485 2012
  641.5'636--dc23

                                                                                    2012024015

ISBN 978-1-61519-062-1
Ebook ISBN 978-1-61519-160-4

Cover design by Susi Oberhelman
Cover and interior photographs by Cara Howe
Author photograph by Kari Giordano
Food and prop styling by María del Mar Sacasa | ENNIS, Inc.
Photo assistance from Jeri Lampert
Photo production by Lukas Volger
Text design by Pauline Neuwirth, Neuwirth & Associates, Inc.

Manufactured in China
Distributed by Workman Publishing Company, Inc.
Distributed simultaneously in Canada by Thomas Allen and Son Ltd.
The Experiment edition first published October 2012
10 9 8 7 6 5 4 3 2

To Ed, as always

Contents

Salads and Salad Dressings

Main-Course Salads

Soups and Stews

Frittatas, Eggs, and Timbales

Savory Pies, Tarts, Pizzas, Etc.

Pasta, Polenta, and Other Grains

Baked Dishes

Curries and Accompaniments

Tofu and Tempeh

Companion Dishes

Desserts

CAKES

PIES AND TARTS

PUDDINGS

The Basics

Menus

Introduction

When I was approached to have my first cookbook reissued, I was delighted. I would get a chance to share once again the recipes that I love and know others will appreciate, but also to breathe new life into the work by updating it with new trends that are worth embracing. When it was first published, *Vegetarian Pleasures* was in a menu format. At that time vegetarian cooking was rather new to the burgeoning cooking scene in the U.S. Menu guidance became the focus to give readers the confidence to make plant-based meals that were nutritionally balanced. But a lot has changed in the food world over the past twenty-five years, and American cooks have become increasingly confident about nutrition and meal planning. As a result, this new format groups recipes into chapters— such as Soups and Stews; Salads and Salad Dressings; Pasta, Polenta, and Other Grains, etc.—and invites readers to construct their own menus. For those who want menu guidance, menu suggestions are offered at the end of the book.

Having the opportunity to reissue my first cookbook is especially gratifying because I am continually approached by fans of the book who wish to purchase copies for their family and friends. This collection includes a variety of seasonal dishes that are simple to prepare, even for the novice cook, and the broad appeal of the dishes makes this cookbook a reliable friend in the kitchen with recipes for everyone to enjoy.

What an exciting time it is for those of us who love vegetables and favor vegetable-centered cooking. Everywhere we turn there is a new appreciation for the health benefits of vegetables and for the aesthetic contribution that fresh vegetables make to the menu. In fact, a meal without brightly colored fresh vegetables in some form seems lacking. It is also heartening to see how mainstream the vegetarian option has become in the twenty-first century. A plant-based diet is recommended by many high-profile nutritionists and medical professionals as a sure way to prevent and reverse heart disease, diabetes, and other lifestyle-related diseases. Gone are the concerns that a meatless diet might lack the necessary protein and nutrients for growth and strength. In fact, the vegetarian diet not only can provide all the essential nutrients for a healthy diet, but surpasses a traditional meat-centered cuisine with its generous supply of fiber and antioxidants. Maintaining a low-fat meatless diet along with regular exercise is considered the best strategy for improving one's health.

So now that we all agree about how indispensable vegetables have become, let's look at how to make meals that appeal to vegetarians and non-vegetarians alike. It's all about variety and balance. Meal planning should take into account a number of factors: the heaviness and lightness of dishes, color compatibility, flavor complexity, and nutritional balance. For example, if you are going to serve a Mexican entrée that is protein filled, cheesy, and red, then a light vegetable side dish such as sautéed spinach or simply prepared green beans would offer balance with weight (light), color (green), and nutrition (low protein/high vitamins and minerals).

I also seek balance in my diet in general. Because we know that it is ideal to maintain a low-fat regimen but also know that this approach can backfire if one feels deprived as a result, I have worked out this ratio: I eat low-fat food about 90 percent of the time, and allow myself indulgences 10 percent of the time. Of course this is not something to be mathematically calculated, but you get the idea. Eat dessert very infrequently, but when you do, let it be rich and satisfying (and a small portion!).

This book is a celebration of good food. I have written five cookbooks and am fortunate to have won a James Beard award. My recipes are designed for the busy cook who wants to link the pleasures of good eating with health and a respect for life. Throughout this book I encourage you to relax in the kitchen and have fun with the recipes. I am quite specific in explaining techniques and guiding you through each recipe—that is my style because I am a teacher and want my readers and students to feel prepared to face the task at hand; but that is only half the story of becoming a good cook. Developing a playful, relaxed approach to cooking is essential to becoming successful in the kitchen. It's all about getting a "feel" for the recipe and having that spirit infuse your cooking. Here are some tips for helping you become a confident, relaxed cook.

A Secret to Relaxed Cooking

- Read the entire recipe beforehand.
- Take out all the ingredients you need and place them nearby or in front of you.
- Do all the advance preparation you can before you actually begin cooking: for example, chopping nuts, cutting vegetables, measuring ingredients, etc.
- Take out and prepare any pans or dishes that you need for the recipe.
- Pour yourself a glass of wine.

Tips and Tools

TIPS

I have learned many tricks from having spent so much time in the kitchen cooking for family and friends and developing countless recipes, and I'd like to share them with you.

WASHING GREENS: Although many stores sell salad and cooking greens with labels saying they have been triple washed, I still like to wash my greens just before I use them. The salad spinner is a cook's best friend when it comes to this task, and mine gets plenty of use. No kitchen should be without one. The funny thing is, however, that many people misuse theirs. If you put the greens in the basket and rinse them under the faucet, sand or dirt can still remain trapped in them. This is especially problematic with garden or farmer's market leafy vegetables. The way to thoroughly clean greens is to place them in the bottom part of the salad spinner and fill it with plenty of cold water. Swish around the greens to loosen any dirt, then pick them up with your hands and place them in the basket. Discard the water. Repeat this step if the water is very dirty. Spin the greens until dry.

DAIRY PRODUCTS: When yogurt or milk is called for in these recipes, it is smart to choose low-fat varieties to cut down on fat intake. The dishes will be as nicely textured and satisfying, and you'll have created a more healthful version. There are times, however, when I use cream and butter in a recipe because I'm looking for a richer quality. These dishes are intended for a special occasion—meant as a treat rather than for frequent consumption. It's all about balance: eat low-fat food for most of your meals and allow an occasional rich dish just for the pleasure of it.

FRESH VEGETABLE ALTERNATIVES: Although freshness is always my guidepost when choosing vegetables, sometimes it is just not practical or possible, especially since I live in New England. Long winters limit the availability of much produce, especially peas, corn, and good-quality tomatoes. Fortunately there are acceptable alternatives for these vegetables. Frozen peas and corn are good choices because they are flash frozen at their peak and retain crispness when thawed. Many brands of canned tomatoes, especially imported Italian varieties, use tomatoes picked at their ripest. These tomatoes are just fine for cooked dishes, such as sauces, soups, and casseroles.

CANNED BEANS: Another liberty I often take is using canned beans rather than cooking dried beans from scratch. This is mostly because of time constraints rather than availability. When I became a parent and saw my free time evaporate, I adopted some shortcuts in the kitchen that streamlined my cooking style without compromising quality. Canned beans proved a godsend. The nutritional make-up—primarily protein and iron—is not diminished as a result of canning, and there are brands that offer organic, additive-free beans that are not overcooked. I always rinse beans in a strainer before adding them to a dish; this improves their flavor and texture.

FRESH HERBS: Fresh herbs are a wonderful addition to American cooking, something for which we are grateful to the Europeans, and their inclusion into the mainstream was long overdue. However, it is not always prudent to purchase fresh herbs if we don't intend to use them up before they get spoiled. It can be expensive and wasteful. I have found a clever way to capture the bright flavor and color of fresh of basil and cilantro, two herbs that I love and use most, by freezing them as purées. Here's how to do it: Wash and spin dry a bunch of either herb. Place in the blender with 2 cloves of garlic and just enough olive oil to make the mixture purée when blended. For the cilantro, add a teaspoon of vinegar; this heightens its flavor. Blend until smooth. Pour the purée into a small plastic container with a tight-fitting lid. A small deli container works well. Freeze until ready to use. When that time comes, place a warm towel or a dish of warm water beneath the container just until it causes the frozen purée to melt a tiny bit and shrink from the sides of the container, which should take a few minutes or so. Open the container and flip out the frozen disk. Using a vegetable (potato) peeler, shave the purée onto whatever you wish, such as enchiladas or any Mexican dish for the cilantro, or pasta and soup for the basil. Return the disk to the container and refreeze. The purée will keep up to a year and still be wonderful.

COOKING RICE: Properly cooked rice, whether it is brown rice or white rice, is not at all gummy and has grains that are separate yet tender. To achieve this consistency, it is important that the proper amount of water is used and that the rice is never stirred during the cooking process. My favorite habit when cooking rice is to always double the recipe and save the extra amount for another day. I cut back the cooking liquid by ¼ cup when I cook a double amount because it needs less to compensate for the added weight in the pot. To reheat cold rice for another meal, sprinkle on a few tablespoons of water and reheat on the stovetop in a covered pan over low heat or in a 350°F oven in a covered baking dish.

SALAD DRESSING: Although there are now countless varieties of commercial salad dressings available, nothing quite compares to the fresh flavor of a homemade dressing. This is one place where I feel the extra time needed to make a dressing is worth every minute, no matter how busy I am. But because I serve salad with almost every meal, I often want to have some on hand in a crunch. Doubling or tripling my salad dressing recipes has become a standard practice for me in order to achieve this. I have a few glass jars with screw top lids that I have saved for this purpose. Jam jars or small canning jars are good choices for mixing dressing ingredients.

TOOLS

A well-equipped kitchen can definitely make cooking more pleasurable than having to make do with inadequate tools. But having said this, I am not one to fill my kitchen with all the latest gadgets. I choose judiciously between tools that are worthwhile and ones that are gimmicks. I like an uncluttered kitchen, so only tools that are well made and essential are on my must-have list.

Pans:
- A set of saucepans and lids (preferably stainless steel with aluminum bottoms)
- A large stockpot for pasta and soup
- A cast iron grill pan—great for grilling vegetables
- 8- and 12-inch skillets

Knives:

- 8-inch chef's knife made of high-carbon steel
- 6-inch utility knife
- Paring knife
- Large serrated bread knife
- A steel for sharpening or a Chef's Choice electric knife sharpener (highly recommended)

Baking dishes and baking pans:

- Assorted casserole dishes (13 × 9 × 2 and 12 × 7 × 2) or oval gratins (3 quart and 2½ quart)
- 8 × 8- and 9 × 9-inch baking pans
- Muffin pans—standard and jumbo size
- Baking sheets—with sides and without sides

- Glass pie plate (good conductor of heat and helps with browning)
- 9- or 10-inch tart pan with removable sides
- 8 glass custard cups

Odds and ends:

- Large colander
- Vegetable steamer—a simple stainless steel collapsible one works fine
- Garlic press (great for when garlic is uncooked and needs to be fine, such as in salad dressings)
- Cutting boards (a separate one for cutting garlic and onions)
- Stainless steel mixing bowls

KEY TO SYMBOLS

▶ If a recipe is noted in a Menu at the end of the book, it is noted within the recipe. These are simply meant as helpful suggestions.

Ⓖ Indicates that more detailed information can be found in the Glossary.

SimplySatisfying

I'M A FAN OF A GOOD BREAKFAST. ALTHOUGH I DO ENJOY

brunch on occasion (which is served later in the morning

and has more formal fare), I especially enjoy a hearty break-

fast that offers a combination of classic favorites. Pancakes

Breakfast Favorites

and fruit; granola, muffins, and fruit; French toast, yogurt,

and fruit—that's right, for my liking, fruit needs to be part of

every breakfast to offer a wholesome balance. Don't hesitate

to include some of the egg dishes, such as the frittatas, that

are in the Frittatas, Eggs, and Timbales chapter. They also are

great breakfast choices.

Maple Pancakes

I like my pancakes to have crispy edges. The secret? Put a little butter on the pan instead of oil. These pancakes are at once wholesome and light. To keep the finished pancakes hot while you cook the remaining batter, heat a cookie sheet in a 300°F oven, and spread out the cooked pancakes on it as they are completed. They won't get soggy as they often do when you stack them in the oven. A side of fresh fruit with a pancake breakfast offsets the starchiness of the pancakes.

SERVES 4

2½ cups whole wheat pastry flour (or 1¼ cups whole wheat flour
    and 1¼ cups unbleached white flour)
1 tablespoon baking powder
1 teaspoon salt
2 eggs, beaten
2 cups milk
2 tablespoons pure maple syrup
6 tablespoons melted butter, slightly cooled, plus extra for the pan
Pure maple syrup G

1. Mix the flour, baking powder, and salt together in a large bowl.

2. Beat the eggs with the milk and maple syrup in a medium-size bowl until well mixed. Add to the dry ingredients along with the melted butter and stir just until blended. It's all right if the batter is lumpy; do not overmix. Let sit for 10 minutes before cooking.

3. Heat a large skillet (or a small one if you prefer to cook 1 medium-size pancake at a time) over medium heat with a little butter to coat the bottom. Test the pan's readiness by adding a drop of batter—it should sizzle immediately. Spoon some batter into the pan to make the pancakes the size you want. Flip them over once the surface is covered with broken bubbles. They should be a nice golden brown. Repeat with the remaining batter.

4. Serve with maple syrup. (If your maple syrup has been chilled, then heat it slightly so it doesn't make your pancakes cold.)

> NOTE: This recipe can be halved successfully if you are serving only 2 people.

French Toast with Orange and Brandy

Everyone seems to have his or her own idea about which type of bread makes the best French toast. I prefer French bread sliced on the diagonal, but whole wheat bread is a close second. Both are delicious topped with warm maple syrup.

SERVES 4   ▶ **BREAKFAST AND BRUNCH MENU 2**

5 eggs
⅔ cup milk
⅓ cup sugar
Grated rind of 1 large orange
½ teaspoon cinnamon
2 tablespoons brandy, or 1½ teaspoons vanilla extract
12 to 16 slices slightly stale French bread (sliced diagonally ¾ inch thick),
    or 8 slices regular bread
Butter for frying
Warm pure maple syrup **G**

1. Beat the eggs thoroughly in a large bowl. Add the milk, sugar, orange rind, cinnamon, and brandy, and mix well. Pour into a shallow dish like a pie plate if your bowl doesn't have a good flat bottom.

2. Add a few slices of bread and let soak, turning occasionally, for at least 5 minutes if it's French bread, or 2 minutes if it's regular sliced bread.

3. Put a little butter in a large skillet and heat over medium heat until hot. It should sizzle when a drop of water is flicked on it. Fry the bread on both sides until golden brown and piping hot. Serve immediately or keep warm in the oven (300°F) while you prepare the rest. I like to serve these with a pat of butter on each toast and pass the maple syrup at the table.

Egg and Pepper Croustades

Egg and Pepper Croustades

This is an attractive and unusual way to serve eggs. Crisp, buttery toasted bread squares serve as shells for creamy scrambled eggs. Have everything that you plan to serve with the croustades ready when you begin. You will need about half a loaf of unsliced homemade-type white bread, or you can use French bread.

SERVES 4   ▶ **BREAKFAST AND BRUNCH MENU 3**

4 slices white loaf bread (1 inch thick), or 8 slices French bread (1 inch thick)
1½ tablespoons melted butter, plus 2 tablespoons
2 red, orange, and/or yellow bell peppers, cored and very finely diced
8 eggs
¼ cup milk
¼ teaspoon dried oregano
Freshly ground pepper to taste

1. Preheat the oven to 300°F.

2. Remove the crusts from the bread. Bit by bit tear out the center of each slice, leaving a ¾-inch wall, or a ½-inch wall if using French bread. Save the crusts and centers to make Bread Crumbs (page 294). Lightly brush the bread all over with the melted butter, and place the slices on a cookie sheet.

3. Bake for 5 minutes or until lightly golden all over. Turn off the oven and keep the hollowed-out bread warm in it.

4. In a large skillet melt 1 tablespoon of the butter over medium heat and sauté the green peppers until very tender, about 7 minutes.

5. Meanwhile, in a large bowl beat together the eggs, milk, oregano, and pepper just until blended. Don't incorporate too much air into the eggs.

6. Reduce the heat under the skillet to low. Add the egg mixture and stir constantly until creamy and just the consistency you like for scrambled eggs. Be sure not to overcook them. Use a tablespoon to stir for the creamiest results.

7. Place a croustade on each plate and spoon equal amounts of eggs into the centers, spreading some to the edges also. Cut the remaining tablespoon of butter into bits and place on top of the eggs. Serve immediately.

Granola

Some granolas are filled with nutritious ingredients but somehow aren't particularly appetizing. This is the best granola I've tasted. It has a deliciously sweet cinnamon flavor—though not overly sweet—and just the right balance of textures. It is very easy to make, but you must watch it carefully during the second half of cooking, for it burns easily. For a delicious change try Granola served with yogurt and a little honey or maple syrup.

MAKES 3 TO 3½ QUARTS ▶ **BREAKFAST AND BRUNCH MENU 1**

½ cup oil
½ cup honey
6 cups rolled oats (non-instant oatmeal)
⅔ cup bran or wheat germ
½ teaspoon salt
1 tablespoon cinnamon
2 cups unsweetened dried coconut
½ cup sesame seeds or sunflower seeds
2 cups chopped walnuts
⅔ cup raisins
⅔ cup dried cranberries

1. Preheat the oven to 350°F. Combine the oil and honey in a large pot and heat until blended; do not boil it. Add all of the remaining ingredients except the raisins and cranberries, and stir until thoroughly mixed.

2. Bake in 2 or 3 batches. Place one-half or one-third on the baking sheet, and cook for 10 minutes. For the next 5 to 10 minutes occasionally toss the granola with a spatula to prevent it from burning. Be especially attentive to the sides, where it burns more easily. When ready the granola will be lightly browned but still somewhat soft; it becomes crisp when cooled.

3. Remove the pan from the oven and scrape this batch into a large bowl. Add half or a third of the raisins and cranberries—depending on the size of the batch—toss well, and cool completely before storing in covered jars or tins. Repeat this procedure with the remaining mixture and dried fruit. This granola will keep for 2 to 3 months in a tightly covered container in the refrigerator.

Roasted Home-Fried Potatoes and Onions

Roasting home fries rather than frying them is by far the easiest way to prepare these tasty potatoes, and the results are just as impressive.

SERVES 4 TO 6   ▶ **BREAKFAST AND BRUNCH MENU 5**

6 medium waxy or all-purpose boiling potatoes, peeled and cut into ½-inch dice
3 tablespoons oil
2 medium onions, diced
1 teaspoon paprika
Salt to taste
Freshly ground pepper to taste

1. Preheat the oven to 400°F.

2. Combine all the ingredients in a large bowl and toss to coat evenly. Spread the mixture on a large baking sheet so that the vegetables rest in one layer.

3. Bake until tender and golden, about 30 to 40 minutes, tossing the vegetables after 20 minutes.

Sweet Potato Home Fries

These are a nice change from the usual home fries that are made with white potatoes, and the beautiful orange color of the sweet potatoes will brighten up any breakfast (or dinner) plate. After about 30 minutes of cooking the potatoes will be tender, but to get them brown and crispy, you must keep cooking them another 20 to 30 minutes. It's worth the extra time.

SERVES 4 ▶ **BREAKFAST AND BRUNCH MENU 3**

4 medium sweet potatoes or yams (about 1½ pounds), peeled and cut into 1-inch chunks
¼ cup oil
2 large onions, cut into 1-inch dice
Salt to taste
Freshly ground pepper to taste

1. Preheat the oven to 400°F.

2. Combine all the ingredients in a large bowl and toss well. Spread the mixture onto a large baking sheet in one layer.

3. Cook 50 to 60 minutes, or until brown and crispy, tossing every 20 minutes.

Oatmeal Scones

These are my favorite scones; they are light and buttery and have a delightful chewy texture from the oatmeal. You can also serve them for mid-afternoon tea along with fruit, butter, or jam.

MAKES 8 LARGE SCONES ▶ **BREAKFAST AND BRUNCH MENU 3**

1 cup rolled oats (non-instant oatmeal)
½ cup buttermilk **G** or plain low-fat yogurt
½ cup whole wheat flour
½ cup unbleached white flour
2 tablespoons firmly packed light brown sugar
1½ teaspoons baking powder
½ teaspoon baking soda
¼ teaspoon salt
4 tablespoons chilled butter
1 to 2 eggs

1. Preheat the oven to 400°F. Butter a baking sheet. Combine the oats and buttermilk or yogurt in a large bowl and let soak for 15 minutes.

2. In a separate bowl mix the flours, sugar, baking powder, baking soda, and salt until well blended. Cut the butter into the mixture with a pastry blender until the mixture resembles coarse meal yet still shows little chunks of butter.

3. Beat 1 egg lightly and add to the oatmeal mixture; blend well. Stir in the flour mixture and mix just until evenly moistened, then gather into a ball. If it is too dry add a little more buttermilk or yogurt. Turn the mixture onto a lightly floured board and knead 5 times. Form into a circle about ¾ inch thick, and with a knife that has been dipped into flour cut the circle into 8 wedges. Place them a few inches apart on the baking sheet. At this point you can refrigerate them, covered, for up to 8 hours before baking.

4. For an attractive glazed look beat an egg with a teaspoon of water and brush some of this egg wash on each scone, if desired. Bake for 15 to 17 minutes, or until evenly golden. Serve immediately with fruit preserves and/or butter, or eat plain.

Blueberry Muffins

These large, fat muffins are filled with blueberries. The secret to all muffins and other quick breads is to mix just until moistened and no more. This recipe makes eleven instead of a dozen so that each muffin cup is filled right to the top.

MAKES 11 MUFFINS   ▶ **BREAKFAST AND BRUNCH MENU 1**

2 cups whole wheat pastry flour
    (or 1 cup whole wheat flour and 1 cup unbleached white flour)
½ cup sugar, plus extra for sprinking on top
2½ teaspoons baking powder
½ teaspoon salt
2 cups blueberries (unthawed if frozen)
2 eggs
½ cup milk
1 teaspoon vanilla extract
4 tablespoons melted butter, slightly cooled

1. Preheat the oven to 425°F.

2. Generously butter 11 cups of a medium-size muffin pan (or pans). Make sure also to butter the top surface of the pan because the muffins will spill over during cooking.

3. Combine the flour, sugar, baking powder, and salt in a large bowl and mix well. Add the berries and gently toss to coat them.

4. Beat the eggs, milk, and vanilla together, and carefully mix the liquid into the blueberry mixture just until moistened.

5. Add the melted butter and mix just until blended. Spoon some batter into each muffin cup so that they are filled to the top. Sprinkle some sugar onto the top of each muffin.

6. Bake for 15 minutes, or until a knife inserted in the center of a muffin comes out dry. Let sit on a wire rack for 10 minutes before removing them from the pan. (If you want an extra sparkle, then sprinkle a little sugar on top of your muffins again as soon as they come out of the oven.) Serve hot.

> NOTE: These Blueberry Muffins do freeze and reheat well, so if you are going to be pressed for time, or if you have any leftovers, wrap them in foil or plastic once they are thoroughly cooled, then freeze them in a plastic bag. Reheat them unthawed in a 350°F oven for 15 minutes, or until hot throughout.

Irish Soda Bread

When I was in Ireland I was served soda bread in every bed-and-breakfast house I stayed in (some ten to fifteen of them), and each one was different from the last. This is my favorite version, and one that is always eaten all up in one day in our house.

MAKES 1 LOAF, ABOUT 20 SLICES   ▶ BREAKFAST AND BRUNCH MENU 5

2½ cups unbleached white flour
½ cup whole wheat flour
½ cup sugar
¾ teaspoon salt
2 teaspoons baking soda
4 tablespoons butter, cut into bits
1 cup raisins
2 tablespoons caraway seeds
1½ cups buttermilk **G** or plain low-fat yogurt
Milk to brush on top

1. Preheat the oven to 350°F. Butter an 8-inch round cake pan and set aside. (If your dish is glass, then set the oven at 325°F.)

2. In a large bowl combine the flours, sugar, salt, and baking soda. Mix well.

3. Add the cut-up butter and toss. With your fingertips rub the butter into the flour mixture until it resembles coarse meal. Add the raisins and caraway seeds and mix well.

4. Add the buttermilk or yogurt and stir until the dough is evenly moistened, but don't overwork it. If the dough is too dry add a little more buttermilk or yogurt until it is the right consistency for kneading.

5. Turn the dough onto a lightly floured board and knead for 1 minute, or just until it is pliable; it will be sticky. Put it in the prepared cake pan and cut an X on top. (The easiest way to do this is to snip the dough with large scissors.) Brush the top of the dough with milk.

6. Bake for 60 minutes, or until golden brown. Remove the bread from the baking dish and let cool on a wire rack. Cool thoroughly before slicing.

NOTE: To avoid a crust that is too hard I put Irish Soda Bread in a plastic bag for the last half of the cooling time. I find it slices more easily when the crust is tender.

Prune Butter

This Czechoslovakian specialty is my favorite topping for scones, muffins, and toast. It is sweet and richly flavored, so a little goes a long way. This makes a nice gift when given in an attractive jar.

MAKES ABOUT 4 CUPS   ▶ BREAKFAST AND BRUNCH MENU 3

¾ pound pitted prunes
2 cups water
½ cup orange juice
Juice of 1 lemon
2 cups sugar
Dash salt

1. Combine everything in a heavy-bottomed medium saucepan and bring to a boil. Reduce to a simmer and cook for 30 minutes.

2. In batches purée the prune mixture in the blender or food processor and return it to the pot. Simmer another 20 minutes, or until the mixture is thick and smooth. To test whether or not it is thick enough, remove the pan from the heat, then drop a spoonful of the prune butter on a small plate. Chill it for 5 minutes. Remove and check to see if a rim of water has separated from around the prune butter. If so, it is too watery and should cook an additional 10 minutes. Test again. If no water has separated then it is done.

3. Let cool to lukewarm, then spoon into glass jars or containers with tight-fitting lids. Chill until ready to use. Prune butter will keep, refrigerated, for a few months.

Fresh Fruit with Yogurt Lime Sauce

A quick, light dish that can be prepared in any season. Pick the best fruit that you can get and strive for an attractive color combination. If you cannot get strawberries for the sauce, then try mashed banana, although the color will not be as striking.

SERVES 6   ▶ **INFORMAL MENU 7**

SAUCE
  4 strawberries, hulled
  2 tablespoons honey
  Juice of 1 lime
  1½ cups plain low-fat yogurt

FRUIT
  A combination of 3 or more of the following:
    Blueberries
    Strawberries
    Diced melon
    Diced mango
    Sliced banana
    Diced papaya
    Orange sections
    Sliced kiwi
    Finely diced apple
    Pineapple chunks
    Diced pears

  Mint sprigs for garnish

1. In a small bowl mash the 4 strawberries with the honey and lime juice to form a paste. Stir in the yogurt, cover, and chill for at least 2 hours and up to 48 hours before serving.

2. Put a mixture of fruit in each serving dish and spoon on some sauce, or arrange an attractive fruit platter using hollowed-out melon or pineapple halves and serve the sauce in a sauceboat. Garnish with mint sprigs.

Orange and Grapefruit Sections with Kiwi

If you cut the peel off citrus fruit and section it with a knife instead of your hands, it will be infinitely more delicate and colorful. To test the ripeness of kiwis, lightly press your thumb on the skin—they should feel tender, not mushy or hard.

SERVES 4

4 large navel oranges
3 pink grapefruits
2 ripe kiwis

1. To section the oranges and grapefruits cut a slice off the top and bottom of each fruit to expose the flesh. Stand the fruit upright and cut off the skin from top to bottom. One by one hold a piece of fruit in your hand and with a small sharp knife cut away each section of fruit from its membrane. Do this over a bowl to collect any juice that drips, and let each section fall into the bowl. Squeeze out all of the juice from the remaining membrane into the bowl.

2. Peel the kiwis, cut them into ¼-inch-thick slices, and add them to the bowl. Serve at room temperature in smaller bowls or decorative goblets.

Cantaloupe with Strawberries and Lime

This simple preparation is one of my favorite ways to liven up the breakfast table with very little effort.

SERVES 4 ▶ SUMMER MENU 7

1 medium ripe cantaloupe
½ lime
12 strawberries

1. Cut the cantaloupe in half vertically and scoop out the seeds. Cut each half vertically in half again. With a sharp knife cut the fruit away from the skin, keeping each quarter in one piece. Put the fruit back on the skin.

2. Still keeping the fruit on the skin, make a lengthwise cut down the center, then cut crosswise into 1-inch rows.

3. Place the cantaloupe quarters on individual dessert plates. Slice the lime vertically into 4 wedges. Garnish each cantaloupe top with 3 strawberries and a lime wedge.

SETTING THE TONE FOR A MEAL BY CHOOSING THE right appetizer requires that you take a few things into account. If you have a cheesy entrée, then select a light, cheese-free starter to nibble on. If your main course does

Starters

not contain a lot of vegetables, then a dip with crudités can add balance to the meal. Time management can be another factor. When your entrée is quick to prepare, then this can be an opportunity to experiment with a pâté or other more elaborate starter. Whatever you choose, seek balance, and you will set the right tone for the main affair.

Cauliflower and Cashew Croquettes

These croquettes are rich and luscious, with a crisp coating on the outside and a creamy filling of cauliflower and cashews within. Leftover cold croquettes make a great finger food for picnics; they go with almost anything—such as cold soups, salads, and marinated pasta dishes.

SERVES 4

4 cups finely chopped cauliflower (not minced)
1 cup raw cashews*
3 tablespoons butter
¼ cup plus 1 tablespoon unbleached white flour
¾ cup milk
1 egg yolk plus 1 egg
½ cup grated Parmesan cheese
½ teaspoon salt
Liberal seasoning freshly ground pepper
1¼ cups Bread Crumbs (page 294)
Oil

If you cannot get raw cashews, you can substitute roasted, unsalted cashews, in which case you do not have to toast them.

1. Steam the cauliflower until very tender, then put it into a large bowl to cool. (If you boil it be sure to drain it very well.)

2. Toast the cashews in a 350°F oven in a shallow dish such as a pie plate, stirring often until they are golden, about 10 minutes. Be careful not to burn them. With a large knife chop them into small pieces. (Do not put them in a blender or food processor; they will be chopped too fine.) Add to the cauliflower and mix.

3. Melt the butter in a small saucepan, then whisk in the flour and cook this roux over low heat for 2 minutes, whisking constantly. Whisk in the milk and cook another 3 to 4 minutes, or until the mixture is very thick. Remove from the heat and let cool for 5 minutes.

4. Beat in the egg yolk, Parmesan cheese, salt, and pepper. Scrape this mixture onto the cauliflower and cashews and stir until well mixed. Cover and chill until cold, at least 1 hour, and up to 24 hours.

5. Lightly beat the egg in one bowl and put the bread crumbs into another. Form about ¼ cup of the cauliflower mixture into an oblong shape about 2 inches by 3½ inches. Don't worry about its shape being perfect at this point; it will be easier to form once it is coated with the bread crumbs.

Roll in the egg, then the bread crumbs. Repeat with the remaining mixture; you should get 12 croquettes. (They can be breaded up to 1 hour in advance and kept at room temperature. Don't chill once they are breaded or moisture will collect and they won't fry well.)

6. Heat about ¼ inch of oil in a large skillet until it is hot but not smoking. Fry the croquettes in batches until they are golden all over, then drain on paper towels. Serve immediately or keep hot in a 350°F oven.

NOTE: Although I prefer them fried, you can bake the croquettes instead. Lightly grease a baking dish and place them in one layer. Bake in a 425°F oven for 30 minutes, or until golden all over. Turn the croquettes over after the first 15 minutes.

Tzatziki

This is a simple Greek dip that has a pungent garlic flavor. It is especially good served with hot pita bread triangles.

MAKES 1¼ CUPS ▶ SUMMER MENU 1

½ medium cucumber
1 cup yogurt
2 cloves garlic, minced
1 tablespoon minced fresh dill
¼ teaspoon salt
1 teaspoon minced fresh parsley

1. Peel the cucumber and slice in half lengthwise. With a spoon, scrape out the seeds and discard. Grate the cucumber on a grater, then spoon into a clean cotton kitchen towel. Gather the towel into a ball and gently squeeze out all the liquid that is in the grated cucumber. Place the cucumber in a medium-size serving bowl.

2. Stir in the yogurt, garlic, dill, and salt and garnish with the minced parsley. Chill for at least 30 minutes before serving to develop the flavor.

Yogurt Herb Cheese Spread

This Middle Eastern method of making fresh cheese out of yogurt is easy and fun. You simply place the yogurt in a cheesecloth-lined strainer and let it drip until the yogurt reaches the consistency you want; the longer it drips, the firmer it gets. To make a creamy dip let it drain for 1 hour; for a ricotta cheese (spread) consistency, 4 hours; and for a cream cheese consistency let it drain at least 12 hours or overnight. My recipe makes a tangy, creamy spread that is delicious on crackers or thin toasts. It doesn't take long to prepare, although it must drain for at least 4 hours, then after it is mixed with the herbs it should sit a few hours to blend the flavors.

MAKES ABOUT 1 CUP ▶ SUMMER MENU 8

2 cups plain low-fat yogurt
1 clove garlic, minced
1 tablespoon olive oil
½ teaspoon fresh thyme, or ¼ teaspoon dried
1 tablespoon minced fresh basil, or ¼ teaspoon dried
½ teaspoon fresh oregano, or ¼ teaspoon dried
Salt to taste
Freshly ground pepper to taste

1. Line a strainer with cheesecloth and place the strainer over a large bowl. Spoon the yogurt into the center of the strainer and place the setup in the refrigerator. Let sit for 4 to 12 hours. Occasionally check the consistency. The cheese is ready when it has the consistency of ricotta cheese.

2. Place the yogurt cheese in a small bowl. Mix in all of the remaining ingredients. Cover and chill for at least 2 hours before serving. Serve as a spread on toasted French bread slices or crackers.

Ricotta Basil Spread

This spread is reminiscent of the filling of traditional cheese ravioli and lasagna—so luscious and satisfying.

MAKES 1½ CUPS ▶ QUICK MENU 3

1 cup ricotta cheese (preferably part-skim)
¼ cup grated Parmesan cheese
1 tablespoon milk
1 clove garlic, minced
2 tablespoons minced fresh basil, or 1 teaspoon dried basil
¼ cup minced fresh parsley
Salt to taste
Freshly ground pepper to taste

Beat all the ingredients together by hand—except 1 teaspoon of minced parsley—in a medium bowl until very smooth. Scrape into a serving bowl and garnish with the remaining parsley. Cover and chill at least 30 minutes before serving. Use as a spread on toasted French bread or crackers, or as a stuffing in raw pepper strips.

NOTE: If you would like to make this into a dip, increase the milk to 3 tablespoons and the parsley to ½ cup. Put all the ingredients in the blender and blend until smooth. It will make an attractive jade-colored dip.

Guacamole

This dip deserves the popularity that it has gained. Though it's delicious served with crackers or crudités, I think it's even more appetizing when served with corn chips.

MAKES 1¼ CUPS ▶ **ELEGANT MENU 8**

2 ripe avocados (preferably Hass variety)
Juice of ½ lemon or lime
1 tomato, seeded and minced
1 tablespoon minced onion
2 tablespoons sour cream
Salt to taste
½ jalapeño pepper, seeded and minced Ⓖ, or Tabasco to taste
Lemon slice, lime slice, or tomato wedges for garnish

1. Slice the avocados in half vertically and remove the pit. Insert the handle of a spoon between the skin and the flesh and move it around to separate them.

2. In a medium bowl mash the avocado with a fork until smooth. Add all of the remaining ingredients (except the garnish) and mix. Cover and chill for at least 1 hour.

3. Spoon into a serving dish and add the garnish of your choice.

Indian Eggplant Dip

This is a richly flavored, spicy dip that is very easy to prepare. It is one of my favorite appetizers, and a good choice to acquaint newcomers to the flavors of curry. I highly recommend serving it with hot pita bread triangles so you can scoop it up, but it also works well as a spread on crackers.

MAKES 1¼ CUPS ▶ INFORMAL MENU 14

1 medium eggplant (1¼ pounds)
3 tablespoons butter or Ghee (page 300)
2 teaspoons ground coriander
½ teaspoon turmeric
¼ teaspoon cumin seeds
⅛ teaspoon cayenne pepper
1 clove garlic, minced
½ cup finely chopped tomato
½ teaspoon salt
3 tablespoons yogurt
2 tomato wedges for garnish
Fresh coriander or parsley sprigs for garnish

1. Preheat the oven to 400°F. Cut the stem end off the eggplant and discard. Prick the eggplant with a fork in a few places to prevent it from exploding when cooking, and place it on a pie plate or baking dish. Bake for 1 to 1½ hours, or until the eggplant collapses and is very soft. Let sit for 10 minutes or so, or until cool enough to handle.

2. Meanwhile, heat the butter or ghee in a medium skillet. Add the coriander, turmeric, cumin seeds, cayenne, and garlic, and "toast" these spices for 2 minutes, stirring often. Add the tomato and cook 2 minutes more. Remove from the heat.

3. Scoop out the pulp of the eggplant into a medium bowl and mash very well. Add the spiced tomato mixture, salt, and yogurt, and mix well. Cover and chill at least 1 hour or overnight.

4. Spoon into a serving dish and garnish with the tomato wedges and the coriander or parsley sprigs. Serve with hot pita bread triangles.

Pesto on Toasted French Bread

Pesto is usually served as a sauce on pasta and sometimes is used to enhance vegetables. But by far the most luscious way to enjoy pesto that I know of is to spread it on slices of toasted French bread and have them as an appetizer.

MAKES 12 SLICES ·   ▶ **INFORMAL MENU 11**

> 12 slices French bread (½ inch thick)
> ½ cup Pesto (page 296) or Winter Pesto (page 297)

1. Toast the French bread under the broiler on a cookie sheet until lightly golden on both sides.

2. Spread about 2 teaspoons of pesto on each slice. Serve within 20 minutes.

> NOTE: If you want to take this on a picnic, then pack the pesto in a container and place the warm toasted French bread in a plastic bag. Spread when you get there.

Pesto on Toasted French Bread

Hummus

Although there are some store-bought varieties of hummus that are good, none compares to this luxurious version. For a delicious lunch, try spooning leftover hummus over sautéed vegetables that have been stuffed into pita bread.

MAKES ABOUT 2½ CUPS ▶ ELEGANT MENU 6

16-ounce can chickpeas, drained, rinsed, and drained again
3 cloves garlic, minced
½ cup fresh lemon juice (about 3 lemons)
¾ cup tahini Ⓖ
½ teaspoon salt
½ cup cold water
Olive oil
Paprika

1. In a blender or food processor combine the chickpeas, garlic, lemon juice, tahini, and salt. Blend and slowly pour in the water. Turn off the machine and scrape down the sides as necessary. If the hummus is too thick, add 1 tablespoon more water at a time until desired consistency is achieved.

2. Pour into a serving dish, cover, and chill until ready to serve. Just before serving drizzle a little olive oil on top (don't mix) and sprinkle on some paprika. Serve with warm pita bread triangles.

Stuffed Red Pepper Strips with Ricotta Basil Spread

I love the vivid, contrasting colors of red, white, and green in this appetizer. It is very simple to prepare yet looks impressive. If red peppers at the market aren't firm and glossy, substitute green or yellow bell peppers.

SERVES 4　　　　　　　　　　　　　　　　　　　　　▶ QUICK MENU 7

1 recipe Ricotta Basil Spread (page 24)
2 large red bell peppers

1. Prepare the Ricotta Basil Spread and reserve 2 teaspoons of minced parsley for garnish.

2. Core the peppers and slice each into 6 vertical strips. Spread the inside of each strip with an equal portion of the spread, then garnish each strip with some minced parsley. Arrange the strips on a serving plate in a circular pattern to resemble a flower. Serve at room temperature for maximum flavor.

> NOTE: You could also make this recipe using 6 sweet baby peppers, cored and with the tops removed.

Stuffed Mushrooms with Feta and Dill

This Greek-inspired filling marries well with the rich flavor of the mushrooms to make these morsels a real standout.

SERVES 4
▶ QUICK MENU 11

½ cup walnuts, finely chopped
½ cup Bread Crumbs (page 294)
1 heaping tablespoon finely chopped fresh dill
¾ cup finely crumbled feta cheese
2 tablespoons milk
Freshly ground pepper to taste
16 large mushrooms
2½ tablespoons olive oil

1. Preheat the oven to 375°F. Mix the walnuts, bread crumbs, dill, feta, milk, and pepper together in a medium bowl.

2. Wipe the mushrooms very clean with a damp cloth, then remove the stems and reserve for another use, such as a pizza topping or to flavor rice. Divide the mixture evenly and stuff each mushroom cap, pressing in the stuffing firmly.

3. Generously butter a baking dish that will hold all of the mushrooms and place them in it, then drizzle the olive oil over each one. *May be prepared to this point up to 24 hours in advance, covered, and chilled.* Bake for 20 minutes, or until the mushrooms are juicy and the tops are lightly browned. Serve immediately.

Stuffed Mushrooms with Blue Cheese

The toasted flavor of the sunflower seeds nicely complements the blue cheese in this stuffing. This version is more cheesy and just as delicious.

SERVES 4   ▶ ELEGANT MENU 11

2 tablespoons raw sunflower seeds
12 large mushrooms
¼ cup crumbled blue cheese
¼ cup cream cheese
2 tablespoons milk
2 tablespoons fine bread or cracker crumbs

1. Preheat the oven to 400°F. Put the sunflower seeds in a baking dish large enough to hold the 12 mushrooms (to save you from dirtying an extra pan) and toast them in the oven until lightly golden, about 7 minutes.

2. Remove the stems from the mushrooms and reserve for another use. Wipe the mushroom caps clean with a damp cloth.

3. Mash the blue cheese, cream cheese, and milk in a medium bowl until smooth. Stir in the toasted sunflower seeds and bread crumbs.

4. Fill each mushroom cap with this mixture. Butter the baking dish and arrange the mushroom caps within. *May be prepared to this point up to 24 hours in advance, covered, and chilled.* Bake for 15 to 20 minutes, or until golden on top and juicy. Serve immediately.

Deep-Fried Cheese-Filled Polenta Balls

Deep-Fried Cheese-Filled Polenta Balls

Polenta is a wonderful grain dish to become familiar with because it is so quick to make, and it goes well with most vegetables and sauces. This is a sumptuous appetizer that is richly varied in texture, with a crispy coating on the outside, light and moist polenta within, and a creamy center of melted cheese.

MAKES 12 BALLS (4 TO 6 SERVINGS)   ▶ ELEGANT MENU 9

1½ cups water
½ cup cornmeal
1 egg, beaten
½ cup grated Parmesan cheese
¼ cup plus 2 tablespoons unbleached white flour
¼ teaspoon salt
3 ounces semisoft cheese (such as Italian Fontina, Muenster, or Monterey Jack)
¾ cup Bread Crumbs (page 294)
Oil for frying

1. To make the polenta: Bring the water to a boil in a small saucepan, then very slowly add the cornmeal, beating constantly with a wire whisk. Reduce the heat to a simmer and cook, whisking constantly, until the polenta tears away from the sides of the pan, about 10 minutes. Pour onto a plate and chill until cold, about 20 to 30 minutes.

2. Put the polenta in a medium bowl and mash with a fork. Add the egg, Parmesan cheese, flour, and salt, and mix well. *May be prepared to this point up to 24 hours in advance, covered, and chilled.*

3. Cut the cheese into 12 cubes, about ½-inch each. Form the polenta mixture into balls about 1½ inches in diameter and insert a cube of cheese into the center, making sure to cover the cheese completely. This will be messy but manageable. Roll the balls in the bread crumbs to coat completely. You can let them sit at room temperature for up to 30 minutes before cooking.

4. Pour enough oil into a medium saucepan to reach a depth of 2 inches and heat until it is very hot but not smoking. (The best way to test if the oil is hot enough is to drop in a bread crumb; it should immediately rise to the top.) Fry 4 or 5 balls at a time, turning occasionally to brown all over. It should take about 3 to 4 minutes to brown them. Remove with a slotted spoon and drain on paper towels. Serve immediately.

Cheese and Onion Filo Triangles

This is a light and flaky Turkish appetizer of filo dough shaped into a triangle and stuffed with a mixture of melted cheese and onion. It is a good choice for entertaining because it can be made in advance and frozen.

MAKES 12 ▶ **SUMMER MENU 7**

....

2 medium onions, finely diced
1 tablespoon olive oil
½ pound Monterey Jack cheese, cut into small cubes (about 2 cups)
6 tablespoons butter, melted
8 sheets filo dough (12 x 16 inches)

1. In a medium skillet sauté the onions in the olive oil until tender, about 10 minutes. Remove from the heat and transfer to a small bowl. Let cool.

2. Preheat the oven to 400°F. Have the onions, cubed cheese, and melted butter in front of you. Place the 8 sheets of filo in front of you, cover them with a sheet of wax paper, then cover the wax paper with a damp towel to prevent the dough from drying out. Return any remaining filo to the refrigerator well wrapped.

3. Remove 1 sheet of filo from the stack, cover the stack again, and with a pastry brush lightly brush the surface of the dough with melted butter. Place a second sheet of filo on top. Brush it lightly with butter, making sure to get the edges. (Always keep the remaining stack of filo covered.) Using the tip of a pointed knife cut the buttered sheets of filo into 3 even lengthwise strips.

4. Place not more than 1 tablespoon each of the cubed cheese and sautéed onion near the corner of 1 strip. Gently fold this corner to make a triangle, covering the filling, and continue to fold the triangle as you would a flag, that is, folding the triangle in half in such a way that the triangular shape is maintained.

5. Lightly brush the top and bottom of the triangle with melted butter and place it on a baking sheet. Repeat this procedure with the 2 remaining strips.

6. Repeat steps 3, 4, and 5 until the 8 sheets of filo have been used. You should have 12 triangles. *May be prepared to this point up to 8 hours in advance, covered, and refrigerated.*

7. Bake for 15 minutes, or until golden all over. (To freeze uncooked triangles, place them in the freezer uncovered on a platter. Once frozen, remove them from the platter, wrap them in plastic or foil, and return to freezer. Do not defrost before baking.)

Baked Stuffed Artichokes with Pine Nuts and Lemon Herb Sauce

These scrumptious artichokes are not difficult to prepare, and they look stunning. They resemble open flowers because some of the stuffing is pushed between the leaves and it keeps the petals apart. Since they are rather filling, I like to serve them just before a hearty soup rather than a regular main course. To test an artichoke's freshness you should squeeze the top of the artichoke and listen for a squeaky sound. If it sounds dull, then it is past its prime.

SERVES 4   ▶ INFORMAL MENU 16

    4 medium to large artichokes
    ½ lemon
    ¼ cup pine nuts
    6 slices white bread, or 4 slices white bread and 2 slices whole wheat bread
    ¼ cup minced fresh parsley
    ½ teaspoon dried tarragon
    ¼ cup grated Parmesan cheese
    ½ teaspoon salt
    Freshly ground pepper to taste
    2 cloves garlic, minced
    1 tablespoon butter
    ¼ cup olive oil
    ½ cup dry white wine

  SAUCE
    ½ cup plain yogurt
    ½ cup Mayonnaise (page 298)
    3 tablespoons lemon juice
    ½ teaspoon mixed dried herbs (I like tarragon, basil, thyme, and oregano)
    Freshly ground pepper to taste

1. Bring a large (6-quart) pot of water to a boil. Meanwhile rinse the artichokes under cold running water, then cut off the stems so they can sit upright. With a sharp knife (preferably serrated) slice off 1½ inches from the top of each artichoke. Rub the newly exposed area with the lemon half to prevent discoloration. With scissors trim ½ inch off the top of each leaf, and continue to rub each newly exposed area with the lemon. Drop the artichokes into the boiling water and cook, covered, for 20 minutes.

2. Meanwhile make the stuffing. Preheat the oven to 375°F. Toast the pine nuts in one layer in a shallow pan for about 10 minutes, tossing occasionally. Be careful not to burn them; they should be a pale golden color. Put them in a medium bowl and keep the oven on.

3. Put some water in a large bowl and soak half of the bread slices for 10 seconds. Drain out the water then squeeze the bread in your hands to remove *all* of the remaining water. Add the squeezed bread to the pine nuts and crumble with your fingers. Repeat with the remaining bread.

4. Stir in the parsley, tarragon, Parmesan cheese, salt, and pepper. Sauté the minced garlic in the butter for 2 minutes—do not let it brown—and add to the stuffing mixture, tossing to mix.

5. After the artichokes have cooked for 20 minutes, remove them from the pot and invert onto a paper towel until cool enough to handle. Gently make an opening in the center of each artichoke and pull out a few of the innermost leaves, then scoop out the choke—the fuzzy, hairy center—with a teaspoon until it is completely removed. Discard the choke and those innermost leaves.

6. Divide the stuffing into 4 equal portions and stuff the center of each artichoke, and also push bits of stuffing between the leaves in a symmetrical fashion. *May be prepared to this point up to 8 hours in advance, covered, and chilled.*

7. Place the stuffed artichokes in a medium-size baking dish or a pie plate and pour the oil over them. Pour the wine into the dish, then cover the dish with foil. Bake for 45 minutes, then remove the foil and baste the artichokes. Bake *uncovered* for an additional 15 minutes, or until a leaf near the center pulls out easily when grasped with the fingertips.

8. Meanwhile make the sauce. Combine all of the ingredients in a small bowl and beat until smooth. Let sit for at least 30 minutes before serving. (You can cover and chill it.) Serve cool or at room temperature, but not cold.

9. When the artichokes are done, let them sit for 10 minutes before serving; they will be easier to handle and more flavorful if not served piping hot. To eat the artichokes spoon some sauce onto the side of your plate. Pull a leaf out of the artichoke and dip the end that was attached into the sauce. Pull the artichoke leaf through your teeth and the tender meat will easily come off. When all of the leaves have been "scraped" in this manner you will be left with the artichoke bottom, the best part of this experience. Dip the bottom into the sauce and enjoy! Of course, don't forget to eat the stuffing as you go along.

Pâté de Legumes

Here is a rich pâté that resembles a meat pâté in texture, but it is much more nutritious and lower in fat. It can be served sliced with crusty French bread on the side, or used as a sandwich spread. Because this recipe makes a large loaf, I like to freeze a portion of it; but whatever you do it is so delicious you can be sure none will go to waste.

MAKES 1 LARGE LOAF (8 TO 10 SERVINGS)

6 cups water
2 cups lentils, rinsed and picked over
2 cups diced green beans
¼ cup olive oil
4 medium onions, diced
4 cloves garlic, minced
1 cup Bread Crumbs (page 294)
½ cup minced fresh parsley
3 eggs, beaten
1½ tablespoons dry sherry
1 tablespoon tamari or other soy sauce
½ teaspoon salt
A few dashes cayenne pepper
Pinch thyme
Liberal seasoning freshly ground pepper

1. In a medium saucepan bring the water to a boil. Add the lentils and cook, uncovered, for 20 minutes. Stir occasionally.

2. Add the diced green beans and cook 20 minutes more, or until the green beans are very tender. Stir occasionally. Drain this mixture well in a colander and return it to the pot (off the heat).

3. Heat the olive oil in a medium skillet over low heat. Add the onions and garlic and sauté, stirring often, for 20 minutes, or until the onions are very tender.

4. Add the onions to the pot containing the lentils, and mix. Add all of the remaining ingredients and mix well.

5. Preheat the oven to 375°F. Purée the lentil mixture in the blender or processor in batches until very smooth. Scrape down the sides of the blender as necessary. Taste to adjust seasoning.

6. Generously butter a 1½-quart loaf pan. Line with wax paper and generously butter the wax paper. Pour in the pâté and smooth over the top. Cover with buttered wax paper or aluminum foil.

7. Set the pan into a larger baking dish and fill the outer dish with enough hot water to reach one-third up the sides of the loaf pan. (This *bain-marie,* or water bath, ensures gentle, moist cooking.)

8. Place the pans in the oven and bake for 1½ hours, or until a knife inserted in the center comes out clean.

9. Remove from the oven, and lift out the loaf pan. Uncover and let it sit for 20 minutes.

10. Place a large plate or platter over the pâté and invert it onto the plate. Lift off the pan, then carefully remove the wax paper. Let the pâté cool for 15 minutes or so, then wrap it in foil and chill for at least 4 hours and up to 4 days. Serve chilled or at room temperature, but not warm. You can also freeze the pâté for up to 2 weeks, wrapped in foil and placed in a plastic bag.

> NOTE: Place a slice of pâté on a small serving plate and garnish with a few sprigs of parsley or watercress. Serve with crusty French bread, crostini, or Melba toast. In addition, serve some chopped raw onion and mayonnaise on each plate. You could also serve it spread on warm toast with mayonnaise on top.

Three-Layered Vegetable Pâté with Herb Mayonnaise

Here is a delicious and impressive pâté made up of layers of carrot purée, minced leeks, and minced spinach. It is not as complicated to prepare as it appears, and a little goes a long way. I like to simplify the preparation by cooking the vegetables on one day and assembling the pâté on the next day. Whichever way you choose to do it, this beautiful pâté is well worth the effort. In addition to serving it as an appetizer, I also like to serve it for lunch along with a cup of soup and well-made crusty bread. Read about purchasing spinach under Spinach Custard Ring with Tomato Cream Sauce (page 118).

MAKES 1 LARGE LOAF (ABOUT 10 SERVINGS) ▶ ELEGANT MENU 5

CARROT LAYER

    1 pound carrots (9 medium), thinly sliced
    2 eggs
    ¼ cup heavy or whipping cream
    1 tablespoon honey
    ½ teaspoon ground coriander
    ⅛ teaspoon cinnamon
    ½ teaspoon salt
    Liberal seasoning freshly ground pepper
    ½ cup Bread Crumbs (page 294)

LEEK LAYER

    4 medium to large leeks (with 2 inches of green top)
    2 tablespoons butter
    2 eggs
    ¼ cup Bread Crumbs (page 294)
    ¼ cup heavy or whipping cream
    ½ teaspoon salt
    Liberal seasoning freshly ground pepper

SPINACH LAYER

    2 pounds loose fresh spinach (weight with stems), or two 10-ounce packages fresh spinach,
        cleaned thoroughly and stemmed, or two 10-ounce packages frozen chopped spinach
    2 eggs
    ½ cup heavy or whipping cream
    ¼ cup Bread Crumbs (page 294)
    ¼ cup grated Parmesan cheese
    1 tablespoon minced fresh basil, or 1 teaspoon dried basil

½ teaspoon salt

A few dashes cayenne pepper

HERB MAYONNAISE

1 cup Mayonnaise (page 298)

¾ cup yogurt

¼ cup minced fresh parsley

½ teaspoon mixed dried herbs (I like crushed fennel seed, basil, thyme, and tarragon)

Freshly ground pepper to taste

Parsley sprigs for garnish

1. Butter a 1½-quart loaf pan and line with wax paper. Butter the wax paper.

2. Cook (preferably steam) the carrots until *very* tender, then drain thoroughly. Purée them in a blender or food processor along with the eggs, cream, honey, coriander, cinnamon, salt, and pepper until *very* smooth. Stir in the bread crumbs, then spoon into the loaf pan and smooth over the top.

3. Cut the roots off the leeks and cut off all but 2 inches of the top green part. Slit each one lengthwise almost all the way through to the other side, then open each leek and thoroughly rinse under cold running water to rid them of all of their dirt. Finger through the leaves to find hidden dirt. Pat dry and then thinly slice; you need 6 cups sliced.

4. In a large skillet melt the butter and sauté the leeks for 10 minutes, or until tender. Beat the eggs in a medium bowl, then add the leeks, bread crumbs, cream, salt, and pepper, and mix well. Spoon this mixture over the carrot layer, then smooth over the top.

5. Put the spinach in a large pot with just the water that clings to it, and cook until it wilts. Drain in a colander and let sit until cool enough to handle. Squeeze the spinach in your hands until *all* of the liquid is removed. (If you are using frozen spinach then either let it thaw completely and squeeze dry, or cook until thawed and squeeze dry.) Mince the spinach *very* fine (do not purée it).

6. Beat the eggs in a medium bowl, then add the spinach, cream, bread crumbs, Parmesan cheese, basil, salt, and cayenne pepper, and mix well. Spoon this mixture over the leek mixture and smooth over the top.

7. Preheat the oven to 350°F. Cover the top of the pâté with a sheet of buttered wax paper, then cover that with a sheet of foil. Place the loaf in a larger baking pan, and pour in enough hot water to reach halfway up the sides of the loaf pan. Bake for 1½ hours, or until a knife inserted in the center of the pâté comes out clean. Remove the loaf pan from the water bath, peel away the foil and wax paper, then cool on a wire rack for 1 hour.

8. To unmold place a large plate or platter over the pâté and invert. Remove the loaf pan, then peel away the wax paper. Let sit for 20 minutes at room temperature, then cover with foil and chill for at least 2 hours and up to 48 hours before serving.

9. Meanwhile make the herb mayonnaise. Combine all of the ingredients (except the parsley sprigs) in a medium bowl and stir until well blended. Cover and chill at least 1 hour before serving to thicken and develop the flavors.

10. To serve, slice the pâté into ¾-inch-thick slices and place each slice on a small serving plate. Spoon a few spoonfuls of herb mayonnaise next to the pâté and garnish the sauce with a sprig of parsley.

Three-Layered Vegetable Pâté

LETTUCE SELECTIONS HAVE IMPROVED SO MUCH OVER the past twenty years that the salad course can rival any other part of the meal and with little effort. Because I am so fond of salad, I have never adopted the custom of serving

Salads and Salad Dressings

the salad after the entrée, as is customary in Europe. Often I am full and end up eating much less salad when it is the closer to a meal. But I know that many people prefer to offer salad at the meal's conclusion, and most of these salads, particularly the leafy green ones, will nicely cleanse the palate. Aim for balance when you select one of these salads to accompany your meal. Factor in richness, color, the season, and flavor compatibility to make a good match.

Indonesian Salad with Spicy Peanut Dressing

This dressing, reminiscent of satay sauce, is sure to become one of your favorites. It has that intriguing balance of spicy, sweet, and tangy flavors that characterizes so much of Southeast Asian cooking.

SERVES 4 TO 6   ► INFORMAL MENU 1

2 small cucumbers, peeled and sliced ¼ inch thick
2 cups finely shredded cabbage
1 cup fresh bean sprouts
3 radishes, thinly sliced
3 scallions, sliced into 1-inch lengths

DRESSING
⅔ cup crunchy natural peanut butter
3 tablespoons milk
Juice of ½ lemon
½ teaspoon minced fresh ginger
2 cloves garlic, minced
1 teaspoon honey
Dash cayenne pepper
Salt to taste
3 to 4 tablespoons water

1. Place all of the salad ingredients in a bowl, reserving some radish slices for garnish, and toss.

2. To make the dressing: In a medium bowl beat the peanut butter and milk together with a fork until well blended; it will be very thick.

3. Add all of the remaining ingredients for the dressing and mix well. Use the greater amount of water if the sauce is too thick. Taste to correct seasoning.

4. Divide the salad evenly among the serving plates. Top each portion with a few spoonfuls of dressing and garnish with a slice of radish. Serve the remaining dressing at the table so more can be added if desired.

Arugula and Boston Lettuce Salad

The incomparable flavor of arugula can easily be overpowered by a strong salad dressing. The best way to accentuate its wonderful flavor is to use only a light dressing of lemon juice and olive oil with a sprinkling of Parmesan cheese.

SERVES 4 ▶ **INFORMAL MENU 10**

1 head Boston lettuce, washed and spun dry
1 bunch arugula, washed, stems removed, and spun dry
¼ cup olive oil
1½ tablespoons lemon juice
1 tablespoon grated Parmesan cheese
Salt to taste
Freshly ground pepper to taste

1. Tear the lettuce into bite-size pieces and each arugula leaf in half, and place the greens in a large salad bowl.

2. Sprinkle on the olive oil. Toss to coat. Sprinkle on the lemon juice and toss well. Sprinkle on the Parmesan cheese and toss again. Season with a little salt and freshly ground pepper and serve immediately.

> NOTE: The size of a lettuce head and a bunch of arugula will vary, so use your judgment as to whether or not you need more or less dressing.

Spinach Salad with Creamy Dill Dressing

Spinach Salad with Creamy Dill Dressing

Spinach and dill are natural companions and this salad proves the rule.

SERVES 6
▶ INFORMAL MENUS 5 AND 8

12 ounces fresh spinach, washed, stems removed, and spun dry
½ medium red onion, thinly sliced
2 cups (6 ounces) sliced mushrooms
1 hard-boiled egg, minced
Creamy Dill Dressing (page 73)

1. Tear the spinach into bite-size pieces and place in a large bowl.

2. Separate the onion into rings and slice in half any that are too large. Add to the spinach.

3. Add the mushrooms and minced hard-boiled egg, and toss.

4. Just before serving pour on the salad dressing and toss.

Garden Salad with Creamy Garlic Tofu Dressing

You need a crunchy mixture of vegetables to hold up to this dense, creamy dressing, and that's just what this salad provides. I like these flavors and textures so much that I sometimes stuff this salad into pita bread to make a pocket sandwich.

SERVES 4 TO 6

1 medium head romaine lettuce, washed and spun dry
1 medium carrot, grated
1 small cucumber, peeled and sliced
2 scallions, sliced into 1-inch lengths
2 ounces alfalfa sprouts
¼ cup sunflower seeds (preferably roasted)
Creamy Garlic Tofu Dressing (page 72)

1. Tear the lettuce into bite-size pieces and put into a large bowl together with the carrot, cucumber, and scallions. Toss thoroughly.

2. Serve the salad in individual bowls and top each serving with alfalfa sprouts and sunflower seeds. Pass the salad dressing at the table in a sauceboat.

Fresh Pea Salad Rémoulade

I love to eat fresh peas raw; they are so sweet and delicate, and have a delightful crunchiness. The pungency of this dressing provides a nice contrast, making this salad very special.

SERVES 4   ▶ **INFORMAL MENU 3**

⅓ cup Mayonnaise (page 298)
1 teaspoon Dijon mustard
2 tablespoons minced red onion
1 teaspoon capers
½ teaspoon minced fresh tarragon, or ¼ teaspoon dried tarragon, crumbled
1 tablespoon minced fresh parsley plus additional parsley for garnish
Freshly ground pepper to taste
1 cup freshly shelled raw peas (1 pound whole peas)
½ head green or red leaf lettuce, washed and spun dry
1½ tablespoons lemon juice
⅓ cup olive oil
Salt and freshly ground pepper to taste

1. In a medium bowl combine the mayonnaise and mustard and beat until smooth. Add the onion, capers, tarragon, parsley, and freshly ground pepper. Stir to mix.

2. Add the peas, stir, and set aside.

3. Tear the lettuce into small pieces and place in a large bowl.

4. In a small bowl combine the lemon juice, olive oil, and salt and pepper to taste. Mix well. Pour onto the lettuce leaves and toss until well coated.

5. Place equal portions of the lettuce on 4 small serving plates. Top each portion with a mound of the pea mixture. Garnish with minced parsley. Serve immediately.

Mango and Avocado Salad with Raspberry Vinaigrette

Mango and avocado complement each other nicely in this delectable salad. The avocado is blanketed with the vinaigrette while the mango adds a sweet contrast. If you aren't familiar with mangoes, this is a good way to become acquainted. When ripe, they will be tender to the touch and will have a rose or yellow blush on them.

SERVES 4   ▶ **ELEGANT MENU 3**

VINAIGRETTE

3 tablespoons Raspberry Vinegar (page 301) or red wine vinegar
⅓ cup olive oil
¼ teaspoon salt
Freshly ground pepper to taste

2 ripe avocados (preferably Hass, or black pebbled-skin variety)
1 ripe mango
8 red leaf lettuce leaves, washed and patted or spun dry
¼ cup thinly sliced red onion

1. To make the vinaigrette put the vinegar, oil, salt, and pepper in a small jar with a tight-fitting cover, and shake vigorously. Pour the vinaigrette into a medium bowl.

2. Cut the avocados in half vertically. Remove the seeds and discard. Insert the handle of a teaspoon between the skin and the flesh of each avocado and gently move it all around the circumference until the flesh is free from the skin. Slice each half into 4 lengthwise slices, then add the slices to the vinaigrette. Toss gently to coat well.

3. Peel the mango with a small sharp knife. The seed of the mango does not free itself from the flesh as the avocado seed does, so cut 12 lengthwise slices cutting toward the seed, then gently cut them away from the seed.

4. Lay 2 lettuce leaves on each of 4 serving plates. Remove the avocado from the vinaigrette and alternate slices of avocado and mango (4 avocado, 3 mango) on the lettuce leaves. Sprinkle on a horizontal row of the onion. Pour an equal amount of the vinaigrette over each serving. Serve immediately.

Mango and Avocado Salad with Raspberry Vinaigrette

Avocado and Bathed Bread Vinaigrette

The combined flavors of the perfectly ripe avocado and thin slices of toasted French bread in this garlicky vinaigrette are incomparable. Black pebbly skinned Hass avocados are the best variety because they are the creamiest.

SERVES 4 ▶ **INFORMAL MENU 2**

½ cup Classic Vinaigrette (page 71)
2 cloves garlic, minced
6 slices French bread (about ¼ inch thick)
2 ripe medium avocados (preferably Hass, or black pebbled-skin variety)

1. In a small bowl mix the vinaigrette with the minced garlic and set aside.

2. Toast the French bread slices until golden on both sides. Cut each slice into 1-inch strips, then into bite-size pieces.

3. Slice the avocado in half vertically and remove the pit. Insert the handle of a teaspoon between the skin and flesh of each avocado half and move it around the avocado until the flesh is released from the skin. Discard the skin.

4. Arrange 4 small serving plates in front of you. Allow half an avocado for each person. Slice each half into 6 slices and arrange them on the serving plate with equally divided pieces of toasted French bread.

5. Drizzle the vinaigrette equally over the 4 portions and let sit for 5 minutes before serving.

Asparagus Vinaigrette

I have tried all methods of preparing asparagus to ensure even cooking—dicing the stalks, tying them together with a string and cooking them upright, cutting a cross in the stalks to encourage quicker cooking, etc., and none of them has ever been satisfactory to me; the bottom half of the asparagus still remains slightly tough. The one foolproof method to ensure tender, evenly cooked asparagus is to peel the bottom half of each one with a paring knife—not a vegetable peeler. Although you do lose some nutrients by peeling away that top layer, you gain by being able to use almost the whole asparagus.

SERVES 4   ▶ **INFORMAL MENU 9**

1 pound asparagus

VINAIGRETTE
⅓ cup olive oil
1½ tablespoons red wine vinegar
2 cloves garlic, minced
½ teaspoon Dijon mustard
¼ teaspoon salt
Liberal seasoning freshly ground pepper

1 hard-boiled egg yolk, minced

1. Cut off only the very tough bottoms on the asparagus, and with a sharp paring knife carefully peel the bottom half of each one. Bring about 1 inch of water to a boil in a large skillet, lay the asparagus in the water, and cover the pan. Cook for about 4 to 5 minutes, or until tender but not mushy. (They will continue to cook a little more while cooling.) Drain very well and arrange on a large serving platter or on individual serving dishes.

2. To make the vinaigrette combine all of the dressing ingredients in a jar with a tight-fitting lid and shake vigorously. Pour over the asparagus and refrigerate, uncovered, until chilled.

3. When ready to serve, roll the asparagus spears around in the dressing to coat them, then sprinkle the egg yolk over them in a horizontal strip. Serve cool or at room temperature—not cold.

Cucumber and Grated Carrot Salad in Creamy Dill Dressing

Here is a simple, refreshing salad that is a nice change from a traditional lettuce-based salad. It's all about the crunch.

SERVES 4 ▶ QUICK MENU 4

2 medium cucumbers
2 medium carrots
Creamy Dill Dressing (page 73)

1. Peel the cucumbers and slice them in half lengthwise. Scoop out the seeds with a spoon and discard them. Slice the cucumbers into ¼-inch-thick slices and divide them equally among serving plates.

2. Peel the carrots and grate them.

3. Drizzle the dill dressing over the cucumbers and top each serving with grated carrot.

Spicy Cucumber Salad

Here's another cucumber salad; this one goes particularly well with Asian meals. This is a very simple salad with a delicious, piquant sauce. You could improvise by substituting for one of the cucumbers a red bell pepper or some crisp snow peas, if you'd like.

SERVES 4 ▶ QUICK MENU 9

DRESSING

    1 tablespoon tamari or other soy sauce
    1 tablespoon Chinese rice vinegar (or white vinegar)
    1 tablespoon peanut oil
    1 teaspoon sugar
    2 teaspoons Asian sesame oil Ⓖ
    Dash Tabasco

    3 medium cucumbers

1. Mix the dressing ingredients together in a medium bowl.

2. Peel the cucumbers. Cut in half lengthwise and scoop out the seeds with a spoon. Discard the seeds. Slice the cucumbers ½ inch thick.

3. Add to the dressing and toss very well. Serve immediately, or chill and let marinate for up to 2 hours. Don't marinate any longer or the cucumbers will get soggy.

Marinated Tofu, Cucumber, and Radish Salad

Cold tofu is delicious when marinated in a flavorful sauce and mixed with crunchy vegetables. It is not often that you get protein in the salad course and with so little effort.

SERVES 4 ▶ SUMMER MENU 5

½ pound firm tofu, cut into ¾-inch cubes
2 cucumbers
8 radishes, thinly sliced
1 tablespoon tamari or other soy sauce
2 tablespoons Chinese rice vinegar (or other vinegar)
2 tablespoons peanut oil
½ teaspoon sugar
Freshly ground pepper to taste

1. Half-fill a medium saucepan with water and bring to a boil. Toss in the tofu and blanch for 1 minute. (This improves its texture.) Remove with a slotted spoon to paper towels to drain. Let cool. Put in a medium serving bowl.

2. Peel the cucumbers. Slice in half lengthwise and scrape out the seeds. Discard them. Cut each half in half again lengthwise and slice into ½-inch-thick pieces. Add to the tofu, along with the radishes, and toss.

3. Mix together the remaining ingredients and pour over the tofu mixture. Toss well. Cover and chill up to an hour before serving; the salad gets too soggy if left any longer. Serve cool, not cold.

Marinated Vegetables with Sesame Dressing

The current popularity and widespread availability of Asian sesame oil is a great boon for sesame lovers like me. In this salad it has a pronounced—though not overpowering—flavor and provides a welcome change from the more common garlic-herb flavors of many marinated dishes.

SERVES 6   ▶ SUMMER MENU 8

DRESSING
    3 tablespoons Chinese rice vinegar (or other vinegar)
    2 tablespoons tamari or other soy sauce
    2 tablespoons peanut oil
    1 tablespoon Asian sesame oil Ⓖ
    1 clove garlic, minced
    ¼ teaspoon dried red pepper flakes
    ¼ teaspoon sugar

    3 medium carrots, cut diagonally into ⅛-inch slices
    2 medium cucumbers
    2 large red bell peppers, cored and cut into 1-inch squares
    3 ounces fresh snow peas, strings removed, cut into 1-inch pieces
    1 tablespoon sesame seeds
    3 scallions, cut diagonally into ⅛-inch slices

1. Put the dressing ingredients in a jar with a tight-fitting lid and shake vigorously.

2. Bring a medium pot of water to a boil. Blanch the carrots in boiling water for 4 minutes, or until tender yet still crunchy. Cool under running water, then pat very dry. Put in a medium to large serving bowl.

3. Peel the cucumbers and slice them in half lengthwise. With a small spoon scrape out the seeds and discard them. Cut the cucumbers into slices ¼ inch thick and add to the serving bowl.

4. Add the red pepper squares and snow peas and toss. Add half the dressing and toss to coat well. Cover and chill at least 2 hours and up to 48 hours. Keep the remaining dressing at room temperature. *(Note: If you are going to make this more than 2 hours in advance, don't add the sliced cucumbers until 2 hours before serving.)*

5. Meanwhile, toast the sesame seeds in a small saucepan over medium heat until they begin to get fragrant. Stir often and do not let them burn.

6. Before serving add the sliced scallions and the remaining dressing and toss well. Garnish with the sesame seeds. Serve cool, not cold.

Fresh Mozzarella, Roasted Pepper, and Black Olive Salad

Fresh Mozzarella, Roasted Pepper, and Black Olive Salad

This "salad" has an intriguing array of flavors and textures. Roasting the peppers until the skin is charred provides a nice smokiness, contrasting with the sweetness of the mozzarella and the saltiness of the olives.

SERVES 4   ▶ INFORMAL MENU 13

1 large red bell pepper
1 large green bell pepper
8 ounces fresh mozzarella cheese
16 black olives (preferably kalamata)
2 teaspoons minced fresh oregano or 1 teaspoon dried
Freshly ground pepper to taste
¼ cup plus 2 tablespoons olive oil (preferably extra virgin)

1. Roast the bell peppers on a long-handled fork over a gas flame or on the burner of an electric stove until they are blackened. (Or you can put them on a cookie sheet and broil until charred.) Place them in a paper or plastic bag, tightly closed, for 10 minutes; the steam will make the skin peel off more easily. Under cold running water scrape off the skin with your fingers or a knife, then core the peppers and cut into strips about ¾ inch wide.

2. Slice the mozzarella into thin slices.

3. On 4 serving plates or 1 large platter place the pepper strips, mozzarella slices, and olives in a nice arrangement. Sprinkle the oregano and ground pepper evenly over everything, then drizzle on the olive oil. Let sit for 30 minutes at room temperature before serving in order to soften the oregano and let it absorb some of the olive oil.

Moroccan Tomato and Roasted Pepper Salad

I became interested in Moroccan cooking after reading Paula Wolfert's recipes and writings on Moroccan food. This colorful "salad" has a refreshing soupy consistency and is redolent of cumin and lemon.

SERVES 6 ▶ ELEGANT MENU 10

3 medium green bell peppers
5 medium ripe tomatoes, peeled, seeded, and cubed Ⓖ
2 tablespoons minced onion
¼ teaspoon dried red pepper flakes
2 cloves garlic, minced
2 tablespoons minced fresh parsley
Juice of 1 lemon
¼ cup olive oil
1 teaspoon ground cumin
Salt to taste
Freshly ground pepper to taste

1. Roast the green peppers over the flame on a gas stove or on the burner of an electric stove until the skin is evenly charred. (Roasting the peppers under the broiler cooks them too much for this dish.) Place them in a plastic or paper bag, close it, and let them sit for 10 minutes to facilitate removing the skin. Scrape the skin off with a knife under cold running water, then pat the peppers very dry. Core them, cut into bite-size pieces, and put in a medium bowl.

2. Add all of the remaining ingredients and toss gently. Marinate at least 1 hour before serving and serve at room temperature. If you are going to marinate the salad longer, cover and chill, and bring to room temperature before serving. Because of its soupy consistency, I like to serve this salad in bowls, although it is traditionally eaten with the fingers.

New Potato and Dill Salad

New potatoes are not a variety of potato but are any tiny, waxy potatoes that have been freshly dug. I prefer red-skinned for this salad because of their decorative color, although you could substitute any round white boiling potato with successful results.

SERVES 6 ▶ SUMMER MENU 8

3 pounds red-skinned new potatoes (about 13 small to medium)
¼ cup hot Vegetable Stock (page 290)
3 scallions, thinly sliced

DRESSING
¼ cup red wine vinegar
1 teaspoon Dijon mustard
⅔ cup olive oil
1 teaspoon salt
Freshly ground pepper to taste
1 clove garlic, minced
¼ cup coarsely chopped fresh dill

1. Scrub the potatoes very well with a vegetable brush. Leaving the skin on, cut each one in half. (If some are considerably larger than others, cut them so that the pieces are of equal size.)

2. Bring a large (6-quart) pot of water to a boil. Add the potatoes and cook, covered, for about 25 minutes, or until they are tender—not mushy—when carefully pierced with a knife. Drain in a colander.

3. Cut each potato piece into bite-size pieces and put in a large serving bowl. Pour on the hot vegetable stock and toss gently. Add the sliced scallions and toss again.

4. Mix all of the ingredients in a medium jar with a tight-fitting lid. Shake vigorously. Pour the dressing over the potatoes and toss carefully but thoroughly. Cover and chill for about 30 minutes before serving. Serve cool or at room temperature, but not cold.

NOTE: If you make this dish a day in advance be sure to bring it near room temperature before serving, and taste to adjust the seasonings.

Mixed Vegetable Slaw

Mixed Vegetable Slaw

Here is a delicious grated raw vegetable salad made primarily with cabbage and winter squash (I prefer butternut). This salad has a crunchy texture, sweet flavor, and brilliant color, and I think it is far superior to traditional cole slaw.

SERVES 6 TO 8

3 cups grated butternut (or Hubbard) squash (about 1 pound)
3 cups finely shredded cabbage
1 medium to large carrot, grated
1 medium green bell pepper, finely shredded or julienned by hand (not on a grater)
1 cup raisins

DRESSING
1 cup Mayonnaise (page 298)
⅔ cup plain yogurt
2 teaspoons sugar
2 teaspoons Raspberry Vinegar (page 301) or red wine vinegar
½ teaspoon salt
Freshly ground pepper to taste

1. Mix the squash, cabbage, carrot, green pepper, and raisins together in a large bowl.

2. Mix the ingredients for the dressing in a small bowl and pour onto the vegetable mixture. Toss to coat well, cover, and chill for at least 1 hour before serving.

NOTE: If you prefer larger pieces of vegetables in your slaw, use a mandoline to cut the squash into very thin ribbons, as shown in the photo opposite.

Summer Fruit Salad

A luscious fruit salad that develops a beautiful rosy color as it sits. You can improvise, but I have found this to be the best combination of fruits. It is great for dessert, breakfast, or a light lunch.

SERVES 6

SAUCE

2 cups plain yogurt
3 tablespoons honey
¾ teaspoon cinnamon

½ pint strawberries, hulled and halved
2 ripe bananas, sliced ½ inch thick
½ pint blueberries
2 ripe peaches, peeled and sliced ½ inch thick
½ ripe cantaloupe, cut into ½-inch cubes

1. In a large bowl combine the ingredients for the sauce and mix well.

2. Set aside 6 strawberry halves for garnish. Toss the remaining strawberries and the other fruit with the sauce. Chill for at least 1 hour before serving and up to 24 hours. Serve each portion garnished with a strawberry half.

Simple Salad with Lemon-Soy Dressing

This is a light and simple salad with an aromatic, piquant dressing, tossed at the last minute with a sprinkling of Parmesan cheese and garnished with red onion rings.

SERVES 4　　　　　　　　　　　　　　　　　　　　▶ INFORMAL MENU 4

1 small head romaine lettuce, or ½ large head, thoroughly washed and spun dry

DRESSING (MAKES ⅔ CUP)
2 cloves garlic, minced
2 tablespoons lemon juice (about ½ lemon)
1 teaspoon tamari or other soy sauce
½ cup olive oil
Dash salt
Freshly ground pepper

¼ cup grated Parmesan cheese
1 small red onion, sliced

1. Tear the lettuce into small pieces and place in a large bowl.

2. Combine the garlic, lemon juice, soy sauce, oil, salt, and pepper in a jar with a tight-fitting lid. Shake vigorously. *Extra dressing may be kept covered in the refrigerator for up to 1 week.* Pour on the salad. Toss until well coated. Add the Parmesan cheese and gently toss again.

3. Separate the rings of the onion slices and garnish the salad with these rings. Serve immediately.

Mixed Green Salad

Let your imagination and what's in the market (or garden) determine what will be put into this salad. Try the less known greens, such as Belgian endive, watercress, arugula, radicchio, and alfalfa sprouts.

SERVES 4

8 cups mixed salad greens (such as red and green leaf lettuces, romaine lettuce, spinach, watercress, and arugula), rinsed, spun dry, and torn into bite-size pieces
½ cup slivered red onion
1 large carrot, grated

A combination of any of the following:
thinly sliced zucchini
Belgian endive, separated into leaves
radicchio, leaves torn in half
alfalfa sprouts

Dressing: Classic Vinaigrette (page 71); Creamy Garlic Tofu Dressing (page 72); or Creamy Dill Dressing (page 73)
¼ cup crumbled blue cheese (optional)

1. Put the greens in a large salad bowl and add the onion, carrot, and whatever else you choose.

2. Just before serving pour on half of the dressing and toss well. If more is needed add some more, but be sure not to overdo it or you will have a soggy salad.

3. Sprinkle on the blue cheese if desired. Serve immediately on individual salad plates.

Classic Vinaigrette

Here's an all-purpose vinaigrette that has a perfect balance of flavors.

MAKES ABOUT 1 CUP

> 3 tablespoons red wine vinegar
> 1 teaspoon Dijon mustard
> 2 cloves garlic, minced
> ¾ cup olive oil
> Salt to taste
> Freshly ground pepper to taste

Put all of the ingredients into a jar with a screw top and shake well. *May be kept covered in the refrigerator for up to 1 week.*

Creamy Garlic Tofu Dressing or Dip

The texture of tofu changes dramatically when it is puréed in the blender and makes an unusually smooth and flavorful salad dressing, dip, or sandwich spread.

MAKES 1½ CUPS   ▶ QUICK MENU 2

....

½ pound firm or soft tofu, patted dry
2 tablespoons lemon juice (about ½ lemon)
¼ cup olive oil
4 tablespoons water (use only 2 for the dip or spread)
1 tablespoon tamari or other soy sauce
2 to 3 cloves garlic, chopped

1. Place all of the ingredients in a blender or food processor and purée until very smooth. (Use more or less garlic depending on your taste.) You may need to turn off the machine and scrape down the sides a few times.

2. If too thick for salad dressing, then add a little more water until desired consistency is reached. *May be kept covered in the refrigerator for up to 4 days.*

Creamy Dill Dressing

In produce stands now fresh dill is nearly as commonplace as fresh parsley. This is fortunate because dill loses much of its flavor when dried. I love to use it in salads, breads, dips, marinades, and spreads, so I try to always have some on hand. The most convenient way to do this, I have found, is to wash it and gently pat it very dry (or spin dry), then tear the feathery part from its stem (discard the stems), and keep it chilled in a covered container until ready to use. It will last 5 to 7 days this way.

MAKES 1 CUP ▶ QUICK MENU 4

½ cup plain yogurt
½ cup Mayonnaise (page 298)
1 teaspoon red wine vinegar
2 teaspoons olive oil
1 clove garlic, minced
1 tablespoon minced fresh dill
Freshly ground pepper to taste

Mix all of the ingredients together in a medium bowl until well blended. Chill until ready to use. *May be kept covered in the refrigerator for up to 1 week.*

MORE OFTEN THAN NOT, SUMMERTIME IS WHEN I'LL serve a main-course salad. I can do the cooking in the morning to avoid heating up the kitchen during the hottest time of day, and I appreciate the lightness of these meals when

Main-Course Salads

the weather is hot. Another time that I turn to these entrée salads is when I need a dish for a potluck dinner. They travel well and are popular with vegetarians and meat eaters alike. It is easy to round out the meal with some good crusty bread.

Curried Rice Salad with Apples and Cashews

This is a stunning, beautifully colored salad served on contrasting spinach leaves and topped with toasted coconut. It would make a wonderful luncheon, dinner, or buffet dish.

SERVES 4 ► SUMMER MENU 1

1½ cups brown rice, cooked and well chilled (about 4 cups cooked, page 292)
⅓ cup raisins
½ cup raw cashews, toasted*
1 medium carrot, very thinly sliced
1 small firm, tart apple (such as Granny Smith or Jonagold), cored and diced

DRESSING
½ cup plain yogurt
½ cup Mayonnaise (page 298)
2 teaspoons curry powder
2 cloves garlic, minced
½ teaspoon minced fresh ginger
Dash cayenne pepper

3 cups fresh spinach leaves, washed and stemmed
⅓ cup Classic Vinaigrette (page 71)
¼ cup unsweetened dried coconut, toasted**

Raw cashews may be toasted in a moderate (350°F) oven for 10 to 15 minutes, or until lightly browned. Otherwise dry-roasted, unsalted cashews may be used.

**To toast coconut place in a saucepan and heat over medium heat. Toss often until it is fragrant and begins to get lightly browned. Be careful not to burn it.*

1. In a large serving bowl toss the cold cooked rice, raisins, cashews, carrot, and apple together, mixing well.

2. In a medium bowl mix together thoroughly the yogurt, mayonnaise, curry powder, garlic, ginger, and cayenne pepper. Add to the rice mixture and toss to coat. Taste to correct seasoning; it may need salt. Chill at least 2 hours before serving.

3. Just before serving toss the spinach with the vinaigrette to coat lightly. Serve the rice salad on a bed of spinach either on one large platter or on individual serving plates. Garnish with the toasted coconut.

Cold Sesame Noodles with Broccoli and Cashews

This is my version of the traditional Chinese dish. Because it is so rich and satisfying, I prefer to serve it as a main course as one would serve other pasta salads.

SERVES 4 ▶ SUMMER MENU 5

1 bunch broccoli, florets only, cut into small pieces
12 ounces thin spaghetti or vermicelli
1 tablespoon plus 1 teaspoon Asian sesame oil Ⓖ
¾ cup unsalted roasted cashews (see Notes)
⅓ cup Asian sesame paste Ⓖ
2 teaspoons hot spicy oil Ⓖ
3 tablespoons tamari or other soy sauce
1 tablespoon Chinese rice vinegar (or other vinegar)
¼ cup peanut oil
4 cloves garlic, minced

1. In a medium saucepan bring water to a boil and blanch the broccoli for 2 minutes. Drain and immerse in cold water until thoroughly cold. Pat dry with a towel until very dry and set aside.

2. Boil the noodles for a few minutes, or until al dente. Drain in a colander very well and pat with paper towels. Place the noodles in a large serving bowl and add 1 teaspoon of the sesame oil. Toss thoroughly.

3. Add the broccoli and cashews and toss again.

4. In a separate small bowl stir the sesame paste with a fork until smooth (see Notes). Add the spicy oil, soy sauce, vinegar, remaining sesame oil, peanut oil, and garlic, and stir to blend.

5. Add the sauce to the noodles and toss well. The salad can be served immediately, or covered and chilled for up to 48 hours. Serve cool, not cold.

> NOTES: You can use raw cashews and toast them in the oven (400°F) until golden. When you purchase sesame paste it will probably have separated in the jar. It is best to put all of it in a bowl and whisk until smooth. Return it to the jar and measure the amount needed.

Wild Rice and Artichoke Salad

Wild rice, though very tasty, is also very expensive, so I save it for special occasions and stretch it a bit by cooking it with brown rice. Although this salad does not take a lot of time to prepare, you should cook the rice in the morning or the night before so it can get thoroughly chilled.

SERVES 4 ▶ SUMMER MENU 9

¾ cup wild rice

¾ cup brown rice, rinsed

3 cups water

1 tablespoon oil

½ teaspoon salt

One 6-ounce jar marinated artichoke hearts, drained and halved

1 red bell pepper, cored and cut into ½-inch pieces

3 scallions, thinly sliced

1 medium carrot, very thinly sliced

DRESSING

⅔ cup olive oil

3 tablespoons red wine vinegar

1 teaspoon Dijon mustard

1 clove garlic, minced

½ teaspoon poultry seasoning

1 teaspoon dried thyme

¼ teaspoon dried basil

¼ teaspoon dried oregano

½ teaspoon salt

Liberal seasoning freshly ground pepper

1 small head leaf lettuce (such as Boston or red or green leaf), washed, dried, and torn into bite-size pieces)

1. Rinse the wild rice in a strainer under cold running water. Put in a medium bowl and pour on boiling water to cover. Let soak for 30 minutes, then drain thoroughly.

2. Rinse the brown rice in a strainer and put in a medium saucepan along with the drained wild rice, 3 cups of water, oil, and salt. Cover and bring to a boil. Reduce the heat to a simmer and cook until all of the liquid is absorbed, about 45 minutes. Do not stir the rice at any time. When done put in a large bowl and chill until very cold, about 2 hours.

3. When the rice is cold add the artichokes, red pepper, scallions, and carrot, and toss well.

4. To make the marinade combine all of the dressing ingredients in a jar with a tight-fitting lid and shake vigorously. Pour over the salad and toss well. Chill for 2 hours or up to 24 hours. To serve, arrange equal portions of lettuce on 4 large plates and mound on the rice salad.

Tabbouleh

Traditional tabbouleh is more like a parsley and mint salad with a little bulgur thrown in. I prefer to let the bulgur dominate and have the herbs play a supporting role. This nutritious and substantial salad has just the right balance to me.

SERVES 6 TO 8   ▶ ELEGANT MENU 6

1½ cups bulgur **G**
2 medium tomatoes, seeded and very finely diced
3 tablespoons minced fresh parsley
3 scallions, thinly sliced
3 tablespoons minced fresh mint
3 tablespoons lemon juice
½ cup olive oil
Salt to taste
Freshly ground pepper to taste
12 to 16 small lettuce leaves (such as Boston or red or green leaf)

1. Rinse the bulgur in a sieve under cold running water. Empty it into a medium bowl and cover with boiling water by 2 inches. Let soak for 30 minutes, or until tender when tasted.

2. Line a sieve with cheesecloth and drain the bulgur into it. (This might have to be done in batches.) Bring up the edges of the cheesecloth and squeeze to extract all of the moisture.

3. Put the bulgur into a mixing bowl and add all of the remaining ingredients except the lettuce, Toss to blend thoroughly. Cover and chill for at least 1 hour and up to 48 hours. To serve, arrange 2 lettuce leaves on each small serving plate and spoon on the tabbouleh.

Bulgur Salad with Tarragon and Vegetables

This bulgur salad is filled with vegetables and is milder, though no less delicious, than herb-filled tabbouleh.

SERVES 4

1½ cups bulgur Ⓖ
1 cup (4 ounces) diced green beans
2 cups (6 ounces) sliced mushrooms
½ tablespoon butter
1 red bell pepper, cored and cut into ½-inch pieces
1 scallion, thinly sliced
2 tablespoons minced fresh parsley

DRESSING

½ cup olive oil
2 tablespoons red wine vinegar
3 cloves garlic, minced
2 teaspoons minced fresh tarragon
¼ teaspoon dried oregano
½ teaspoon salt
Freshly ground pepper to taste

Mesclun (optional)

1. Rinse the bulgur in a sieve under cold running water, then place in a medium bowl and pour boiling water over it to cover by 2 inches. Soak for 30 minutes, or until tender when tasted. Drape a cheesecloth over a sieve and pour in some of the bulgur. Gather up the edges of the cheesecloth and squeeze out all the moisture from the bulgur. Dump it out into a large bowl and repeat with the remainder.

2. Steam the green beans until tender but still slightly crunchy, about 10 minutes. Cool under cold running water then pat dry. Add to the bulgur. Sauté the mushrooms in the butter and add to the bulgur. Add the red pepper, scallion, and parsley, and stir to mix.

3. Place all of the dressing ingredients in a small jar with a tight-fitting lid and shake well. Pour over the bulgur mixture and toss until well coated.

4. Chill at least 2 hours and up to 24 hours. Taste to correct the seasoning before serving. Serve as is or on a bed of mesclun.

Tomatoes Stuffed with White Beans and Pesto

Creamy-textured white beans cloaked in fragrant pesto are offset by the welcome acidity of juicy tomatoes. Use perfectly fresh ripe summer tomatoes that are both flavorful and tender for this dish.

SERVES 4   ▶ SUMMER MENU 6

16-ounce can white beans (Great Northern or navy), drained and rinsed
½ cup Pesto (page 296) or Winter Pesto (page 297)
¼ teaspoon salt
Freshly ground pepper to taste
½ medium red onion, minced, plus 1 tablespoon for garnish
½ celery rib, minced
4 large ripe tomatoes

1. Toss the beans in a medium bowl with the pesto, salt, pepper, onion, and celery. Taste to adjust the seasoning. Chill for at least 1 hour, or until cold.

2. Meanwhile slice off the top of each tomato and scoop out the pulp with a spoon. Discard. Invert the tomatoes on a plate and allow to drain.

3. Stuff equal amounts of the bean mixture into each tomato. Garnish with the remaining onion.

NOTE: You can prepare this dish in advance and refrigerate it, covered, but be sure to remove it 30 minutes before serving. Tomatoes lose their flavor if served cold.

Marinated Pasta and Vegetable Salad

I like the mixture of whole wheat and white pasta in this salad; the whole wheat rotini adds extra flavor and nutrients. You could substitute all white rotini with successful results, but I don't recommend using all whole wheat because its flavor is too strong. Whenever I have served this salad to a large crowd, it has been very popular. Children are attracted to it because of the playful shape of the rotini, which entices them to eat it with their fingers.

SERVES 6 ▶ SUMMER MENU 4

½ pound whole wheat rotini (short spiral-shaped pasta)*
½ pound white rotini
3 cups sliced mushrooms
1 tablespoon olive oil
3 cups broccoli florets**
1 cup peas (fresh or frozen)
15 cherry tomatoes
½ cup chopped fresh parsley
¼ cup finely diced red onion

DRESSING

⅔ cup olive oil
3 tablespoons red wine vinegar
4 cloves garlic, minced
½ teaspoon dried basil
¼ teaspoon dried oregano
¼ teaspoon dried tarragon, crumbled
¼ teaspoon dried red pepper flakes
1 teaspoon salt
Liberal seasoning freshly ground pepper

One-half pound of rotini is about 3½ cups uncooked. Whole wheat rotini can be purchased at health food stores and some specialty food shops.

**The broccoli stalks can be used in Lemon-Glazed Broccoli Stalks Julienne (page 221).*

1. Cook both pastas together in a large pot of rapidly boiling water until al dente. Drain in a colander and run under cold water. Drain again thoroughly, then put into a large serving bowl.

2. Sauté the mushrooms in the olive oil until tender and brown, then add to the pasta and toss.

3. Steam the broccoli until tender yet still bright green. Immerse in cold water to stop further cooking, then drain very well. Pat dry with a towel and add to the pasta.

4. If you are using fresh peas, steam them just until tender, about 5 minutes, or add them raw for a nice touch if they are particularly young and sweet. If you are using frozen peas thoroughly defrost them, or place in a sieve and pour hot water over them; they do not need further cooking. Pat dry, then add to the pasta.

5. Add the cherry tomatoes, parsley, and onion and mix well.

6. Combine all of the ingredients for the dressing in a jar with a tight-fitting lid and shake vigorously. Pour onto the pasta and toss until well coated. Cover and chill for 2 hours or up to 48 hours. Bring to room temperature before serving.

Tempeh Salade Niçoise

This salad, like traditional Salade Niçoise, is a meal in itself. In France, much to my bewilderment, I was often served Salade Niçoise packed in a bowl with its dressing on the side. Served in such a manner it is impossible to toss, or to get at the lettuce without causing the toppings to land in your lap and the olives to roll across the table. To prevent such a disaster in my home, I like to arrange it decoratively on large dinner plates and pour on the dressing before serving it. See if you agree.

SERVES 4   ▶ SUMMER MENU 3

8 ounces tempeh Ⓖ, cut into ½-inch cubes
1½ cups Classic Vinaigrette (page 71)
2 tablespoons Mayonnaise (page 298)
1½ cups diced green beans
1 large head lettuce (Boston, green or red leaf, Bibb, or other soft lettuce),
    washed and spun dry
2 hard-boiled eggs, minced or quartered
1 small red onion, sliced
2 medium ripe tomatoes
16 to 20 black olives (preferably kalamata)
2 teaspoons capers
1 cup alfalfa sprouts

1. Steam the tempeh in a vegetable steamer for 20 minutes. Put in a medium bowl and toss with ¼ cup of the vinaigrette, then toss with the mayonnaise and chill for at least 20 minutes.

2. Blanch the green beans in boiling water for 3 minutes, or until tender yet slightly crunchy. Drain and cool thoroughly in cold water. Drain again, pat dry, then toss with 2 tablespoons of the vinaigrette.

3. Tear the lettuce into bite-size pieces and divide evenly among 4 dinner plates. Mound one-quarter of the tempeh in the center of each plate.

4. Evenly divide and decoratively arrange the green beans, hard-boiled eggs, onion, tomatoes, and olives on each plate. Top with the capers and sprouts. Drizzle some of the remaining vinaigrette over, and serve immediately with the remaining dressing alongside.

HAVING A COLLECTION OF WONDERFUL SOUP RECIPES is essential for the serious home cook. On a cold fall or winter evening, sometimes a meal of soup, salad, and bread is the only choice that will warm your bones. A good vegetable stock as the base for many soups is necessary, but it needn't

Soups and Stews

be made from scratch if time is an issue. There are now many store-bought organic vegetable stocks that will work well, and there are also powdered vegetable stock bases that can be purchased in natural food markets that will create a good stock. The chilled soups in this chapter are delightful in the summer months when you want light food that requires minimal time in a hot kitchen. Think of them when you want to supplement a main-course salad meal, or serve them with a favorite sandwich.

Iced Plum Soup

Choose sweet, flavorful plums for this soup and allow them to get perfectly ripe. I often take this on a picnic, transporting it in a glass jar with a screw top and then serving it in cups.

SERVES 4 AS A FIRST COURSE   ▶ **SUMMER MENU 3**

9 to 10 ripe plums (about 2 pounds), washed
½ cup dry red wine
½ cup water
½ teaspoon ground coriander
⅛ teaspoon ground allspice
¼ teaspoon salt
1 tablespoon honey
½ cup heavy cream
1 cup sour cream
Mint sprigs for garnish

1. Fill a medium saucepan half full of water and bring to a boil. In batches blanch the plums for 10 seconds. Remove them with a slotted spoon to your work surface. Discard the water when all have been blanched. Peel the plums and put the skins in the saucepan along with the red wine and the ½ cup of water. Bring to a boil, cook 5 minutes, then remove from the heat.

2. With a slotted spoon remove the skins and put in a strainer and rest it over the pan. Press out as much liquid as you can, then discard the skins. (Cooking the skins flavors and colors the soup.)

3. Make sure the plums don't have any skin adhering to them. Cut them into bite-size pieces and discard the pits. Add them to the wine mixture along with the coriander, allspice, salt, and honey. Bring to a boil and simmer for 10 minutes.

4. In the container of the blender or food processor purée the mixture with the heavy cream. Pour into a large bowl. Chill at least 1½ hours, or until very cold.

5. Before serving whisk in the sour cream until perfectly blended. Serve chilled, garnished with a mint sprig on each serving.

Gazpacho

Nothing celebrates summer like a bowl of chilled gazpacho prepared when tomatoes are at their peak. Only the most flavorful garden specimens will do.

SERVES 6 AS A FIRST COURSE   ▶ SUMMER MENU 4

5 medium tomatoes, cored
2 medium cucumbers
1 small onion, diced
1 large green bell pepper, cored and cut into ¼-inch dice
2 cloves garlic, minced
⅓ cup red wine vinegar
⅓ cup olive oil
½ cup Vegetable Stock (page 290), tomato juice, or water
A few dashes Tabasco
Salt to taste
Freshly ground pepper to taste
Croutons (see Note)

1. Roughly chop all of the tomatoes. Peel both cucumbers and cut in half lengthwise. Remove the seeds with a teaspoon and discard them. Roughly chop 3 of the cucumber halves and add to the tomatoes along with the diced onion. In batches purée this mixture in a blender or food processor until almost smooth but not liquefied. Pour into a large serving bowl.

2. By hand finely dice the remaining cucumber half and add to the soup. Add all of the remaining ingredients except the croutons and stir to blend. Chill at least 2 hours before serving. Taste to adjust seasoning. Serve well chilled, garnished with the croutons, in individual soup bowls.

NOTE: To make croutons remove the crusts from a few slices of bread. Lightly toast them in a toaster. Rub both sides with a garlic half (you will probably need a couple of them). Then, using a pastry brush, brush both sides lightly with olive oil. Cut the bread into ½-inch cubes and lay them on a cookie sheet. Dry them out until they are crisp in a 350°F oven that has just been turned off. Toss occasionally. They will get harder as they come to room temperature.

Cold Yogurt Cucumber Soup

This Turkish soup is ideal for a summer meal because no cooking is involved and it is so refreshing and satisfying. It is also wonderful served as a first course to a Middle Eastern meal. Do use fresh dill if you can get it; it really defines the dish.

SERVES 4 AS A MAIN COURSE   ▶ SUMMER MENU 7

....

        3 cups plain yogurt
        ½ cup water
        2 medium cucumbers
        3 tablespoons olive oil
        1 tablespoon red wine vinegar
        2 cloves garlic, minced
        2 tablespoons minced fresh dill, or 1 tablespoon dried dill
        1 tablespoon minced fresh parsley
        ½ teaspoon salt
        Freshly ground pepper to taste
        ½ cup walnuts, finely chopped

1. In a large bowl whisk together the yogurt and water.

2. Peel the cucumbers and slice them in half lengthwise. Scrape out all of the seeds with a spoon and discard them. Dice the cucumbers and add to the yogurt.

3. Add all of the remaining ingredients and stir well.

4. Chill for at least 1 hour and up to 48 hours before serving.

Cold Cucumber and Watercress Soup

This classic French soup gets its body from the silkiness of the puréed cucumbers and its kick from the peppery watercress. This soup becomes more flavorful as time passes, so don't hesitate to make it 24 to 48 hours in advance.

SERVES 4 TO 6 AS A FIRST COURSE　　　　　　　　　　　▶ SUMMER MENU 6

2 tablespoons butter
2 medium onions, diced
4 medium to large cucumbers, peeled, halved lengthwise and seeded, and sliced ½ inch thick
2 cups Vegetable Stock (page 290)
2 teaspoons minced fresh tarragon, or 1 teaspoon dried tarragon, crumbled
1 teaspoon vinegar
½ teaspoon salt
Freshly ground pepper to taste
1 bunch watercress, washed and patted dry
1 cup sour cream

1. In a medium saucepan melt the butter over medium heat and sauté the onions for 5 minutes.

2. Add the sliced cucumber, vegetable stock, tarragon, vinegar, salt, and pepper. Cover the pot and bring to a boil. Cook over medium heat for 20 minutes, or until the cucumbers are very tender. Stir occasionally.

3. Meanwhile remove a few perfect-looking watercress sprigs for garnish, wrap them, and chill them until ready to use. Tear off all of the remaining watercress leaves from their stems and discard the stems. Mince the watercress leaves and set aside.

4. When the cucumbers are very tender purée the soup in a blender or food processor in batches. Pour the soup into a large bowl and stir in the minced watercress. Let cool for 15 minutes.

5. Whisk in the sour cream, and chill the soup until it is ice cold, at least 3 hours. Serve garnished with the reserved watercress sprigs.

Chilled Summer Borscht

There seem to be as many versions of borscht as there are species of plants. I like cold borscht to be smooth and spicy and topped with sour cream. My husband looks forward to this soup each summer, and so in our house this recipe serves only two!

SERVES 6 AS A FIRST COURSE   ▶ SUMMER MENU 9

8 medium beets (or two 16-ounce cans)
1 cup beet cooking liquid
1½ cups tomato purée
Juice of 2 lemons
A few dashes Tabasco
1 small onion, minced
Salt to taste
Freshly ground pepper to taste
1 cup sour cream
Minced fresh parsley for garnish

1. Cut the beet greens off the beets, leaving 1 inch of their stems attached, and leave on the root ends. This ensures that the beets won't bleed profusely and you'll get optimum color. Scrub with a vegetable brush under cold running water to remove all the dirt. If using canned beets, reserve 1 cup of beet liquid and proceed with step 3.

2. If the beets are approximately the same size, then put them in a large pot and cover with water (otherwise cook them in stages, that is, start cooking the larger ones first and add the smaller ones after a while). Bring to a boil and cook, covered, for about 1 hour, or until tender when carefully pierced with a sharp knife. Drain very well and reserve the beet liquid. Let sit until cool enough to handle, then peel them.

3. Coarsely chop the beets and put them in a blender or food processor with all of the remaining ingredients except the sour cream and parsley, and blend until smooth. If the soup is too thick add a little more of the reserved liquid. Pour into a bowl and chill very well. It is a good idea to chill your serving bowls also.

4. When ready to serve, taste to adjust the seasoning. Serve in bowls and top with a spoonful of sour cream and some minced parsley.

> NOTE: If you have fresh-looking beet greens, then serve them as a side dish at another meal. Rinse them very well, steam or sauté them, then stir in some sour cream.

Lentil Soup

A popular vegetarian soup that is high in protein and iron and low in fat. Like many soups it improves with age, so try making it the day before you plan to serve it.

SERVES 6 TO 8 AS A MAIN COURSE

3 tablespoons olive oil
2 large onions, finely diced
4 cloves garlic, minced
2 green bell peppers, finely diced
10 cups Vegetable Stock (page 290)
2 carrots, thinly sliced
1½ cups lentils, picked over and rinsed
½ teaspoon dried thyme
Liberal seasoning freshly ground pepper
1 teaspoon salt
28-ounce can imported plum tomatoes with their juice, finely chopped
10-ounce bag fresh spinach or 1 pound loose fresh spinach (stems removed), finely
    chopped; or 10-ounce package frozen chopped spinach, thawed
2 tablespoons butter

1. Heat the oil in a large stockpot over medium heat. Add the onions, garlic, and green peppers, and sauté for 10 minutes.

2. Add all of the remaining ingredients except the spinach and butter, and bring to a boil. Reduce the heat to a simmer and cook, stirring occasionally, for 45 minutes, or until the lentils are tender.

3. Add the chopped spinach and cook for 5 more minutes, or until it has wilted and become tender. Taste to adjust the seasoning and add the butter just before serving. Stir until melted.

Kale and Vegetable Soup

This meatless version of the traditional Portuguese soup Caldo Verde is both distinctive and substantial. Kale gives the soup a wonderful flavor and texture, and along with the kidney beans provides a good source of iron.

SERVES 6 AS A MAIN COURSE

½ cup olive oil
3 large onions, diced
4 cloves garlic, minced
2 bay leaves
10 cups Vegetable Stock (page 290)
16-ounce can diced tomatoes with their juice
16-ounce can kidney beans, drained and rinsed
1½ teaspoons paprika
⅛ teaspoon cayenne pepper
1½ teaspoons salt
Liberal seasoning freshly ground pepper
1 pound fresh kale (total weight with stems),* cleaned and stemmed
3 medium potatoes, unpeeled and diced
2 tablespoons butter

* Extra kale can be served another time in Sautéed Greens with Garlic (page 217).

1. In a large stockpot heat the olive oil over medium heat. Add the onions, garlic, and bay leaves, and cook for 10 minutes, stirring often.

2. Add the vegetable stock, tomatoes, kidney beans, paprika, cayenne pepper, salt, and pepper and bring to a boil.

3. If there are any coarse ribs on the kale leaves, then rip the leaves off and discard the ribs. Roughly chop the kale. You should have 8 to 10 cups.

4. Add the kale and potatoes to the soup and cook 30 minutes, or until the beans and potatoes are tender. If the soup is too thick add additional stock.

5. Remove the bay leaves and discard. To give the soup a wonderful creamy consistency remove about 2 cups of it and purée it in the blender. Return it to the pot.

6. Before serving add the butter and stir to melt.

Cauliflower and Pasta Soup

A thick, rich soup that doesn't demand much time to prepare. This soup is an exception to the soup rule in that it should not be prepared well in advance because the cauliflower and macaroni risk being overcooked and becoming mushy. Serve with a good whole-grain bread to add more protein to your meal.

SERVES 6 AS A MAIN COURSE ▶ INFORMAL MENU 16

2 tablespoons butter
¼ cup olive oil
6 cloves garlic, minced
2 medium onions, diced
2 tablespoons tomato paste
10 cups Vegetable Stock (page 290)
1 tablespoon tamari or other soy sauce
1 bay leaf
¼ teaspoon dried oregano
¼ teaspoon dried basil
¼ teaspoon dried thyme
1½ teaspoons salt
Liberal seasoning freshly ground pepper
1 medium cauliflower (2 pounds)
1 cup macaroni
2 eggs, well beaten
¼ cup minced fresh parsley
Grated Parmesan cheese

1. In a large stockpot over medium heat melt the butter with the olive oil. Add the garlic and onions, and cook for 10 minutes, stirring often.

2. Add the tomato paste and cook for 1 minute. Add the vegetable stock, soy sauce, herbs, salt, and pepper, and bring to a boil. *May be prepared to this point up to 48 hours in advance. Bring to a boil before proceeding with the next step.*

3. Cut the cauliflower into bite-size pieces. When the soup is boiling add the cauliflower and macaroni. Bring the soup to a boil again, reduce the heat, and cook for 20 minutes, or until the cauliflower and macaroni are tender, not mushy. Stir occasionally or the macaroni will stick to the bottom.

4. Raise the heat and bring the soup to a rolling boil and add the beaten eggs. Keep stirring until fine shreds form, about 30 seconds. Stir in the parsley. Serve in soup bowls with a liberal amount of grated cheese on each serving.

Curried Red Lentil Soup

This soup is quick and easy to prepare and is one of my favorites. The red lentils (actually tiny orange lentils) turn a golden color when cooked and have a rich, buttery flavor. If you have the red lentils and spices on hand, this is a fine soup to prepare on a moment's notice.

SERVES 4 AS A MAIN COURSE

1½ cups red lentils
4 cups water
1 tablespoon oil
½ teaspoon salt
2 medium potatoes, peeled and cut into ½-inch dice
4 tablespoons butter
1 medium onion, diced
2 cloves garlic, minced
1 teaspoon turmeric
1½ teaspoons ground cumin
1½ teaspoons ground coriander
⅛ teaspoon cayenne pepper
Additional butter

1. Rinse the lentils in a strainer under cold running water. Pick them over and discard any stones, etc. Put them in a medium-size saucepan along with the water, oil, and salt. Bring to a boil and cook, uncovered, for 20 minutes over medium heat. Stir occasionally. (If a lot of foam rises to the surface, scoop it off with a spoon.)

2. Add the diced potatoes and stir to blend.

3. In a small skillet melt the butter. Add the onion, garlic, and all of the spices. Cook for 3 minutes, or until the onions begin to get tender.

4. Add to the soup, stir, and cook until the potatoes are tender, about 20 more minutes. If the soup is too thick, thin with a little water.

5. Taste to correct the seasoning. Serve with a small pat of butter on each serving.

> NOTE: Although this soup is delicious if served immediately, it is more flavorful if prepared at least an hour before serving, then reheated.

Peasant Cabbage Soup

A thick, flavorful soup that is easy to prepare and would satisfy any appetite. It is served over a slice of toasted French bread and melted cheese, and finally topped with grated Parmesan cheese. For best results prepare the soup a few hours before serving to develop the flavor.

SERVES 6 AS A MAIN COURSE

½ cup olive oil
4 medium onions, diced
4 cloves garlic, minced
2 bay leaves
3 cups (8 ounces) sliced mushrooms
1 small cabbage (1½ pounds), shredded (7 to 8 cups shredded)
2 medium potatoes, unpeeled and diced
12 cups Vegetable Stock (page 290)
2 teaspoons tamari or other soy sauce
4 tablespoons butter
½ teaspoon dried thyme
1 teaspoon salt
Liberal seasoning freshly ground pepper
12 slices French bread (1 inch thick)
1 clove garlic, cut in half
3 cups (about 12 ounces) grated Gruyère or Swiss cheese
Freshly grated Parmesan cheese

1. In a large stockpot heat the olive oil over medium heat. Add the onions, garlic, and bay leaves, and cook for 10 minutes, stirring often. Add the mushrooms and cook for 10 more minutes.

2. Add all of the remaining ingredients up to the French bread. Bring to a boil, then reduce the heat to a simmer. Cook, stirring occasionally, for about 1 hour, or until the vegetables are tender.

3. Meanwhile rub the slices of the French bread with the garlic halves. Toast them under the broiler on both sides until golden. Be careful not to burn them. You can let them sit at room temperature to harden.

4. When the soup is ready to be served, taste it and adjust the seasoning. Remove the bay leaves. Place 2 slices of French bread in each serving bowl. Top with a generous amount of Swiss cheese, then ladle the soup over it. Sprinkle on some grated Parmesan cheese. Serve additional Parmesan cheese at the table.

> NOTE: If you have individual soup crocks, you can serve this as you would French onion soup. Ladle the soup into each crock, top with a slice of French bread, then Swiss cheese. Broil until melted.

Elegant Yam Soup

This sherry-scented soup is quick to make and very tasty. Its smooth texture and rich orange hue give it an elegant tone, making it an inviting first course when served at a special autumn or winter meal.

SERVES 6 AS A FIRST COURSE

3 cups Vegetable Stock (page 290)
5 large yams (about 2 pounds), peeled and diced
¾ cup heavy or whipping cream
2 tablespoons butter
¼ cup dry sherry
A few dashes cayenne pepper
Salt to taste
Freshly ground pepper to taste
Additional butter

1. Combine the vegetable stock and yams in a medium saucepan, bring to a boil, and cook until very tender, about 20 minutes.

2. In batches purée the mixture in a blender or food processor until smooth, and return it to the saucepan. Stir in the remaining ingredients and heat through. Serve piping hot with a pat of butter on each serving.

Cream of Fennel Soup

This is a smooth and creamy soup with a mild anise flavor. The fennel that is usually available in this country is the variety known as *finocchio*, or Florence fennel. It has a large bulbous root with long stalks and feathery leaves. It can be eaten raw (in salads, for example), but has a much sweeter and more delicate flavor when cooked.

SERVES 3 TO 4 AS A MAIN COURSE

3 large fennel bulbs (about 3 pounds with stalks)
5 tablespoons butter
1 medium onion, diced
1 large potato, peeled and diced
3 cups Vegetable Stock (page 290)
½ teaspoon salt
Freshly ground pepper to taste
½ cup milk
1 cup sour cream

1. Cut the tops off the fennel and reserve a few sprigs of the feathery part as a garnish for each serving. Cut the root end off the bulb, then cut each bulb into quarters. Slice the quarters into pieces ½ inch thick. You should have 8 to 9 cups.

2. In a large stockpot melt 3 tablespoons of butter over medium heat. Add the onion and sauté for 5 minutes. Add the fennel and potato and sauté for 5 more minutes, stirring often.

3. Add the vegetable stock, salt, and pepper, and bring the soup to a boil. Cover the pot, reduce the heat to a simmer, and cook for 20 to 30 minutes, or until the vegetables are very tender.

4. Purée the soup in a blender or food processor, then pour it through a medium-mesh sieve into a medium saucepan.

5. Stir in 2 tablespoons butter, and after it has blended stir in the milk. Whisk in the sour cream until blended. Taste to adjust the seasoning. Serve piping hot, with the reserved sprigs of fennel for garnish.

NOTE: Leftover fennel sprigs can be placed in a plastic bag and refrigerated for future use as a salad addition.

Pumpkin Bisque

This is a perfectly smooth soup with a delicate pumpkin flavor that is reminiscent of winter squash. Pumpkins intended for cooking should be small (preferably not over 5 pounds) to ensure a sweet flavor and smooth texture. For this soup be sure to use a good-flavored homemade or your favorite store-bought vegetable stock and include a few dashes of cayenne pepper for a hint of spiciness.

SERVES 4 AS A MAIN COURSE

1 small sugar or pie pumpkin (about 2½ pounds)
2 tablespoons butter
1 medium carrot, grated
2 medium onions, diced
2 cloves garlic, minced
½ teaspoon salt
5 cups Vegetable Stock (page 290)
A few dashes cayenne pepper
1 medium tomato
½ cup sour cream
Additional butter

1. Slice off the top and bottom of the pumpkin and set it upright. From top to bottom cut off the skin as you would cut off the peel of an orange. Cut the pumpkin in half and scoop out the seeds. Discard them. Cut the pumpkin into 1½-inch chunks.

2. In a medium saucepan melt the butter, then add the carrot, onions, and garlic, and cook for 10 minutes over medium heat.

3. Add the pumpkin, salt, vegetable stock, and cayenne pepper, cover the pan, and bring to a boil. Drop the whole tomato in for 30 seconds, then remove with a slotted spoon. Peel off the skin and discard it. Cut the tomato in half horizontally, then squeeze out the seeds and discard them. Mince the tomato and add to the soup. Reduce the heat to a simmer and cook, uncovered, for 30 minutes, or until the pumpkin is very tender.

4. Purée the soup in batches in a blender or food processor until it is very smooth. Return the soup to the pot and whisk in the sour cream. Taste to adjust the seasoning. Serve in bowls with a pat of butter on each serving.

Miso Soup

A very nutritious and attractive light soup featuring miso, the wonder food of the soybean family, that could be part of a light meal with a salad, or could serve as a first course to an Asian meal. Boiling soup with tofu is poured over fresh raw spinach, thereby quickly cooking it and allowing it to retain its bright green color.

SERVES 4 AS A MAIN COURSE ▶ ELEGANT MENU 2

¼ pound spinach (5 to 6 cups loosely packed), washed and patted dry
6 cups water
½ cup miso **G**
2 teaspoons Asian sesame oil **G**
1 tablespoon tamari or other soy sauce
Freshly ground pepper to taste
½ pound firm tofu, cut into ½-inch dice
2 scallions, very thinly sliced

1. Cut the spinach into shreds and divide it evenly among the serving bowls.

2. Bring the water to a boil in a medium saucepan. Remove about a cup of the water (a coffee mug is easy to use) and mix the miso into it until it is dissolved. (You must dilute the miso this way or it will remain lumpy.) Return the liquid to the pot and stir to blend.

3. Add the oil, tamari, and the pepper. Bring to a boil again and add the tofu. Cook 1 minute. *May be prepared to this point up to 24 hours in advance and chilled.*

4. Ladle the boiling soup into the serving bowls over the raw spinach and stir lightly. Top each serving with sliced scallions. Serve immediately.

Vegetarian Chili

This recipe can be easily doubled or tripled and, therefore, is a good choice for serving at a large informal gathering. The bulgur adds a meaty flavor and texture so be sure to include it. Try serving it with cornbread for a delicious combination.

SERVES 4 AS A MAIN COURSE　　　　　　　　　　　　　　▶ INFORMAL MENU 8

⅓ cup oil
2 large onions, diced
6 cloves garlic, minced
1 tablespoon chili powder
1 tablespoon ground cumin
1 teaspoon dried oregano
⅛ teaspoon cayenne pepper
2 bay leaves
½ cup bulgur **G**
28-ounce can diced tomatoes
Three 16-ounce cans kidney beans, drained and rinsed
1 tablespoon tamari or other soy sauce
3 cups water
1 teaspoon salt
Liberal seasoning freshly ground pepper
2 tablespoons butter
½ cup finely chopped red onion

1. In a large (6-quart) pot heat the oil. Put in the onions and garlic and sauté for 10 minutes.

2. Add the chili powder, cumin, oregano, cayenne pepper, bay leaves, and bulgur, and cook for 2 minutes (no less), stirring frequently.

3. Add the tomatoes with their juice, the kidney beans, soy sauce, water, salt, and pepper. Cook over low heat for 30 minutes, or until the chili is thick and fragrant. Stir occasionally. Just before serving add the butter and stir until melted. Taste to adjust the seasoning. If you like it spicier add a few dashes of cayenne pepper. Serve with chopped onion on each portion.

Fragrant Vegetable Stew with Corn Dumplings

This is one of my most treasured recipes, and one that my stepdaughter asks me to make for her when she wants a special treat. Buttery corn dumplings top clove-scented vegetables to make this a wonderfully fragrant and colorful stew. The dumplings take only a few minutes to prepare, so don't be dissuaded by their inclusion.

SERVES 6 AS A MAIN COURSE   ▶ INFORMAL MENU 5

¼ cup olive oil

3 medium onions, diced

3 cloves garlic, minced

2 bay leaves

4 whole cloves

¼ teaspoon cayenne pepper

10 cups Vegetable Stock (page 290)

1½ teaspoons salt

Freshly ground pepper to taste

28-ounce can diced tomatoes

¾ cup minced fresh parsley

3 medium parsnips, peeled, halved lengthwise, and thinly sliced

2 medium carrots, peeled, halved lengthwise, and thinly sliced

2 medium potatoes, peeled and cut into ½-inch dice

12-ounce box frozen baby lima beans

2 cups corn, fresh or frozen (10-ounce package)

3 tablespoons butter

DUMPLINGS

¾ cup unbleached white flour

¼ cup whole wheat flour

2 tablespoons cornmeal

2 teaspoons baking powder

½ teaspoon salt

1 teaspoon sugar

1 tablespoon chilled butter

½ cup corn, thawed if frozen

⅔ cup cold milk

1. Heat the oil in a large pot and sauté the onions and garlic for 5 minutes. Add the bay leaves, cloves, and cayenne pepper, and sauté for 1 more minute.

2. Add the vegetable stock, salt, pepper, tomatoes, ½ cup of the parsley, parsnips, carrots, potatoes, and lima beans and cook 45 minutes, or until the vegetables are tender.

3. Meanwhile prepare the dumplings. Combine the flours, cornmeal, baking powder, salt, and sugar in a medium bowl, and mix well. Cut in the butter until small crumbs are formed, then stir in the ½ cup corn and milk just until evenly moistened. Do not overmix. Cover and chill until ready to use. (The chilled batter will keep up to 24 hours.)

4. Add the 2 cups corn, 3 tablespoons of butter, and remaining ¼ cup of parsley to the stew, and cook 10 minutes more. Remove the bay leaves. *May be prepared to this point up to 24 hours in advance, covered, and chilled. Reheat to boiling before proceeding with the next step.*

5. Keeping the soup at a simmer, drop the dumpling mixture in by tablespoonfuls and cover the pot. (You'll get 6 to 8 dumplings.) Cook for 15 to 20 minutes, or until a toothpick inserted in the center of a dumpling comes out clean. Serve the stew with 1 dumpling to each bowl.

Indonesian Curried Vegetable Stew with Coconut Milk

This is a meatless version of a delicious and exquisite-looking Indonesian stew. It is bright golden yellow with flecks of green and fiery red interlaced. The coconut milk gives this a satiny smoothness, and adds a rich, faintly sweet flavor.

SERVES 4 TO 6 AS A MAIN COURSE ▶ INFORMAL MENU 1

3 tablespoons oil
2 medium onions, finely chopped
1 small fresh red chile pepper, seeded and minced **G**, or ⅛ teaspoon cayenne pepper
4 cloves garlic, minced
2 teaspoons minced fresh ginger
2 teaspoons ground coriander
1 teaspoon ground cumin
1 teaspoon turmeric
½ teaspoon freshly ground pepper
Grated rind of 1 lemon
1½ cups (4 ounces) sliced mushrooms
3 cups Vegetable Stock (page 290)
2½ cups homemade coconut milk **G** or canned light coconut milk
1 teaspoon salt
2 large potatoes, peeled and diced
1½ cups fine egg noodles (or vermicelli broken into 1-inch lengths)
2 cups small broccoli florets*
Juice of 1 lemon
Lemon wedges (1 per serving)

Broccoli stalks can be used in Lemon-Glazed Broccoli Stalks Julienne (page 221).

1. Set all of the ingredients in front of you before you begin cooking. In a medium saucepan heat the oil and add the onions and chili. Sauté for 5 minutes, or until the onions begin to get golden. Add the garlic and ginger, stir, then add all of the spices and the lemon rind. Cook for 3 minutes, stirring often.

2. Add the mushrooms and cook for 5 minutes, then add the vegetable stock, coconut milk, and salt.

3. Bring the contents to a boil and add the potatoes. Cook, uncovered, for about 10 minutes, stirring occasionally, or until the potatoes are almost tender.

4. Add the noodles, let the mixture return to a boil, then add the broccoli. Cook for about 5 minutes, stirring frequently, or until the noodles are tender but slightly firm to the bite. The broccoli should retain its bright green color.

5. Add the lemon juice and stir to blend. Serve in bowls with lemon wedges on the side.

> NOTE: If you are preparing this stew in advance, add the broccoli in step 4 but do not cook it. Chill until ready to serve. Reheat over low heat and add a few tablespoons of water if it is too thick. Stir frequently.

Curried Chickpea and Ginger Stew

This stew is a real winner—the chickpeas are a natural match for the curry while the potatoes soak up the spices and add an appealing contrast in texture.

SERVES 4 AS A MAIN COURSE

¼ cup oil
2 medium onions, diced
3 cloves garlic, minced
2 tablespoons minced fresh ginger
2 teaspoons ground coriander
¼ teaspoon ground cardamom
⅛ teaspoon cayenne pepper
15-ounce can chickpeas, drained and rinsed
16-ounce can diced tomatoes with their juice (2 cups)
1 medium carrot, diced
1 medium potato, diced
1 teaspoon salt
4 cups water
3 tablespoons butter
Lemon wedges (1 per serving)
Yogurt (optional)

1. In a large stockpot heat the oil with the onions, garlic, ginger, coriander, cardamom, and cayenne pepper. Sauté, stirring frequently, for about 7 minutes, or until the onions are tender.

2. Add the chickpeas, tomatoes, carrot, potato, salt, and water, and bring to a boil. Cook for 30 minutes, stirring often, or until the vegetables are tender.

3. Swirl in the butter, and taste for seasoning.

4. Spoon into bowls and serve with a lemon wedge on the side. This dish is especially delicious with yogurt; serve a bowlful so each person can add his or her own if desired.

THE MUCH-MALIGNED EGG OF THE 1980S AND 1990S HAS been vindicated; eggs are now recognized as an important part of a balanced diet when eaten in moderation. The cholesterol in eggs does not go directly to your bloodstream, as once was thought. It's saturated and trans fats that are the real culprits.

Frittatas, Eggs, and Timbales

The frittatas and curried eggs in this chapter are equally good options for breakfast, lunch, or dinner, while the timbales are ideal for elegant meals when you want a rich, sophisticated entrée. I think that organic, free-range eggs—particularly from a local farm—are the only eggs worth buying. They are more flavorful, more healthful, and the chickens were raised in humane conditions. It is easy to find these high-quality eggs now, and the difference in cost is negligible.

Moo Shu Vegetables with Mandarin Pancakes

This shredded egg and vegetable dish served with Mandarin Pancakes is an irresistible adaptation of the traditional Chinese dish. The recipe works well for entertaining because, unlike most Chinese dishes, both the filling and the pancakes can be prepared in advance and reheated. To help organize yourself, it is a good idea to prepare the vegetables while the tiger lily buds and cloud ears are soaking.

SERVES 4 ▶ ELEGANT MENU 2

Mandarin Pancakes (see next recipe)

SAUCE
¼ cup tamari or other soy sauce
½ cup water
2 tablespoons Chinese rice wine or dry sherry
2 slices fresh ginger (1 inch wide)

FILLING
½ cup dried tiger lily buds
1 tablespoon dried cloud ears (tree ears)
1 tablespoon Chinese rice wine or dry sherry
2 tablespoons tamari or other soy sauce
1 teaspoon cornstarch
1 teaspoon sugar
2 teaspoons minced fresh ginger
2 cups finely shredded cabbage (6 ounces—about ¼ of a small head)
2 cups (6 ounces) thinly sliced mushrooms
½ cup (about ½ of an 8-ounce can) finely chopped water chestnuts
6 scallions, shredded
¼ cup peanut oil
4 eggs, well beaten
2 teaspoons Asian sesame oil Ⓖ
Salt to taste
Freshly ground pepper to taste

1. Make the Mandarin Pancakes and set them aside.

2. To make the sauce: Boil the soy sauce, water, rice wine, and ginger in a small saucepan for 1 minute. Remove the ginger and discard. Pour into individual small dishes and set aside.

3. To make the filling: In a small bowl add enough hot water to cover the tiger lily buds. Soak for 30 minutes, then rinse in a sieve under cold running water and drain. Cut off and discard any hard ends on the buds, and cut the buds in half. Set aside.

4. In the meantime cover the cloud ears with hot water and soak for 30 minutes. Rinse in a sieve under cold running water and drain. Finely chop and set aside.

5. In a small bowl mix together the rice wine, soy sauce, cornstarch, and sugar and set aside. Warm the Mandarin Pancakes by folding them into quarters and placing them in a steamer, or putting them in a covered baking dish in a 300°F oven.

6. Place the minced ginger, cabbage, fresh mushrooms, water chestnuts, and scallions within easy reach of the stove. Heat a wok or large skillet over medium heat until hot but not smoking. Pour in 2 tablespoons of the peanut oil, and when hot but not smoking add the eggs. Cook, tossing constantly until set, about 3 minutes. Transfer the eggs to a plate and set aside.

7. Add the remaining 2 tablespoons of oil to the pan, and when hot add the ginger and cook for 15 seconds. Add the cabbage and stir-fry for 2 minutes. Add the mushrooms and stir-fry another 2 minutes. Continue stirring and add the water chestnuts, reserved tiger lily buds, and cloud ears. Stir-fry 2 minutes more.

8. Roughly chop the reserved eggs and add. Toss to mix. Stir the soy sauce mixture, pour it in, and continue tossing for another 2 minutes. Add the scallions, toss, then remove from the heat and scrape into a serving bowl. Drizzle on the sesame oil, toss; season with salt and pepper to taste. *May be prepared to this point up to 24 hours in advance, covered, and chilled. Reheat gently in a skillet or wok just until hot.*

9. To serve, each person spoons 1 to 2 tablespoons of the moo shu mixture onto an open pancake, then rolls the pancake over the mixture, folding in one side as he/she goes along. Eat with your hands, and dip the unfolded end into the dipping sauce.

> NOTES: Cloud ears are a dark-brown dried fungi that when soaked become crinkly and gelatinous, resembling floppy ears. They have a smoky taste and somewhat crunchy texture. Tiger lily buds are dried elongated lily buds about 2 to 3 inches long, which are used as a vegetable in Chinese cooking. They must be soaked beforehand, and any hard stems should be cut off after soaking. Stored in a covered container in a cool, dark place, both of these items will last indefinitely. They can be purchased in Chinese food shops and in some supermarkets, health food stores, and specialty food shops.

Mandarin Pancakes

Most countries have to their credit some type of dish using the ubiquitous pancake. In China, Mandarin pancakes are used as wrappers for Peking duck or a moo shu dish made with shredded ingredients. They are similar to Mexican tortillas but are thinner and chewier. They are easy to make, and the ones you don't use freeze very well. Rolling out and cooking them in pairs ensures the thinnest and most delicate pancakes possible. If you have leftover pancakes, you can use them as a wrap for scrambled eggs.

MAKES 12 PANCAKES

1 cup unbleached white flour
½ cup boiling water
1 tablespoon Asian sesame oil **G**

1. Put the flour in a medium bowl. Make a well in the center and pour in the boiling water. Gradually incorporate the water into the flour by stirring with a wooden spoon from the center outward. When the flour and water are mixed, turn the dough onto a lightly floured board or work surface.

2. Knead the dough until it is smooth and elastic, at least 7 minutes. Leave the dough on the board or work surface, cover it with a damp cloth or towel, and let rest for 15 minutes.

3. Cut the dough in half. Roll each half into a 6-inch log. Cut each log into 6 equal pieces. Roll each piece into a round ball, then flatten each ball into a 3-inch circle. Lightly brush some sesame oil on 6 of the circles. Place each oiled circle face down on an unoiled circle. You should now have 6 pairs.

4. On a lightly floured board roll each pair into 6-inch circles, turning the dough occasionally as you roll in order to keep the circles as round as possible.

5. Heat a medium or large skillet over medium heat. Cook the pancakes, 1 pair at a time, for 30 seconds on each side; they should have a few brown flecks on them when they are done. After each pair is cooked, gently separate the halves and stack them. Keep them covered with a dry towel.

6. Serve immediately, or reserve and reheat by folding each pancake into quarters and steaming them in a steamer for about 3 minutes. (A vegetable steamer works well.)

> NOTE: To freeze, thoroughly wrap the stack of pancakes in aluminum foil, then place in a plastic bag. Defrost before using. Reheat as in step 6.

Zucchini, Tomato, and Basil Frittata

A frittata is a type of omelet in which the filling and the eggs are cooked together slowly, and then served cut into wedges. As with most egg dishes, in order for a frittata to be tender and delicate you must not overcook it.

SERVES 4 ▶ QUICK MENU 6

6 eggs
¼ cup milk
¼ cup grated Parmesan cheese
½ teaspoon salt
Liberal seasoning freshly ground pepper
3 tablespoons olive oil
2 medium onions, diced
28-ounce can diced tomatoes, well drained
1 tablespoon minced fresh basil, or 1 teaspoon dried basil
1 small zucchini, halved lengthwise and thinly sliced

1. Preheat the oven to 325°F. Butter a pie plate. (If your plate is glass set the oven at 300°F.)

2. In a large bowl beat together the eggs, milk, Parmesan cheese, salt, and pepper.

3. Heat the oil in a large skillet over medium heat. Add the onions and sauté for 5 minutes. Add the drained tomatoes and basil, and sauté for 10 more minutes (no less), tossing frequently.

4. Add the zucchini and cook until tender yet still slightly crisp, about 5 more minutes.

5. Add this mixture to the eggs and stir to blend. Pour into the prepared pie plate.

6. Bake for 15 to 17 minutes, or until a knife inserted into the center of the frittata comes out almost clean. Cut into wedges and serve immediately.

Roasted Potato, Onion, and Smoked Cheese Frittata

These flavors were meant for each other, but if you don't have smoked cheese on hand, crumbled goat cheese is a wonderful substitute.

SERVES 4

2 medium all-purpose potatoes, peeled and cut into ½-inch dice
3 medium onions, cut into ¾-inch dice
1 tablespoon olive oil
¼ teaspoon salt
Freshly ground pepper to taste
1 teaspoon butter
8 large eggs
½ cup grated smoked Gouda or smoked mozzarella cheese

1. Preheat the oven to 400°F.

2. In a large bowl toss the potatoes and onions with the olive oil and spread onto a large baking sheet in one layer. Cook 25 to 30 minutes, or until brown and tender. Toss after the first 15 minutes. Remove from the oven and sprinkle on the salt and pepper. Let cool.

3. Meanwhile reduce the oven heat to 325°F (or 300°F if you are using a glass pie plate), and butter a pie plate or pan.

4. In a large bowl beat the eggs. Stir in the cooled potato mixture and cheese. Pour into the prepared pie plate.

5. Bake 25 to 30 minutes, or until a knife inserted in the center of the frittata comes out almost clean.

Bombay-Style Curried Eggs

This bright-colored Indian dish is excellent served as a breakfast, lunch, or dinner course, and it takes only minutes to make. It is creamy and spicy, and eggs don't get much better than this.

SERVES 4   ▶ **BREAKFAST AND BRUNCH MENU 4**

8 eggs
¼ cup milk
½ teaspoon salt
Liberal seasoning freshly ground pepper
2 tablespoons Ghee (page 300) or butter
¾ cup finely chopped mushrooms
6 scallions, thinly sliced
½ fresh red or green chile pepper, seeded and minced **G**, or ⅛ teaspoon cayenne pepper
1 teaspoon minced fresh ginger
1 tomato, seeded and finely diced (fresh or canned)
¼ teaspoon turmeric
½ teaspoon ground cumin
Fresh coriander or parsley sprigs for garnish

1. Beat the eggs, milk, salt, and pepper together in a large bowl until well blended but not airy.

2. Heat the ghee or butter in a large skillet over medium heat, and when hot add the mushrooms, scallions, chili or cayenne pepper, and ginger. Sauté, tossing often, until the mushrooms are tender, about 10 minutes.

3. Add the tomato, turmeric, and cumin, and cook 3 minutes more, or until the tomato is heated through and tender. Reduce the heat to medium-low.

4. Pour in the egg mixture and cook, stirring constantly with a large spoon, until the eggs are set yet still very creamy; do not let them dry out. Serve immediately, garnished with coriander or parsley sprigs.

Spinach Custard Ring with Tomato Cream Sauce

This is a stunning dish that is very easy to make. If you don't have a ring mold, you can substitute a loaf pan or soufflé dish, although the ring mold looks especially elegant. When you purchase spinach, check to see that it is free of yellow spots, which are a sign of old age. If you use loose fresh spinach, be sure to buy a full two pounds, because once you've removed the long stems you will be left with closer to 20 ounces.

SERVES 4 ▶ ELEGANT MENU 3

2 pounds loose fresh spinach (weight with stems), or two 10-ounce packages fresh spinach, cleaned and stemmed, or two 10-ounce packages frozen chopped spinach, thawed
4 large eggs
1 cup heavy or whipping cream
1½ teaspoons minced fresh basil, or ½ teaspoon dried basil
½ teaspoon salt
Liberal seasoning freshly ground pepper

SAUCE
¾ cup tomato purée
¾ cup heavy or whipping cream
¼ teaspoon salt
Freshly ground pepper to taste

¼ cup grated Parmesan cheese

1. Put the spinach in a large pot with just the water that clings to it. Cover the pot and cook, over low heat, just until it wilts. Drain in a colander and let cool. When cool enough to handle, squeeze out *all* of the water from the spinach with your hands. Mince it on a cutting board and set aside. (If you are using frozen chopped spinach then, when thawed, squeeze out *all* of its moisture with your hands. Set aside.)

2. Preheat the oven to 375°F. Beat the eggs very well in a large bowl and stir in the cream, basil, salt, pepper, and spinach. *May be prepared to this point up to 8 hours in advance, covered, and refrigerated. Bring to room temperature before proceeding with the next step.*

3. Generously butter a 1½-quart ring mold (or loaf pan or soufflé dish), and fill with the spinach custard. Place this dish in a larger baking dish. Pour enough hot water into the larger dish to reach halfway up the sides of the mold. (This must be done to ensure gentle cooking.)

4. Bake for 20 to 30 minutes, or until a knife inserted in the center of the custard comes out clean. Let sit for 10 minutes before unmolding.

5. While the ring mold is resting, turn the oven up to 450°F. Combine the tomato purée, cream, salt, and pepper, and mix well.

6. Run a knife around the mold and carefully unmold it onto a quiche dish (not a quiche pan with a removable bottom), or any other attractive shallow baking dish. Pour the tomato cream sauce evenly over it, and sprinkle on the Parmesan cheese.

7. Bake for another 15 minutes, or until golden brown.

Noodle Timbales with Pesto Cream Sauce

Timbales are little custards that are so named because their shape resembles a kettledrum— *timbale* in French. These noodle timbales are especially rich and luscious, and need only a salad and side vegetable as accompaniments. They are virtually foolproof and reheat very well.

SERVES 4 ▶ **ELEGANT MENU 7**

2 cups fine egg noodles
6 eggs, well beaten
½ cup heavy or whipping cream
⅓ cup milk
½ cup grated Parmesan cheese
¼ teaspoon salt
Freshly ground pepper to taste

SAUCE
⅓ cup heavy or whipping cream
⅔ cup Pesto (page 296) or Winter Pesto (page 297)

1. Fill a medium saucepan with water and bring it to a boil. Add the noodles and cook until al dente. Drain very well, then put in a large bowl and cool slightly.

2. Add the beaten eggs, cream, milk, Parmesan cheese, salt, and pepper, and mix well. *May be prepared to this point up to 8 hours in advance, covered, and refrigerated.*

3. Preheat the oven to 375°F. Butter eight 1-cup custard cups or small soufflé dishes and fill evenly with the mixture. (Smaller cups can be used but be sure to adjust the cooking time accordingly.) Place the custard cups in a large baking dish and fill the dish with enough hot water to reach one-third up the sides of the cups. (This *bain-marie*, or water bath, ensures gentle, moist cooking and is essential.) Bake for 20 to 25 minutes, or until a knife inserted in the center of one comes out clean.

4. Meanwhile, make the sauce. Combine the cream and pesto in a small saucepan and heat over low heat until piping hot, stirring constantly.

5. Remove the cups from the baking dish, and loosen the timbales by inserting a knife around the edges. Invert them onto a platter (or dry the baking dish they were in and use that if it is suitable), and spoon the sauce over them. Serve immediately.

> NOTE: If you are not going to serve all of the timbales at one sitting, you can keep them in the cups and they will reheat very well the next day. Place them in a saucepan with about an inch of water, cover the pan, and heat over medium heat until hot throughout, about 10 to 15 minutes.

Noodle Timbales with Pesto Cream Sauce

Leek Timbales with White Wine Sauce

Leeks and onions are not interchangeable; the leek has a sweetness that is one of the most captivating of flavors. We make this dish in one of my classes and I have yet to meet a fledgling cook who wasn't won over by this vegetable. When you purchase leeks, choose firm, unblemished ones with healthy-looking tops. Beware of spring leeks; they have oftentimes been wintered over and have developed hard cores. These small savory custards are virtually foolproof to make, and the leeks give a delicious flavor. The custard can be made a day in advance, and leftover timbales reheat very well. What more could you ask of a dish?

SERVES 4   ▶ ELEGANT MENU 11

6 medium to large leeks (with 2 inches of their green tops)
4 tablespoons butter
4 eggs, well beaten
½ cup heavy or whipping cream
⅓ cup milk
½ teaspoon salt
Freshly ground pepper to taste

SAUCE
2 tablespoons butter
2 tablespoons unbleached white flour
1 to 2 teaspoons tomato paste (for color)
1½ cups Vegetable Stock (page 290)
½ cup dry white wine
Freshly ground pepper to taste
Parsley sprigs for garnish

1. Cut the roots off the leeks, then slice them lengthwise down their centers almost through to the other side. Rinse them under cold running water, being careful to clean out all of the dirt that is lodged between the leaves. (Leeks are very dirty, so use your fingers to separate the leaves and look for hidden dirt.) Pat them dry and slice very thin. You need 7 cups.

2. Melt the butter in a large skillet and sauté the leeks until tender, about 15 minutes. Spoon them into a large bowl, add the eggs, cream, milk, salt, and pepper, and mix well. *May be prepared to this point up to 24 hours in advance, covered, and chilled.*

3. Preheat the oven to 375°F. Butter eight 1-cup custard cups or small soufflé dishes and divide the leek mixture evenly among them, filling them no more than three-fourths full. (Of course if your molds are smaller or larger divide the mixture accordingly.)

4. Place the custard cups in a large baking dish and carefully pour in enough hot water to reach halfway up the sides of the cups. Bake for 20 to 30 minutes, or until a toothpick inserted in the center of a timbale comes out dry.

5. Meanwhile make the sauce. Melt the butter in a small saucepan over low heat. Whisk in the flour and cook this roux for 2 minutes, whisking constantly. Be careful not to let it burn.

6. Add a teaspoon of the tomato paste, the vegetable stock, and wine, and whisk until smooth. Bring to a boil and cook an additional 10 minutes, whisking occasionally. If the sauce needs more color add the additional teaspoon of tomato paste. Season with freshly ground pepper and taste to see if it needs salt. If the sauce isn't perfectly smooth, then strain it. *May be prepared up to 24 hours in advance, covered, and chilled. If it is too thick when reheated, thin with a little stock.*

7. Unmold the timbales onto a serving platter and top with the sauce. Garnish the periphery of the platter with parsley sprigs.

THERE IS SOMETHING SO SATISFYING ABOUT PIES, NO matter what form they take. Every ethnicity seems to have some version of a filled shell, and they are equally tempting whether they are eaten with a fork or are finger foods. If you

Savory Pies, Tarts, Pizzas, Etc.

want a pie for dinner and are pressed for time, try the Crustless Broccoli and Cottage Cheese Pie. The trick of making a "crust" by sprinkling bread crumbs in the dish is clever and effective. The crumbs hold the filling together and give the pie a crisp shell, which is what we expect with pies. The other pies in this section, including the pizza "pie," are more time-consuming, but worth the effort. Go to the Companion Dishes chapter to select accompaniments to your pie, and you'll have a meal that provides comfort and satisfaction.

Crustless Broccoli and Cottage Cheese Pie

I love pies or tarts for a main course; they are so substantial and inviting. But they do take time to prepare, so I make this quick version with a bread crumb "crust" when I am in a hurry. Try substituting kale, spinach, or cauliflower with some minced parsley for color if broccoli is not a prime choice at the market.

SERVES 4

3 tablespoons grated Parmesan cheese
¼ cup Bread Crumbs (page 294)
1½ cups cottage cheese
¼ cup milk
1 cup cubed Monterey Jack or Muenster cheese
3 eggs, well beaten
2 cups chopped cooked broccoli florets*
1 tablespoon minced fresh basil, or ¼ teaspoon dried
Dash cayenne pepper
¼ teaspoon salt
Freshly ground pepper to taste
1 tablespoon butter, cut into bits

1. Preheat the oven to 350°F. Generously butter a 9-inch pie plate or quiche pan. Mix the Parmesan cheese and bread crumbs together and pat onto the bottom and sides of the dish—this will form the crust.

2. Mix the cottage cheese, milk, cheese, and eggs together well, then stir in the remaining ingredients (except the butter). *May be prepared to this point up to 8 hours in advance. Cover and chill the crust and filling separately.* Pour into the pie crust and smooth over the top then dot with the butter.

3. Bake for 40 minutes, or until a knife inserted in the center comes out almost dry. Serve immediately.

Use the raw broccoli stalks in Lemon-Glazed Broccoli Stalks Julienne (page 221).

Mushroom Quiche

Many people have become indifferent to quiche because restaurants so often serve soggy versions of it. But a well-made creamy quiche can be a superlative dish, and is equally good for brunch, lunch, or dinner. The secret of a good quiche is the crust; it must be crisp and flaky. If it is undercooked it will be soft and soggy, so be sure to precook it as directed. It would be better to have it slightly overcooked than undercooked.

SERVES 4 TO 6   ▶ **BREAKFAST AND BRUNCH MENU 5**

1 recipe Pâté Brisée with Whole Wheat Flour (page 304)
1½ tablespoons butter
2 cups (6 ounces) thinly sliced mushrooms
1 medium onion, diced
4 eggs
1 cup heavy or whipping cream
½ cup milk
Dash nutmeg
Dash cayenne pepper
½ teaspoon salt
1 cup (4 ounces) grated cheese, either Swiss, Gruyère, or Monterey Jack

1. Make the Pâté Brisée and prebake as directed—13 minutes total. Let cool on a wire rack, and reduce the oven heat to 375°F.

2. Melt 1 tablespoon of the butter in a large skillet. Add the mushrooms and onion, and cook until the mushrooms are brown, about 7 minutes. Remove the pan from the heat.

3. Beat the eggs in a large bowl and add the cream, milk, nutmeg, cayenne, and salt. Mix until well blended. Add the mushroom mixture and mix again.

4. Cover the bottom of the pie crust with the grated cheese. Carefully pour the custard into the pie shell and shake gently to distribute it (see Note). Cut the remaining ½ tablespoon of butter into bits and top the quiche with it.

5. Bake for 20 to 25 minutes, or until it is golden on top and a knife inserted in the center comes out clean. Do not overcook the quiche or it will either become too dry or will separate and become watery. Cool on a wire rack for 15 minutes before serving. Quiche has a better flavor and consistency if served warm rather than hot.

> **NOTE:** When you fill the pie shell don't overfill it with the custard. If there is any leftover custard, bake it in a small buttered dish until set. Serve at once, or chill and reheat within 3 days.

Buttermilk Herb and Onion Tart

Buttermilk, which has the same caloric content as skim milk, adds a delicious piquancy to this tart, and significantly reduces the calories, which would be very high if cream were used. This is a wonderful way to use leftover buttermilk.

SERVES 4

Pâte Brisée with Whole Wheat Flour (page 304)
2½ tablespoons butter
3 medium onions, diced
4 eggs
1½ cups buttermilk (G)
2 cloves garlic, minced
½ teaspoon dried basil
¼ teaspoon dried thyme
¼ teaspoon dried tarragon, crumbled
¼ teaspoon dried oregano
½ teaspoon salt
Freshly ground pepper to taste
1½ cups (6 ounces) grated Monterey Jack or Muenster cheese

1. Prebake the pie crust according to the recipe for Pâte Brisée. Remove from the oven and set aside on a wire rack. Reduce the oven temperature to 375°F.

2. Melt 1½ tablespoons of the butter in a medium-size skillet, add the onions, and sauté for 10 minutes, or until tender but not mushy. Remove from the heat.

3. Beat the eggs in a large bowl until well blended, then beat in the buttermilk, garlic, basil, thyme, tarragon, oregano, salt, pepper, and reserved onions.

4. Evenly distribute the grated cheese over the bottom of the pie crust, then carefully pour in the custard mixture and shake gently to distribute. Cut the remaining tablespoon of butter into bits and place evenly on top of the tart.

5. Bake for 25 to 30 minutes, or until a knife inserted in the center comes out clean. Let sit on a wire rack for 20 minutes before serving. Serve warm, not hot.

Spanakopita

This is one classic dish that cannot be improved upon. The spinach, feta, and dill filling enclosed in crisp, buttery filo is a superb marriage of flavor and texture. It is not as difficult to prepare as it seems—just follow these directions and you can't go wrong. If you are entertaining, take advantage of the fact that the pie can be prepared up to 24 hours in advance; it will be just as crisp.

SERVES 6 TO 8   ▶ **ELEGANT MENU 6**

2 pounds loose fresh spinach (weight with stems) or two 10-ounce packages fresh spinach, washed, stemmed, and thoroughly drained; or two 10-ounce packages frozen chopped spinach, thawed
¼ cup olive oil
3 medium onions, finely diced
¼ cup minced fresh dill, or 2 tablespoons dried dill
¾ teaspoon salt
Freshly ground pepper to taste
⅓ cup milk
¼ pound feta cheese, finely crumbled
1 cup small-curd cottage cheese
4 eggs, well beaten
1 cup (2 sticks) butter, melted
16 sheets filo dough (12 × 16 inches)

1. If using fresh spinach remove the stems and discard. Cook the leaves, covered, in a large skillet with just the water that clings to them (when washed) until the spinach is completely wilted. Put it in a strainer, press out *all* of the liquid with the back of a spoon, and chop the spinach on a cutting board until minced. If using frozen spinach, squeeze it dry to remove *all* the moisture.

2. In a large skillet heat the olive oil over medium heat until hot but not smoking. Add the onions and cook until golden, about 5 minutes, then add the cooked spinach and heat through.

3. Add the dill, salt, and a liberal seasoning of freshly ground pepper, and cook, stirring often, until all of the liquid has evaporated and the spinach has begun to stick to the pan, about 3 minutes.

4. Scrape the mixture into a large bowl and stir in the milk. Cool to room temperature. Add the feta cheese, cottage cheese, and eggs, and mix well.

5. Preheat the oven to 300°F. With a pastry brush coat the sides and bottom of a 12 x 7 x 2-inch rectangular baking dish with some of the melted butter. Line the dish with a sheet of the filo dough and press it firmly into the corners and sides of the dish. There will be some overlap.

6. Brush the entire surface of the filo dough with a little of the melted butter (don't drench it), then lay another sheet of filo on top. Brush this layer with some melted butter and continue this procedure until 8 sheets have been used.

7. With a rubber spatula spread the spinach mixture evenly over the top layer of the dough. Place another layer of filo over the spinach mixture, coat it with some melted butter, and repeat this procedure until the remaining 8 sheets have been used on top.

8. With scissors or a small sharp knife trim the edges of the filo close to the pie (leave ¼-inch rim around it) and brush the top layer of the filo with the remaining melted butter. Make shallow cuts through the first few layers to mark off where you will cut at serving time. (This prevents the top layer from flaking too much afterward.) *May be prepared to this point, covered, and chilled up to 24 hours in advance.*

9. Bake for 1 hour, or until the pastry is evenly golden and crisp. It is best to let the pie sit for 30 minutes or so before serving, for, like quiche, it is more flavorful and has a better texture when served warm rather than hot. To serve cut into squares.

> NOTE: Leftover Spanakopita is great reheated and served as an appetizer, and it is also delicious served room temperature at a picnic.

Vegetarian B'stilla

Moroccan food is little known in this country, and it's interesting to become acquainted with this cuisine's use of spices—such as cinnamon and ground ginger—in main-course dishes. B'stilla is a classic dish that combines sweet and salty flavors. This vegetarian version has an unforgettable combination of sweetness and spiciness. Do try eating it with your fingers—Moroccan style.

SERVES 6 ▶ **ELEGANT MENU 10**

1½ pounds mushrooms
6 tablespoons butter, plus 7 tablespoons melted
1 large onion, minced
2 teaspoons cinnamon
½ teaspoon freshly ground pepper
1 teaspoon ground ginger
¼ teaspoon turmeric
¼ cup lemon juice (about 1½ lemons)
10 eggs, well beaten
Salt to taste
2 tablespoons oil
1½ cups almonds
¼ cup powdered sugar
8 sheets filo dough (12 × 16 inches)
Powdered sugar for garnish
Cinnamon for garnish

1. Wipe each mushroom off with a damp towel or paper towel to remove the dirt, then chop them into medium pieces. Melt 6 tablespoons of butter in a large skillet, then add the onion, ½ teaspoon of the cinnamon, and the pepper, ginger, and turmeric, and sauté for 1 minute. Add the mushrooms and cook for about 5 minutes, or until they give off their juice. Remove with a slotted spoon to a platter and leave the remaining juice in the skillet.

2. Add the lemon juice to the skillet and heat these juices until bubbling. Add the beaten eggs and cook them, stirring constantly, until they resemble moist scrambled eggs. Do not allow them to become dry. Remove them to a platter, add salt to taste, and chill, uncovered, until the eggs are cool.

3. Meanwhile heat the oil in a small skillet, and when hot add the almonds and sauté until golden all over. Be careful not to let them burn. Put them in a blender or food processor and blend until finely chopped. (The almond meal should not be as fine as powder.) Add the remaining

1½ teaspoons of cinnamon, the ¼ cup powdered sugar, and 2 tablespoons of the melted butter, and blend until well mixed.

4. To assemble the B'stilla: Place the filo in front of you and cover with a piece of wax paper and then a damp towel to prevent the dough from drying out. Also set a pastry brush and the remaining 5 tablespoons of melted butter in front of you.

5. Preheat the oven to 425°F. Lightly brush the bottom and sides of a pie plate or 9-inch round cake pan with some melted butter. Lay 1 sheet of filo in the plate, then gently press it into the sides and allow the dough to overlap the edges. (Immediately cover the pile of filo again after removing each sheet.) Quickly and lightly brush the surface of the filo with melted butter; you need not do it perfectly, but be sure to cover the overlapping edges. Repeat this procedure with 4 more sheets of filo.

6. Spoon in the mushroom mixture, top with the cooked eggs, then finely crumble the almond mixture over it.

7. Gather the overlapping edges of the filo and fold over the filling, making sure to keep the round shape of the pie. Now cover the pie with a sheet of filo, allowing it to drape over the sides. Brush lightly with melted butter and repeat with the 2 remaining sheets. Tuck the edges in around the pie, keeping the circular shape, then pour any remaining butter over the top and spread it on evenly. *May be prepared to this point up to 4 hours in advance and chilled.*

8. Bake for 15 minutes, or until evenly golden on top. Remove the pie from the oven, top with a cookie sheet, and invert. Lift off the pie plate and bake the pie on the cookie sheet an additional 15 to 20 minutes, or until golden and crisp.

9. Invert the pie onto a circular plate or platter and sprinkle on some powdered sugar through a sieve. Top with some cinnamon in a lattice pattern.

Tamale Pie

There's something heartwarming about serving a pie for dinner. Tamale Pie is a delicious low-fat, high-protein pie that is made with a cornmeal crust. It is especially quick to make if you use canned beans.

SERVES 4 TO 6

3 tablespoons oil
2 medium onions, diced
1 large green bell pepper, cut into ½-inch dice
1 teaspoon chili powder
½ teaspoon ground cumin
16-ounce can diced tomatoes, well drained (1 cup pulp)
16-ounce can kidney beans (2 cups cooked **G**), drained, rinsed, and drained again
1 cup corn, fresh or frozen
½ teaspoon salt
Liberal seasoning freshly ground pepper

CRUST
2½ cups cold water
1½ cups cornmeal
½ teaspoon chili powder
½ teaspoon salt
1 cup (4 ounces) grated Monterey Jack cheese
1 tablespoon butter, cut into bits

1. In a large skillet heat the oil over medium heat. Add the onions and green pepper, and cook until tender yet still crunchy, about 10 minutes.

2. Add the chili powder, cumin, tomatoes, and beans, and toss well. Cook for 5 minutes, or until the mixture is heated through and begins to get dry.

3. Add the corn, salt, and pepper and cook 1 minute more. Remove from the heat. *May be prepared to this point and chilled up to 24 hours in advance. Bring to room temperature before proceeding with the next step.*

4. To make the crust: Butter a pie plate. Preheat the oven to 350°F. Place the water, cornmeal, chili powder, and salt in a medium heavy-bottomed saucepan. Bring to a boil over medium heat and whisk frequently with a wire whisk until smooth and thick. (As it begins to thicken whisk constantly.) When the mixture begins to tear away from the sides of the pan it is ready, about 5 minutes.

5. Immediately spread two-thirds of the cornmeal on the bottom and sides of the pie plate. Smooth over with a rubber spatula. Top with the bean mixture and smooth over the top. Evenly sprinkle on the cheese. Top with the remaining cornmeal mixture by dropping on small spoonfuls, and use your fingers to spread it out. Top with the butter.

6. Bake for 45 minutes, or until lightly golden. Let sit 10 minutes before serving.

Bean Tostadas

These make a quick meal if you use canned beans, store-bought tortillas, and store-bought salsa; you can also make the tortillas and salsa on a rainy day and have them on hand. In either case try experimenting with toppings such as avocado slices, shredded lettuce, or crumbled fried tofu, just to name a few. This is a great menu for kids—both to make and to eat.

SERVES 4 ▶ QUICK MENU 4

5 tablespoons oil
2 cloves garlic, minced
2 medium onions, finely diced
Two 15-ounce cans kidney beans or black beans (4 cups cooked Ⓖ), drained, rinsed, and drained again
1 cup water
Eight 6-inch wheat tortillas
3 cups (9 ounces) grated Monterey Jack cheese
½ cup sour cream
Salsa

1. Heat 2 tablespoons of the oil in a large skillet over medium heat. Add the garlic and onions and sauté until the onions are tender, about 10 minutes.

2. Add the beans and water and simmer for 5 minutes. Mash half of the beans with the back of a spoon and stir to mix. Keep warm over low heat while preparing the tortillas.

3. Turn the oven on "broil." Brush the tortillas on both sides with the 3 remaining tablespoons of oil. Lay them on a cookie sheet (do this in batches) and broil on both sides until lightly golden.

4. Divide the beans equally and spread on each tortilla. Top with equal amounts of grated cheese.

5. Return to the broiler and broil until the cheese is melted and bubbly.

6. Remove from the oven and spread an equal portion of sour cream in the center of each. Serve immediately and let each person spoon on salsa to taste.

Chalupas

Here is a sensational Mexican delicacy of crisp wheat tortillas covered with jalapeño peppers, melted cheese, and avocado purée. They can be served as a main course as one would serve pizza or tostadas, or they can be made cocktail-size and served as an appetizer. No drink suits them as well as ice-cold beer.

SERVES 4   ▶ INFORMAL MENU 12

3 ripe medium avocados (preferably Hass, or black pebbled-skin variety)
Juice of ½ lemon
3 tablespoons sour cream (or 1½ tablespoons yogurt and 1½ tablespoons mayonnaise)
Salt to taste
Freshly ground pepper to taste
8 wheat tortillas
3 tablespoons oil
4 to 5 seeded and minced jalapeño peppers (pickled, canned, or fresh)Ⓖ
3½ cups grated Monterey Jack cheese (about 12 ounces)

1. Slice the avocados in half vertically and discard the pits. To remove the skin, insert the handle of a spoon between the flesh and the skin and move it all around the avocado until the flesh is released from the skin. Put the flesh in a medium bowl and mash it thoroughly with the lemon juice, sour cream, salt, and pepper. Cover and chill until ready to use, no longer than 3 hours in advance.

2. Preheat the broiler. Brush both sides of the tortillas with the oil and lay them on a cookie sheet; this will have to be done in batches. Broil on both sides until golden. Keep the broiler on. *The tortillas may be prepared up to 2 days in advance. When cool wrap in plastic and keep at room temperature.*

3. Place as many tortillas on the baking sheet as will fit, and top with some of the minced jalapeño peppers. Cover with some of the grated cheese, then broil until the cheese is thoroughly melted. Repeat with the remaining tortillas.

4. Top each chalupa with some avocado purée in the shape of an X (or you can spoon the purée into a pastry bag and pipe it on with a star tube). Serve immediately.

> NOTE: You can create cocktail-size chalupas by using 2- to 4-inch tortillas or by cutting tortillas into small triangles.

Neapolitan Pizza

I make a pizza from scratch and everyone responds with great enthusiasm for this special treat. It's not only the fact that people appreciate the time and effort involved (although it really isn't that time-consuming), but there is a fresh flavor in homemade pizza that is not duplicated in restaurants. This is a memorable pizza with a thin, crisp crust. If you use black or dark pans your crust will be especially crisp, although lighter pans work well also. I prefer a combination of mozzarella and Muenster cheese for heightened flavor.

MAKES ONE 17-INCH RECTANGULAR PIZZA (SERVES 4)

1 cup warm water
1 package dry active yeast
3 tablespoons olive oil
⅔ cup whole wheat flour
1¾ cups unbleached white flour
½ teaspoon salt
1 teaspoon cornmeal
1¼ cups Marinara Sauce (page 295)
1½ cups (6 ounces) grated mozzarella cheese
1½ cups (6 ounces) grated Muenster cheese
4 cups sautéed vegetables, such as mushrooms, peppers, onions, broccoli (optional)

1. Pour the warm water into a large bowl and sprinkle in the yeast. Stir to mix and let sit for 5 minutes.

2. Stir in the oil, then add the flours and salt. Beat with a wooden spoon until well mixed.

3. Turn the dough onto a lightly floured board or work surface and knead for 10 minutes (no less!). Keep lightly flouring the work surface to prevent the dough from sticking.

4. Put the dough in a lightly oiled bowl, then invert the dough so the oiled surface is on top. Cover the bowl with a newspaper and let rise in a warm place (no hotter than 85 °F) for 1½ hours, or until double in bulk. (You can place the bowl in the oven if there is a pilot light, or lightly heat the oven for a few seconds, turn off the heat, then let it sit in the barely warm oven.)

5. Punch down the dough and knead a few times. Lightly flour your work surface, and with a rolling pin roll the dough into a rectangle large enough to fit your baking sheet. Sprinkle the cornmeal on the pan and line with the dough. (The cornmeal prevents sticking and adds extra crispness to the crust.) It is not necessary to form an edge.

6. Preheat the oven to 500°F.

7. Spread a layer of marinara sauce over the dough. Cover the pizza with a mixture of the two cheeses. Top with the sautéed vegetables, if you wish.

8. Bake for 15 to 17 minutes, or until the crust is golden underneath and the cheese lightly browned. (To test the crust insert a knife or spatula under the crust and lift carefully to peek.) Cut into squares and serve immediately.

IT'S DIFFICULT TO IMAGINE WHAT THE AMERICAN kitchen was like before pasta exploded on the scene in the 1980s; it became such a mainstay of the vegetarian and non-vegetarian diet. Many of us then went from eating it almost nightly to now enjoying it with moderation because

Pasta, Polenta, and Other Grains

carbohydrates should be eaten judiciously. When I plan a pasta dinner, though, I want it to be memorable, as are the pastas in this section.

If polenta has not yet become a staple in your kitchen, now is the time to correct that. It is incredibly easy and quick to whip up at a moment's notice, and the toppings, similar to sauces that enhance pasta dishes, are limited only by your imagination. My two favorites are in this section, and are as suitable for a quick supper as they are for an elegant dinner.

Skillet Bulgur and Vegetables with Shredded Basil

This is a tasty dish to turn to when you want something light, low fat, and grainy. Leftovers are good cold and make a good portable lunch the next day.

SERVES 4

1½ cups bulgur **G**
¼ cup oil
2 cloves garlic, minced
2 medium onions, diced
2 small to medium zucchini (1 pound), halved lengthwise and thinly sliced
2 tablespoons finely shredded fresh basil, or 1 teaspoon dried basil
2 medium carrots, grated
2 teaspoons tamari or other soy sauce
½ teaspoon salt
Liberal seasoning freshly ground pepper
1 tablespoon butter, cut into bits

1. Rinse the bulgur in a sieve under cold running water. Place in a medium bowl and pour boiling water over it to cover plus 1 inch. Let soak for 30 minutes, or until tender when tasted. Transfer small batches at a time to a large piece of cheesecloth or a clean kitchen towel and squeeze out all of the liquid, then place in a bowl and set aside.

2. In a large skillet heat the oil over medium-high heat until hot but not smoking. Add the garlic and onions and sauté for 5 minutes.

3. Add the zucchini and basil and cook for 5 minutes, tossing occasionally. Add the carrots and cook for a few more minutes, or until the zucchini is tender but crisp—not mushy.

4. Add the bulgur, soy sauce, salt, pepper, and butter, and cook for 2 to 3 minutes, or until the bulgur is hot. Taste to adjust the seasoning. This dish is delicious as is or served with plain yogurt on the side.

Kasha Topped with Mushrooms in Sour Cream Sauce

Kasha (buckwheat groats) is a delicious grain to become acquainted with. It is very quick to prepare, has a tender, fluffy texture, and is high in protein and iron. The mushrooms in this lightly spiced sauce complement the nutty, roasted flavor of the kasha superbly.

SERVES 4 ▶ **QUICK MENU 10**

1¼ cups kasha **G** (medium granulation)
1 egg, lightly beaten
1 tablespoon butter
2¼ cups hot Vegetable Stock (page 290)
¼ teaspoon salt

SAUCE
3 tablespoons butter
1 large onion, diced
1 pound (6 cups sliced) mushrooms
¼ teaspoon dried thyme
Dash cayenne pepper
Liberal seasoning freshly ground pepper
1 cup sour cream
Minced parsley for garnish

1. Combine the kasha and egg in a medium saucepan and stir over medium heat until the kasha is well coated then begins to look dry, about 3 minutes. Make a well in the center of the pan and melt the butter. Toss it with the kasha, then pour in the hot stock and salt. Reduce the heat to a simmer and cook, covered, until the stock is completely absorbed, about 10 minutes.

2. Meanwhile make the sauce. Melt the butter in a large skillet over medium-high heat, then add the onion and sauté for 3 minutes. Add the mushrooms, thyme, cayenne pepper, and freshly ground pepper, and cook, stirring occasionally, for 10 minutes, or until the mushrooms are brown and juicy.

3. Add the sour cream, stir, and cook 2 more minutes, or until hot and bubbly. Spoon some kasha onto each dinner plate and top with the sauce. Garnish with the parsley and serve immediately.

Penne with Eggplant Sauce

It's amusing to contemplate how much taste is inextricably linked to texture, and the best illustration of this is pasta. Although most pastas are made from the same ingredients, their various shapes will determine the character of the dish they're in. The ingredients in two sauces can be identical, yet if one is served with angel hair pasta and one is served with ziti, the two dishes will taste different. With a robust sauce such as this one with eggplant, garlic, and hot pepper, short, thick pasta is a good match. I love these penne for their quill shape.

SERVES 4   ▶ QUICK MENU 2

1 pound penne
5 tablespoons olive oil
1 medium to large eggplant (about 1½ pounds), peeled and cut into 1-inch dice
4 cloves garlic, minced
¼ teaspoon dried red pepper flakes
35-ounce can diced tomatoes, drained
½ teaspoon salt
Liberal seasoning freshly ground pepper
1½ tablespoons minced fresh parsley

1. Set all of the ingredients in front of you near the stove.

2. Bring a large (6-to 8-quart) pot of water to a boil. Add the penne and cook until al dente, about 12 to 15 minutes.

3. Meanwhile, to begin the sauce, in a large skillet heat 2 tablespoons of the oil over medium-high heat until hot but not smoking. Add *half* of the eggplant and cook until almost tender. Toss frequently and do not add any more oil; just keep tossing if the eggplant begins to stick. When done remove onto a platter. Add 2 more tablespoons of oil and repeat with the remaining eggplant.

4. Add the remaining tablespoon of olive oil to the pan. Add the garlic and red pepper flakes, and cook until the garlic is golden, about 2 minutes, tossing frequently.

5. Add the tomatoes, salt, and pepper, and bring to a boil. Add the eggplant and cook until the sauce has thickened and the eggplant is tender, about 7 to 10 minutes. Keep the sauce hot over low heat if the pasta is not done yet.

6. Drain the pasta in a colander. Return it to the pot or a warm serving bowl and add the sauce. Toss. Add the parsley and toss again. Serve immediately with a bowl of grated Parmesan cheese to pass at the table.

Linguine with Swiss Chard and Garlic

Swiss chard is a delicious member of the beet family. It has a mild beet flavor and is an excellent source of vitamin A. Both the leaves and the ribs are used in this recipe, and if you are a gardener, you'll find that it is one of the easiest vegetables to grow. You could substitute spinach for the Swiss chard with good results, if you like.

SERVES 4   ▶ QUICK MENU 7

        1 pound linguine
        1 to 1½ pounds Swiss chard (about 8 to 10 cups chopped)
        ½ cup olive oil
        2 tablespoons butter
        8 cloves garlic, finely chopped
        ¼ teaspoon dried red pepper flakes
        ½ teaspoon salt
        Freshly grated Parmesan cheese

1. Bring a large (6-quart) pot of water to a boil, add the linguine, and cook until al dente.

2. Meanwhile rinse the Swiss chard under cold running water until it is very clean, then pat very dry with cotton or paper towels. If the ribs are more than ½ inch wide, string them by making a shallow slit in the bottom of each rib and pulling up the strings until they are released. Cut the leaves away from the ribs, chop the ribs into 1-inch pieces, and keep them in a separate pile from the leaves. Chop the leaves into 1-inch pieces.

3. Heat the oil and butter in a large skillet over medium heat, then add the garlic and red pepper flakes, and cook for 2 minutes, stirring often.

4. Raise the heat to medium-high, add the chopped Swiss chard ribs, and cook for 2 minutes, continuing to stir often. Add the leaves and cook for 3 to 5 minutes more, or until the leaves are wilted and tender. Do not overcook; they should retain their bright green color. Add the salt and stir to blend.

5. When the linguine is done drain it thoroughly, then return it to the pot or a warm serving bowl and toss on the chard and its sauce. Serve immediately. Pass a bowl of grated Parmesan cheese at the table and use liberally.

Farfalle with Broccoli Rabe

Broccoli rabe, also called rapini, is a leafy vegetable with small flower clusters resembling broccoli florets. I like to cook it with onions because their natural sweetness balances its slight bitterness. The bow-shaped pasta is worth going out of your way to get; it is delicious, and its bulky shape is a good match for the broccoli rabe sauce.

SERVES 4

1 large bunch broccoli rabe (about 1¼ pounds untrimmed)
2 tablespoons butter
½ cup olive oil
2 large onions, diced
3 cloves garlic, minced
1 pound farfalle (bow-shaped pasta)
½ teaspoon salt
Freshly ground pepper to taste
½ cup grated Parmesan cheese

1. Bring a large pot of water to a boil.

2. Meanwhile chop the coarse stems off the broccoli rabe and discard them. (The remaining stems shouldn't be any thicker than the diameter of a pencil.) Clean it very well by dunking it in a pan of cold water several times. Drain thoroughly, then coarsely chop it. You should have about 6 cups.

3. Melt the butter with the olive oil in a large skillet over medium heat, then add the onions and garlic and sauté, tossing regularly, for 10 minutes. Add the broccoli rabe and cook it, tossing from time to time, until it is tender—about 10 minutes.

4. Meanwhile drop the farfalle into the boiling water and cook until al dente. Taste to make sure.

5. Season the broccoli rabe with salt and pepper. When the farfalle is done, drain it thoroughly in a colander. Return it to the pot or a warm serving bowl and spoon on the greens and their sauce. Toss, sprinkle on the cheese, and toss again. Serve immediately.

Spaghettini with Garlic and Hot Pepper

This is a hot and spicy pasta dish that is rather light and is usually served as is, though one may add a light sprinkling of Parmesan cheese if desired. This is the ideal dish to whip up when simplicity is paramount.

SERVES 4   ▶ **QUICK MENU 11**

....

1 teaspoon salt
1 pound spaghettini
1 tablespoon butter
⅓ cup olive oil
5 cloves garlic, minced
1 small fresh red chile pepper, minced Ⓖ, or ⅓ teaspoon dried red pepper flakes
2 tablespoons minced fresh parsley

1. Bring a large pot of water to a boil. Add the salt and cook the spaghettini until al dente.

2. Meanwhile, melt the butter with the olive oil in a medium skillet; then add the garlic and chili pepper, and cook gently until the garlic is lightly golden, about 3 minutes. Be careful not to burn it.

3. Drain the pasta well, return to the pot or a warm serving bowl, pour on the sauce, and toss well. Add the parsley, toss again, and serve immediately.

Pasta with Uncooked Tomato and Fresh Basil Sauce

This quick summer dish is best prepared at the height of the season, when tomatoes are irresistibly plump and red and fresh basil is available in abundance. This is, to me, one of the best pasta dishes, potent yet simple.

SERVES 4 ▶ SUMMER MENU 2

6 ripe plum tomatoes (about 1 pound)
3 to 4 cloves garlic, minced
1 cup shredded fresh basil leaves (loosely packed)
½ cup chopped fresh parsley
½ cup olive oil
½ teaspoon dried red pepper flakes
½ teaspoon salt
Freshly ground pepper to taste
1 pound pasta, such as linguine, spaghetti, or vermicelli
⅔ cup grated Parmesan cheese

1. Wash the tomatoes and pat them dry. Cut out the cores and discard. Cut each tomato in half horizontally and gently squeeze out the seeds.

2. Dice the tomatoes into 1-inch pieces and place in a medium bowl. Add the garlic, basil, parsley, olive oil, red pepper flakes, salt, and pepper to taste. Toss well. Let marinate at room temperature for at least 2 hours. If you marinate it longer then chill it. *May be prepared to this point in advance, covered, and chilled for up to 24 hours. Bring to room temperature before serving.*

3. Bring a large pot of water to a boil and cook the pasta until al dente. Drain well in a colander and return to the pot or a large serving dish.

4. Immediately toss the Parmesan cheese on the pasta. Pour on the sauce. Toss well and serve immediately. When the dish is served it tends to be warm rather than hot; this is fine and the flavor will gain as a result.

Spaghetti Squash with Broccoli Butter Sauce

Though technically not a pasta, this egg-shaped squash behaves just like it—when cooked, the pulp separates like strands of spaghetti. It is delicious, has considerably fewer calories than spaghetti, and adapts well to most pasta sauces. I prefer it with a delicate sauce, such as this broccoli butter sauce, so as not to overpower its mild flavor. If spaghetti squash is overcooked it will be mushy and lose the texture of individual spaghetti strands. The best way to control this is to undercook when you boil it, then separate it into strands and sauté until tender.

SERVES 2 TO 3 ▶ INFORMAL MENU 17

1 medium spaghetti squash (about 3½ pounds), rinsed off
1 large bunch broccoli
4 tablespoons butter
2 tablespoons olive oil
2 cloves garlic, minced
1 tablespoon minced fresh basil, or 1 teaspoon dried basil
1 tablespoon water
Salt to taste
Freshly ground pepper to taste
Grated Parmesan cheese

1. Bring a large pot of water to a boil, drop in the spaghetti squash, then cover the pan and cook over medium heat for 45 minutes. Remove from the pot and cut it in half crosswise (surprisingly this will give you longer strands). Let sit until cool enough to handle, about 10 minutes, then scoop out the seeds and discard them. With a fork scoop out the pulp and separate it into strands, then put it in a medium bowl. *May be prepared up to 24 hours in advance, covered, and chilled.*

2. Cut the florets off the broccoli, then cut them into small pieces. Save the stalks for another use (such as Lemon-Glazed Broccoli Stalks Julienne, page 221).

3. Melt the butter and olive oil together in a large skillet over medium heat, then add the garlic and cook for 2 minutes. Add the broccoli and basil, toss to coat well, then add 1 tablespoon of water and cover the pan. Cook for 2 minutes, or until the broccoli is about half cooked.

4. Discard any accumulated liquid in the bottom of the squash bowl, then add the squash to the broccoli and toss to blend. Cook, uncovered, for about 10 more minutes, or until the squash is crunchy but not hard. Season with salt and pepper, and serve with grated Parmesan cheese to pass at the table.

Rolled Stuffed Lasagna with Kale in a Tomato Cream Sauce

A delicious alternative to the traditional tomato sauce–laden version of lasagna. In this dish strips of lasagna are covered with a flavorful kale and cheese mixture, then rolled, and finally topped with a delicate tomato cream sauce. The slightly crunchy texture and definite flavor of kale give this lasagna a special character. It is perfect for a special occasion because it can be made in advance and then baked with no fuss.

Avoid kale leaves that are very large and have thick stems; the smaller the leaves the more delicate the flavor and texture. Kale leaves shouldn't be longer than 7 inches or so. If you wish, you can substitute spinach, collards, or mustard greens.

SERVES 4 ▶ ELEGANT MENU 1

1 pound kale (weight with stems)
1 tablespoon oil
8 lasagna noodles
2 tablespoons butter
2 cloves garlic, minced
1 medium onion, minced
1½ cups ricotta cheese
1 cup (about 4 ounces) finely diced mozzarella cheese
½ cup grated Parmesan cheese
¾ teaspoon salt
Freshly ground pepper to taste

SAUCE
4 tablespoons butter
¼ cup unbleached white flour
3 cups milk
⅔ cup tomato purée
⅛ teaspoon nutmeg
½ teaspoon salt
Freshly ground pepper to taste

1. Rinse the kale well by dunking it in a large bowl of cold water. Cut off the stems and discard. If the ribs attached to the leaves are thick then rip the leaves off and discard the ribs. Roughly chop the kale, then place in a large (6-quart) saucepan with a few tablespoons of water. Cover the pot and steam the kale until it wilts and is tender, about 5 minutes. Do not overcook it or it will turn olive brown and develop a strong taste. Drain it in a colander and let cool.

2. Meanwhile fill the same large pot with water and bring to a boil with the oil. Add the lasagna and cook until tender, not mushy. Drain and rinse under cold water to cool quickly. Drain again and toss with a little oil to prevent sticking. Set aside. (Note: You can cook the lasagna noodles the night before and chill.)

3. When the kale is cool enough to handle, squeeze out all of the remaining moisture with your hands. Chop the kale so that it has a fine texture, but not so that it is minced. In a large skillet melt the butter. Add the garlic and onion and sauté for 5 minutes. Add the kale and cook for 5 additional minutes.

4. Place the kale mixture in a large bowl and stir in the ricotta, mozzarella, ¼ cup of the Parmesan cheese, salt, and pepper until well blended. Set aside. Preheat the oven to 350°F.

5. To make the sauce: In a medium saucepan over medium heat melt the butter. Add the flour and whisk until blended. Cook this roux for 2 minutes, whisking frequently. Add the milk, tomato purée, nutmeg, salt, and pepper, and whisk to blend. Cook for 5 minutes, or until the sauce comes to a boil, whisking often. Remove from the heat.

6. To assemble the lasagna: Pour a little of the sauce in a large baking dish to coat the bottom. Lay a strip of lasagna on a work surface and spread one-eighth of the kale mixture evenly over it. It doesn't have to be perfectly covered; the filling will spread when it melts. Roll the lasagna loosely, then lay it seam side down in the baking dish. Repeat with the remaining 7 strips of lasagna. Pour the remaining sauce over and sprinkle on the remaining ¼ cup of Parmesan cheese. *May be prepared to this point up to 24 hours in advance, then covered and refrigerated. Bring to room temperature before baking.*

7. Bake, uncovered, for 30 minutes, or until hot and bubbly.

Stir-Fried Noodles and Vegetables with Sesame Seeds

Don't overcook the vegetables for this dish: the onions and broccoli should be crunchy. As with any stir-fried noodle dish you must use cold cooked noodles to prevent them from sticking together. Be sure to have all of the ingredients in front of you before you proceed.

SERVES 3

2 cups broccoli florets*
¼ cup oil (preferably peanut oil)
2 slices fresh ginger (about 1 inch wide and ¼ inch thick)
½ pound firm tofu, cut into ½-inch cubes and patted dry
2 large onions, quartered vertically and separated
3 cloves garlic, minced
½ pound (weight before cooked) cold cooked noodles such as linguine, spaghetti, or lo mein (6 cups cooked)
2 tablespoons tamari or other soy sauce
1 tablespoon sesame seeds
2 tablespoons Asian sesame oil Ⓖ

The remaining broccoli stalks can be used in Lemon-Glazed Broccoli Stalks Julienne (page 221).

1. In a covered wok or large skillet precook the broccoli over medium heat with ¼ cup water. Cook it until tender yet still bright green, about 3 minutes. Remove the broccoli and set aside. Drain all of the water out of the pan and wipe it dry.

2. Heat the wok or skillet over medium heat. Add the oil, and when hot add the ginger slices. Cook for 5 minutes or until golden. Remove and discard them.

3. Add the tofu to the hot oil and stir-fry until golden, about 5 minutes.

4. Add the onions and garlic and stir-fry for 5 minutes, or until the onions begin to get tender yet are still crunchy.

5. Add the broccoli and toss. Cook 1 minute.

6. Add the cold noodles and toss well. Add the soy sauce and stir-fry for 2 more minutes, or until the noodles are hot.

7. Sprinkle on the sesame seeds and sesame oil. Toss to coat and serve immediately.

NOTE: If you don't have leftover pasta and must cook it especially for this dish, then drain it in a colander and run cold water over it until cold. Drain again and pat dry.

Cuban Black Beans and Rice

The Cubans, along with many other nationalities, made a significant contribution to the culinary world by combining two nutritionally complementary foods—beans and rice. I enjoy all the different variations: Louisiana red beans and rice, Indian dal on rice, Mideast lentils and rice, and various Latin American and Caribbean dishes, but I find this Cuban version the most attractive and flavorful. Black beans in a richly flavored sauce are mounded on rice, then garnished with minced hard-boiled egg, sour cream, and chopped red onion.

SERVES 4 ▶ **INFORMAL MENU 15**

1½ cups dried black beans
3 tablespoons olive oil
3 medium onions, diced
4 cloves garlic, minced
2 bay leaves
½ teaspoon dried oregano
½ teaspoon dried thyme
1 tablespoon tomato paste
¼ teaspoon Tabasco, or to taste
1 tablespoon vinegar (preferably red wine vinegar)
1 cup water
2 green bell peppers, cored and diced
Salt to taste
Freshly ground pepper to taste
Perfect Brown Rice (page 292)*
1 hard-boiled egg, minced
⅔ cup sour cream
½ small red onion, diced

About 40 minutes before the beans are done you can begin cooking the rice in a separate pan, or you can cook it in advance and reheat it in the oven (350°F).

1. Rinse the black beans in a strainer under cold running water and pick out and discard any blemished ones, stones, etc. Soak overnight in water to cover. Or put in a saucepan with water to cover and boil for 2 minutes; turn off the heat, cover, and let the beans sit for 1 hour. Drain very well.

2. Combine the olive oil, onions, and garlic in a medium saucepan and sauté for 2 minutes.

3. Add the drained beans, bay leaves, oregano, thyme, tomato paste, Tabasco, vinegar, and cup of water. Cover, bring to a boil, and simmer on low heat for 1 to 1½ hours, or until the beans are tender yet still retain their shape. Stir occasionally. (You might have to add a bit more water before they are done, depending on how long the beans take to cook. In any event, the sauce should be thick, not dry or watery.)

4. About 10 minutes before the beans are done, add the green peppers, and cook until tender.

5. Taste to adjust the seasoning; it will probably need salt and some freshly ground pepper. *May be prepared to this point in advance, covered, and refrigerated for up to 24 hours. (In this case you will probably have to add a little water when you reheat it to thin the sauce.)*

6. Serve on individual portions of hot brown rice. Garnish with minced hard-boiled egg, top with a spoonful of sour cream, and finally garnish with some diced red onion. Serve immediately.

Risotto of Brown Rice and Mushrooms

Risotto is a rice dish cooked in such a way that the rice makes its own creamy, rich sauce. Preparing it takes time and patience, but it is well worth the effort. It is important to regulate the heat so that you cook the risotto at just the right pace, and you should have everything else for your meal prepared in advance, for risotto must be served immediately.

SERVES 4 ▶ **INFORMAL MENU 13**

4 cups water
1 cup brown rice
3½ cups Vegetable Stock (page 290)
5 tablespoons butter
6 ounces mushrooms, quartered or cut into eighths if very large (2 cups)
¾ cup grated Parmesan cheese
Freshly ground pepper to taste

1. Bring the water to a boil in a medium saucepan. Meanwhile rinse the rice in a sieve under cold running water. Add to the boiling water. Cook, partially covered, for 20 minutes. Drain in a colander.

2. Bring the stock to a simmer in a small saucepan and keep at a very low simmer throughout the cooking of the risotto.

3. Melt 4 tablespoons of the butter in a medium saucepan over medium heat, and sauté the mushrooms for 3 minutes. Add the drained rice and stir to coat all over. Add one ladleful (about ¾ cup) of simmering stock and stir the risotto continuously until the stock is absorbed. The heat should be regulated so that it takes about 5 minutes for the stock to be absorbed.

4. Now add another ladleful of stock and again stir continuously until absorbed. Repeat this process until all but one ladleful of the stock has been used; this will take about 25 minutes. The rice at this stage should be tender yet still *slightly* firm to the bite; if it is too hard add an extra cup of water or stock to the simmering stock, and when it begins to simmer add another ladleful of stock to the risotto and stir until it is absorbed.

5. After the next to the last ladleful has been absorbed, add the Parmesan cheese and remaining tablespoon of butter, and stir to blend. Add the last ladleful of stock and stir until absorbed. Season with pepper and serve immediately.

Goat Cheese Polenta with Braised Greens and Garlic

Greens cooked with hot peppers and garlic are a staple in my house, and here they combine with an ideal companion—a creamy polenta laced with tangy goat cheese. Because polenta is best served as soon as it is cooked, I like to have the greens completely cooked and kept warm on the back burner once I am ready to prepare the polenta.

SERVES 4

1½ pounds mixed greens (kale, escarole, spinach, Swiss chard)
¼ cup olive oil
6 cloves garlic, minced
¼ teaspoon dried red pepper flakes
¼ teaspoon salt

POLENTA
3½ cups vegetable stock
¼ teaspoon salt
1¼ cups cornmeal
2 tablespoons butter
2 tablespoons grated Parmesan cheese
4 ounces (about ¾ cup) crumbled goat cheese

1. Tear any coarse stems off the greens and discard them. Separate thicker greens, such as kale and escarole, from quicker-cooking ones, such as spinach and Swiss chard. Thoroughly wash and spin the greens to get rid of any sand. Keep in separate piles.

2. In a large skillet heat the oil over medium heat. Add the garlic and red pepper flakes and cook until barely colored, not brown. Immediately add the coarser greens with the liquid that clings to them and toss to coat with the garlic mixture. Cover the pan and steam just until wilted.

3. Mix in the remaining greens and cover again. Cook a few more minutes, or until wilted and tender. Season with the salt and keep warm on the back burner.

4. In a medium saucepan bring the vegetable stock and salt to a boil. Very slowly drizzle in the cornmeal, whisking all the while with a wire whisk. Over medium heat continue to whisk until the polenta is thick and creamy, about 5 minutes. Whisk in the butter and Parmesan cheese to blend. Just before serving stir in the goat cheese just until evenly distributed but with some chunks remaining visible.

5. To serve, spoon polenta onto each serving plate and top with the mixed greens.

Polenta Puttanesca

It is a good idea to keep some cornmeal, canned tomatoes, and Parmesan cheese on hand so you can put this polenta together on a moment's notice. Puttanesca sauce is a robust, brazen tomato sauce (*puttana* means whore) and it balances the subtle flavor of the polenta nicely.

SERVES 4 ▶ QUICK MENU 3

SAUCE
⅓ cup olive oil
8 cloves garlic, minced
¼ teaspoon dried red pepper flakes
2 large green bell peppers, cored and cut into ½-inch strips
Two 28-ounce cans diced tomatoes, drained
1½ tablespoons tomato paste
10 imported black olives (1½ ounces, preferably kalamata), pitted and halved
2 teaspoons capers
½ teaspoon salt
Freshly ground pepper to taste

POLENTA
4 cups water
1¼ cups cornmeal (either coarse or regular)
½ teaspoon salt

2 tablespoons butter, cut into bits
⅓ cup grated Parmesan cheese

1. In a large skillet heat the oil over medium heat until hot but not smoking, then add the garlic and red pepper flakes. Cook for 1 minute, or just until the garlic begins to get golden and the oil is fragrant. Be careful not to burn it.

2. Add the green peppers and sauté for 10 minutes, stirring frequently.

3. Raise the heat to medium-high and add the drained tomatoes, tomato paste, olives, capers, salt, and pepper. Cook until the peppers are tender and the sauce is thickened, about 10 minutes. Stir frequently.

4. Meanwhile, make the polenta. In a medium heavy-bottomed saucepan bring the water to a boil. *Very slowly* drizzle in the cornmeal, whisking continuously with a wire whisk all the while it is being sprinkled in. Add the salt and reduce the heat to low. Continue to whisk the polenta until a thick mass develops. (At this point it is better to switch to a wooden spoon.) Stir continuously until the polenta pulls away from the sides of the pan, about 5 to 7 minutes.

5. To serve, spoon equal portions of the polenta onto the center of each serving plate. Top with bits of butter and sprinkle on the Parmesan cheese. Finally top with the sauce. Serve immediately.

> NOTE: If for some reason the polenta cannot be served immediately and it begins to harden in the saucepan, add a small amount of water and, over low heat, whisk the polenta until it is smooth and hot.

BAKED DISHES, OR CASSEROLES, OFFER A MEASURE OF ease that is especially welcome at choice times. They can be completely prepared in advance and cooked at a moment's notice. It is particularly appealing when company is coming

Baked Dishes

to have a meal that is oven ready. These dishes share a homey quality that is hard to resist when you crave a substantial meal with a rustic feel. With each of the recipes I like to serve a salad, which offers a welcome lightness to the menu. Take advantage of the do-ahead steps in the recipes and you'll find the construction of these casseroles to be easy.

Black Bean and Cream Cheese Enchiladas

When I want a stick-to-the-ribs dish I make these hearty enchiladas. Delicate wheat tortillas are filled with black beans and cream cheese and rolled, then topped with a flavorful tomato chili sauce and baked until bubbly.

SERVES 4 ► **ELEGANT MENU 8**

1½ cups dried black beans
2 medium onions, diced
2 cloves garlic, minced
1 teaspoon dried oregano
1 teaspoon ground cumin
2 bay leaves
½ teaspoon salt
Freshly ground pepper to taste

SAUCE
¼ cup olive oil
2 medium onions, diced
2 cloves garlic, minced
28-ounce can diced tomatoes
¼ cup tomato paste
⅓ cup water
1 small can (4 ounces) mild green chiles, drained and finely diced
1 large jalapeño pepper (fresh, pickled, or canned), seeded and minced Ⓖ

8 wheat tortillas (10 if they are 6-inch)
8 ounces cream cheese, cut into 8 (or 10) slices
1½ cups (6 ounces) grated Monterey Jack cheese

1. Rinse the beans in a colander or strainer under cold running water. Pick out any stones, etc. Put the beans in a medium saucepan and cover with water plus 2 inches. Cover the pan, bring to a boil, and cook for 2 minutes. Turn off the heat and let the beans soak for 1 hour.

2. Drain the beans very well by tilting the pan to its side with the cover ajar. Pour in just enough water barely to cover the beans, and add the onions, garlic, oregano, cumin, bay leaves, salt, and pepper. Cover the pan, bring to a boil, then reduce the heat to a simmer. Cook the beans until they are tender, about 1 hour, stirring occasionally. (Note: The point is to have the beans absorb *most* of the liquid by the time they are done so that they have a thick sauce-like consistency. If they aren't done and more water is needed, add just a little and check the beans again when most of it is absorbed. The beans should still retain their shape when they are done.) Discard the bay leaves.

3. Mash about one-quarter of the beans against the sides of the pot and stir to blend them. Set aside to cool.

4. To make the sauce: In a large skillet heat the olive oil. Add the onions and garlic and cook over medium heat for 10 minutes, or until tender and limp, stirring often. Add the tomatoes and all their juice, tomato paste, water, chiles, and jalapeño pepper, and stir to blend. Cook for 5 minutes, or until the sauce has thickened. *May be prepared to this point up to 24 hours in advance. Cover and chill the sauce and beans separately.*

5. Preheat the oven to 350°F. To assemble the enchiladas: Spoon a little of the sauce into the bottom of a large baking dish or 2 medium dishes. Place a tortilla on your work surface and spoon about 2 tablespoons of the bean mixture down the center. (It is good to divide the filling into 8 portions beforehand.) Cut a slice of the cream cheese into 2 or 3 pieces and place on top of the beans. Roll the tortilla and place seam side down in the baking dish. Repeat with the remaining tortillas.

6. Spread the sauce evenly over the enchiladas. Top each enchilada lengthwise with some of the grated cheese. This helps to identify the enchiladas when you are dishing them out. *May be prepared to this point up to 2 hours in advance. Keep covered to prevent the tortillas from drying out.* Bake for 20 to 25 minutes, or until hot and bubbly.

Baked Mexican-Style Beans with Sour Cream and Chiles

Bean lovers take note: the gutsy sauce in this preparation makes these beans irresistible. This would be a good choice for a potluck or party dish, and it can be easily doubled. Serve as is or over hot cooked rice.

SERVES 4 ▶ INFORMAL MENU 2

2 tablespoons olive oil
2 medium onions, diced
2 cloves garlic, minced
28-ounce can diced tomatoes, well drained
1 tablespoon tomato paste
4-ounce can mild green chiles, drained and diced
1 teaspoon chili powder
¼ teaspoon dried oregano
½ teaspoon salt
Freshly ground pepper to taste
Three 15-ounce cans kidney beans, drained and rinsed
1 cup sour cream
2 cups (8 ounces) grated Monterey Jack cheese with jalapeño peppers

1. In a large skillet heat the oil over medium heat, add the onions and garlic, and sauté for 5 minutes. Add the drained tomatoes, tomato paste, chiles, chili powder, oregano, salt, and pepper, and raise the heat to high. Cook, stirring frequently, just until the juice from the tomatoes has evaporated, about 5 minutes.

2. Add the beans to the skillet and toss. Remove the pan from the heat. *May be prepared to this point up to 8 hours in advance, covered, refrigerated, and assembled just before cooking.*

3. Preheat the oven to 375°F. Put half of the bean mixture in a large casserole, cover with half of the sour cream and half of the cheese, add the remaining bean mixture, and top with the remaining sour cream and cheese.

4. Bake for 20 to 25 minutes, or until hot and bubbly.

Baked Eggplant, Chickpeas, and Tomatoes

A myth has developed that says that eggplant must be salted before it is cooked in order to remove its bitterness and/or cut down on its absorption of oil during cooking. I have cooked eggplant in myriad ways and have experimented with both the salted and unsalted methods; I hereupon declare that it makes no difference. I no longer salt eggplant and I have never had a bitter one, nor has the eggplant absorbed any more or less oil as a result. I like to serve crusty bread with the eggplant casserole so that it can be used to mop up all the delicious juices.

SERVES 4 ▶ INFORMAL MENU 9

1 large eggplant (about 1½ pounds)
5 tablespoons oil
2 medium onions, diced
4 cloves garlic, minced
16-ounce can diced tomatoes, well drained
16-ounce can chickpeas, drained and rinsed
Salt to taste
Liberal seasoning freshly ground pepper
⅓ cup minced fresh parsley

1. Preheat the oven to 350°F. Peel the eggplant and slice it lengthwise into ½-inch thicknesses. Cut these slices into ½-inch strips then cubes.

2. Heat 2 tablespoons of the oil in a large skillet over medium heat. When the oil is very hot but not yet smoking add enough eggplant just to make one layer. (You will probably have to do 2 batches, so as not to overcrowd the eggplant.) Fry the eggplant, tossing regularly, until it is browned and tender, though not mushy.

3. Remove the cubes to a platter, put 2 more tablespoons of the oil in the skillet, and when very hot fry the next batch of eggplant in the same manner. Remove to the platter.

4. Put 1 more tablespoon of oil in the skillet and sauté the onions and garlic until the onions are tender, not mushy, about 5 minutes.

5. Add the drained tomatoes and cook for 5 minutes. Add the chickpeas and eggplant and toss well. Season with salt and pepper, and cook 5 more minutes. Spoon into a medium baking dish and stir in the parsley. *May be prepared and chilled up to 24 hours in advance. Bring to room temperature before baking.*

6. Bake for 20 minutes, or until hot and bubbly. Serve immediately.

Baked Chickpeas Provençale

Here is an exquisite-flavored dish laced with rosemary, garlic, and red wine, and topped with a mixture of bread crumbs and more garlic and baked until crispy. Be sure to use the amount of garlic indicated; it mellows with baking and lends a subtle flavor to the sauce.

SERVES 4 TO 6

⅓ cup olive oil
12 cloves garlic, minced
1 teaspoon chopped fresh rosemary, or ½ teaspoon dried rosemary, crumbled
¼ teaspoon dried oregano
2 bay leaves
16-ounce can diced tomatoes
1 tablespoon tomato paste
Two 16-ounce cans chickpeas, drained and rinsed
¾ cup dry red wine
3 medium potatoes, peeled and cut into ½-inch dice
¾ pound cabbage, chopped or thinly sliced (about 4 cups)
½ teaspoon salt
Liberal seasoning freshly ground pepper

TOPPING
½ cup Bread Crumbs (page 294)
1 tablespoon olive oil
2 cloves garlic, minced
½ cup minced fresh parsley
¼ cup grated Parmesan cheese

1. Preheat the oven to 350°F. Heat the olive oil in a large (10 x 10-inch) flameproof casserole over medium heat, then add the garlic, rosemary, oregano, and bay leaves, and sauté for 2 minutes. (Note: If your casserole is not flameproof, then sauté everything in a large skillet and put in a large casserole.)

2. Add the tomatoes with their juice and tomato paste, stir to blend, then add the chickpeas and all of the remaining ingredients except the topping, and stir to mix. *May be prepared to this point up to 24 hours in advance, covered, and chilled.*

3. Cover the casserole, bring to a simmer, then bake for 45 minutes, or until the potatoes are tender. (Occasionally remove the dish from the oven and toss the mixture to ensure even cooking.)

4. Meanwhile prepare the topping. Combine the bread crumbs, olive oil, garlic, parsley, and Parmesan cheese in a small bowl and mix to coat evenly.

5. Remove the casserole from the oven and sprinkle the topping evenly over the top. Return to the oven and bake, *uncovered,* for 15 more minutes. If you desire a browner, crisper crust run the casserole under the broiler for 1 minute, or until golden. Serve immediately.

Baked Macaroni and Cheese with Cauliflower and Jalapeño Peppers

Here two classic favorites are combined—macaroni and cheese and cauliflower in cheese sauce—to make a standout casserole that is rich and satisfying.

SERVES 4 ▶ **INFORMAL MENU 10**

1 cup macaroni, cooked and drained (2 cups cooked)
1 small to medium cauliflower, cut into bite-size florets and steamed until tender
4 tablespoons butter
¼ cup unbleached white flour
2⅓ cups milk
2 cups (8 ounces) grated sharp Cheddar cheese (preferably Wisconsin Cheddar)
1 cup (4 ounces) grated Monterey Jack and jalapeño pepper cheese
½ teaspoon salt
Freshly ground pepper to taste
2 tablespoons Bread Crumbs (page 294)

1. Preheat the oven to 350°F. Make sure the macaroni is well drained. If you want to cook it in advance, then toss it with a little oil to prevent sticking. Make sure the cauliflower is well drained.

2. Melt the butter in a medium saucepan over medium heat. Whisk in the flour and cook this roux for 2 minutes, whisking constantly.

3. Whisk in the milk and cook, whisking often, until it thickens and begins to boil, about 7 minutes. Remove from the heat and stir in the cheeses, salt, and pepper. *May be prepared to this point up to 24 hours in advance. Chill the macaroni, cauliflower, and sauce separately. When ready to cook, heat the sauce and proceed with the next step.*

4. Put the macaroni and cauliflower in a 10-by-10-inch baking dish (or something comparable) and pour on the sauce. Toss gently to mix. Sprinkle on the bread crumbs.

5. Bake for 20 to 25 minutes, or until browned and bubbly.

> NOTE: If you do not have jalapeño pepper cheese then you can use all cheddar cheese and add 1 jalapeño pepper, seeded and minced. (See the Glossary for advice on handling chiles.)

Mexican-Style Stuffed Summer Squash

By the end of each summer many people are hard-pressed to find new ways to prepare the seemingly endless gifts of squash that arrive on their doorsteps from overenthusiastic gardening neighbors. I relish the Mexican flavors of beans, chiles, and sour cream, and think they work sensationally as a stuffing for squash. This dish can be prepared up to 48 hours in advance so it is a good choice for entertaining.

SERVES 4 ▶ INFORMAL MENU 7

4 medium yellow summer squash (8 inches)
2 tablespoons butter
Salt to taste
Freshly ground pepper to taste
2 tablespoons olive oil
2 medium onions, diced
2 teaspoons ground cumin
1 teaspoon dried oregano
1 small fresh jalapeño pepper, seeded and minced **G**
2½ cups cooked kidney beans **G**, drained and rinsed (about one and a half 16-ounce cans)
4-ounce can mild green chiles, drained and chopped
½ cup sour cream
2 cups (8 ounces) cubed Monterey Jack cheese (½-inch cubes)
Minced fresh parsley for garnish

1. Slice the ends off the summer squash and discard. Cut the squash in half lengthwise, and with a teaspoon or melon bailer scoop out the inside of the squash, leaving a thin wall intact. Finely chop the squash centers and set aside.

2. In a large skillet place enough squash halves to fit comfortably and add ½ inch of water. Cover the pan and steam the squash just until tender, about 5 minutes. Repeat with the remaining squash. Drain each one well and place in a shallow buttered baking dish (or two). Cut the butter into bits and place in the hot squash halves. Season with salt and pepper.

3. Drain the water out of the skillet and dry. Add the olive oil and heat over medium heat. Mix in the onions and sauté for 5 minutes. Add the cumin, oregano, and jalapeño pepper, and cook 1 minute. Add the chopped squash centers and cook 5 minutes more, stirring often.

4. Add beans, chiles, and salt and pepper to taste, and cook until the squash is tender. Remove from the heat and let cool 10 minutes. Stir in the sour cream and cheese.

5. Preheat the oven to 350°F. Stuff each squash shell with the filling. Press it in gently. *May be prepared to this point up to 48 hours in advance, covered, and refrigerated. Bring to room temperature before baking.*

6. Bake for 20 to 30 minutes, or until piping hot and bubbly. Garnish with minced parsley before serving.

Walnut Loaf with Burgundy Sauce

Walnut Loaf with Burgundy Sauce

This loaf makes an impressive entrée for a Thanksgiving feast or any special occasion. Being a great fan of leftovers, I particularly look forward to leftover walnut loaf because it makes superb sandwiches, sliced and topped with mayonnaise or Russian dressing.

SERVES 8　　　　　　　　　　　　　　　　　　▶ THANKSGIVING FEAST MENU

> ¾ pound sliced whole wheat bread (about 14 slices)
> ¾ pound (about 2¾ cups) walnuts
> 4 large onions, minced
> 1 bunch fresh parsley, minced (about 2 cups minced)
> 1 green bell pepper, minced
> 1 celery rib, minced
> 3 eggs, beaten
> 1½ teaspoons poultry seasoning
> 1 teaspoon salt
> Pinch dried thyme
> Freshly ground pepper to taste
> 2 tablespoons oil
> 16-ounce can tomatoes, drained and chopped
> 1 bunch fresh parsley for garnish

> BURGUNDY SAUCE
> 7 tablespoons butter
> ¼ cup plus 2 tablespoons unbleached white flour
> ½ cup red Burgundy wine or other dry red wine
> ⅓ cup tamari or other soy sauce
> 3½ cups Vegetable Stock (page 290)
> Freshly ground pepper to taste

1. Preheat the broiler. Lay the slices of bread on a baking sheet and toast under the broiler on both sides until golden. Cool, then grind into bread crumbs in a blender or food processor. Put the bread crumbs in a large bowl.

2. Reduce the oven setting to 375°F. Grind the walnuts in the blender or food processor as you did the bread. Add to the bread crumb bowl and mix well.

3. Add all of the remaining ingredients except the parsley garnish and mix well.

4. Generously butter a 1½-quart loaf pan and spoon the mixture into it. Press it in firmly and smooth over the top. Cover with foil. *May be prepared to this point up to 24 hours in advance and chilled.*

5. Place the loaf pan in a larger pan or baking dish and fill with enough hot water to reach halfway up the sides of the loaf pan. Bake for 2 hours. Let the loaf sit on a wire rack for 10 minutes before unmolding.

6. To unmold, carefully slide a knife around the loaf to loosen it from the pan. Lay a serving platter on top of the loaf pan and invert. Garnish the loaf with parsley sprigs around the platter. Serve sliced, with Burgundy Sauce.

7. To make Burgundy Sauce: In a medium saucepan melt 6 tablespoons of the butter, then add the flour and whisk until smooth. Cook this roux over low heat for 2 minutes, whisking constantly.

8. Add the wine, soy sauce, vegetable stock, and pepper, and whisk to blend. Bring to a boil, whisking constantly, then simmer for 5 minutes, or until the sauce is thickened and fragrant. Just before serving add the remaining tablespoon of butter and stir until melted. Do not boil again. Serve in a sauceboat.

THE COOKING OF AUTHENTIC INDIAN FOOD IS A JOURNEY into the sensual world of spices, aromas, and tantalizing flavors. It can be intimidating at first because prepackaged curry powder was the extent of Americans' exposure to curry for many decades. But once you familiarize yourself with the

Curries and Accompaniments

spices that are commonly used in most curries—turmeric, cumin, coriander, cardamom, cayenne, and ginger—and understand that most dishes begin by cooking these spices in Ghee (page 300) or oil, then you are off to a good start with mastering Indian flavors.

It is customary to serve many different dishes at an Indian meal, so it can be fun to play around with your choices. For a special occasion, however, I always include dal, raita, chutney, and puris with whatever dishes I serve. These accompaniments add a festive touch and complete the meal, Indian style.

Braised Curried Eggplant

When we were in college my sister Jacqueline and I would oftentimes spend days delving into cookbooks to plan some exotic feast, which we would then cook that weekend for friends. Our favorite cuisine was Indian, and the surprises it offered were seemingly endless. She created this dish on the spur of the moment one day, and it has proven to be an enduring favorite.

SERVES 4 ▶ QUICK MENU 8

2 tablespoons Ghee (page 300) or butter
1 onion, diced
2 cloves garlic, minced
1 teaspoon turmeric
2 teaspoons ground coriander
½ teaspoon cumin seeds
¼ teaspoon cayenne pepper (or more to taste)
1 medium to large eggplant (1½ pounds), peeled and cut into 1-inch cubes
3 cups (from 28-ounce can) diced canned tomatoes with their juice
½ teaspoon salt
1 cup frozen peas
1 tablespoon lemon juice

1. Heat the ghee or butter in a medium saucepan over medium heat. Add the onion and garlic and sauté for 10 minutes, or until very tender.

2. Add the turmeric, coriander, cumin seeds, and cayenne pepper, and cook for 2 minutes.

3. Add the eggplant, toss well, and cook for 2 minutes. Add the tomatoes and salt and toss again. Cover the pan and simmer for 25 minutes, or until the eggplant is very tender and some of it is mushy. Remove the cover for the last 5 minutes of cooking. The mixture should be somewhat soupy though not watery. If it is slightly watery then raise the heat and cook uncovered until thickened. *May be prepared to this point up to 24 hours in advance and chilled.*

4. Add the peas and lemon juice and cook 2 minutes more, or until the peas are heated through. They should still retain their bright green color.

Cashew Nut Curry

The cashews in this quick Sri Lanka-style curry become very tender, and the sauce is delicate enough not to overpower their subtle flavor. Raw cashews are the ones to use for this dish.

SERVES 4 ▶ INFORMAL MENU 14

2 tablespoons oil
1 medium onion, diced
½ fresh red chile pepper, seeded and minced **G**, or ⅛ teaspoon cayenne pepper
1 teaspoon turmeric
1 teaspoon ground coriander
¼ teaspoon ground cardamom
2 cloves garlic, minced
½ teaspoon minced fresh ginger
1 cinnamon stick
½ teaspoon salt
8 ounces (about 2 cups) raw cashews
2 medium potatoes, peeled and cut into ½-inch dice
2 cups coconut milk **G**, or 16-ounce can light coconut milk

1. Heat the oil in a medium saucepan over medium heat and add the onion, chili, turmeric, coriander, cardamom, garlic, ginger, and cinnamon stick. Cook for 2 minutes, stirring constantly.

2. Add all of the remaining ingredients and bring to a boil. Lower the heat and simmer, partially covered, for 20 minutes, or until the potatoes are tender and the sauce is thickened. Serve alone or over rice.

Fruited Rice Curry

The contrast of sweet fruit and spicy rice is very appealing in this dish. I sometimes make a simple meal of this with plain yogurt alongside it, or accompany it with a saucy curry, such as Braised Curried Eggplant (page 177).

SERVES 4 ▶ QUICK MENU 8

3 tablespoons oil
1 medium to large banana, sliced ½ inch thick
2 teaspoons minced fresh ginger
½ teaspoon turmeric
1 teaspoon ground cumin
1 teaspoon ground coriander
⅛ teaspoon cayenne pepper
1 medium apple, peeled, cored, and cut into ½-inch dice
8 dried apricots, cut into ¼-inch dice (⅓ cup diced)
2 tablespoons raisins
Grated rind of 1 orange
⅓ cup coarsely chopped pecans or dry-roasted cashews
2½ to 3 cups cold cooked Perfect Brown Rice (page 292), made from 1 cup dry rice
1 tablespoon butter, cut into bits
½ teaspoon salt

1. In a large skillet heat 1 tablespoon of the oil over medium heat. Sauté the banana for 1 minute, or just until lightly golden. Do not allow it to get mushy. Remove and set aside.

2. Heat the remaining 2 tablespoons of oil. Add the ginger and spices and cook for 1 minute. Add the fruit, orange rind, and nuts, and sauté for 5 minutes, stirring often.

3. Add the cold rice, toss well, and cook, stirring frequently, until hot, about 7 minutes. Dot with the butter and add the salt. Add the reserved banana just before serving.

> NOTE: You can prepare this up to 24 hours in advance and reheat in a skillet on the stove, or in a covered baking dish in a 350°F oven. Add the banana just before serving.

Curried Cauliflower and Peas

Curried Cauliflower and Peas

This classic vegetable dish does wonders with cauliflower. Pair it with another dish such as Cashew Nut Curry (page 178), or serve it alongside rice and some plain yogurt for a simple meal.

SERVES 4 ▶ INFORMAL MENU 14

1 large head cauliflower
6 tablespoons Ghee (page 300) or butter
1½ teaspoons turmeric
1½ teaspoons ground cumin
1½ teaspoons cumin seeds
¼ teaspoon cayenne pepper
1½ cups fresh or frozen peas
¼ teaspoon salt

1. Wash the cauliflower and cut it into small florets.

2. Melt the ghee or butter in a large skillet over medium-low heat. Add the spices, stir to blend, and "toast" them for 30 seconds.

3. Add the cauliflower and toss to coat evenly. Add 2 tablespoons of water, then cover and cook for about 15 minutes, or until the cauliflower is almost but not quite tender, stirring occasionally. (If you are using fresh peas add them after 7 minutes.)

4. Add the frozen peas (if you are using them) and the salt, and cook uncovered until the peas and cauliflower are tender, about 3 to 5 additional minutes. *May be prepared up to 24 hours in advance, covered, and refrigerated. Reheat then taste to adjust seasoning.*

Vegetable Kofta

These fried Indian vegetable balls in a fragrant coconut sauce are one of the most delectable Indian dishes. They are somewhat time-consuming but worth it.

SERVES 4 TO 6 ▶ ELEGANT MENU 4

1 cup frozen peas, thawed and mashed
2 large potatoes, peeled, boiled, and mashed
2 medium carrots, finely diced and cooked
2 slices good-quality white bread, moistened with water, squeezed very dry and crumbled
1 tablespoon ground coriander
½ teaspoon turmeric
¼ teaspoon ground cumin
¼ teaspoon cayenne pepper
2 teaspoons sugar
¾ teaspoon salt
Flour for dusting
Oil for frying

SAUCE
¼ cup Ghee (page 300) or butter
1 medium onion, minced
1½ teaspoons minced fresh ginger
1 cinnamon stick
1 bay leaf
½ teaspoon ground cardamom
½ teaspoon turmeric
1½ teaspoons ground coriander
1½ teaspoons ground cumin
¼ teaspoon cayenne pepper
1 large tomato, peeled, seeded, and chopped **G**
2½ cups coconut milk **G**
½ teaspoon salt

1. To make the koftas: Combine the mashed peas, mashed potatoes, cooked carrots, moistened bread, and all of the flavorings in a large bowl and mix well.

2. Place some flour on a plate in front of you. One by one form the mixture into 1½-inch balls, then roll in the flour to coat.

3. Pour enough oil into a large skillet to reach ½ inch up the sides of the pan. Heat the oil over medium heat until hot but not smoking. Fry the balls, turning them often, until they are golden brown and very crisp on the outside. Drain on paper towels and set aside. Discard the oil.

4. To make the sauce: In the same skillet heat the ghee or butter. When hot add the onion and all of the spices, and sauté for 2 minutes.

5. Add the tomato and stir to blend. Add the coconut milk and salt, stir, and boil the mixture for 3 minutes. *May be prepared to this point in advance; cook within 8 hours. Chill the sauce and koftas separately.*

6. Preheat the oven to 350°F. Place the koftas in a large shallow baking dish and pour the sauce over them. Cover and bake for 20 minutes. Alternatively, add the koftas to the sauce in the skillet and cook together, covered, on top of the stove for 20 minutes, or until the sauce has thickened.

Baked Eggplant Stuffed with Curried Vegetables

Eggplant has a very prominent place in Indian vegetarian cooking for its resemblance to meat and because it absorbs spices so well. Although it is not a particularly nutritious vegetable, it can serve as the basis for a very substantial dish. This stuffed eggplant makes a delicious and attractive main course, and it is low in calories. Choose firm, glossy eggplants, and check to see that they are free of bruises.

SERVES 4   ▶ INFORMAL MENU 6

2 small eggplants (about ½ pound each)
3 tablespoons oil
2 medium onions, diced
3 cloves garlic, minced
1 teaspoon minced fresh ginger
1 tablespoon ground coriander
1 teaspoon turmeric
1 teaspoon ground cumin
Pinch cumin seeds
¼ teaspoon cayenne pepper
2 cups (6 ounces) quartered mushrooms
2 medium tomatoes, seeded and chopped, or ¾ cup diced canned tomatoes, drained
1 cup peas, fresh or frozen
½ teaspoon salt
1 cup plain yogurt

1. Wash the eggplants, cut off their stems, and slice them in half lengthwise. Scoop out the pulp with a spoon, leaving a wall of eggplant about ¼ inch thick all around. Roughly chop the pulp and set aside.

2. Preheat the oven to 400°F. Bake the eggplant shells face down on a greased baking sheet for 15 to 20 minutes, or until almost tender. Remove and reduce the heat to 350°F.

3. Meanwhile prepare the filling. Heat the oil in a large skillet over medium heat until it is hot but not smoking. Add the onions, garlic, and ginger, and sauté for 2 minutes. Then add the remainder of the spices and sauté 2 minutes more, stirring often.

4. Add the mushrooms and sauté for 2 minutes, then add the tomatoes and cook 2 minutes more. Add the eggplant pulp and fresh peas if you are using them and cook for 5 minutes, or until the eggplant is almost, but not quite, tender. If you are using frozen peas add them now and cook until the peas are heated through, about 2 more minutes.

5. Turn off the heat under the skillet, add the salt and yogurt, and stir to mix. Fill the eggplant shells with this mixture, then place them in a lightly greased shallow baking dish (a 12 x 2 x 7-inch dish works well). *May be prepared to this point up to 8 hours in advance, covered, and chilled.* Bake for 30 minutes, or until brown on top and piping hot.

Samosas

These Indian deep-fried turnovers are stuffed with a spicy potato filling and have a light crisp exterior. They are wonderful for entertaining because they can be prepared in advance, although they must be cooked just before serving, like most Indian breads.

MAKES 16   ▶ **BREAKFAST AND BRUNCH MENU 4**

FILLING

    1 large potato, peeled
    1 tablespoon Ghee (page 300), oil, or butter
    1 large onion, finely diced
    1 teaspoon minced fresh ginger
    ¼ teaspoon turmeric
    ½ teaspoon ground cumin
    ½ teaspoon ground coriander
    ¼ teaspoon cayenne pepper
    ½ teaspoon salt
    ⅔ cup frozen peas, thawed

DOUGH

    1 cup whole wheat flour
    ½ teaspoon salt
    2 tablespoons Ghee or butter, melted and cooled
    3 to 4 tablespoons water
    2 cups oil for deep frying

1. Cut the potato into quarters and boil just until cooked through. Drain very well and cut into ¼-inch dice.

2. Heat the ghee in a medium skillet over medium heat. Add the onion and sauté for 7 to 8 minutes or until it is clear and limp.

3. Add all of the spices and salt and stir to blend. Cook 1 minute.

4. Add the peas and diced potato, and cook for 2 minutes more, stirring often. Set aside to cool.

5. To make the dough: Put the flour and salt in a medium-size bowl. Add the ghee or cooled melted butter, and with your fingertips blend it into the flour until it is evenly incorporated. Sprinkle on 3 tablespoons of water and stir to blend. Gather the dough into a ball (if it is too crumbly add another tablespoon of water) and knead it for 5 to 7 minutes, or until it is smooth and elastic. Cover with a damp towel and let the dough rest for 15 minutes.

6. Divide the dough in half and roll each half into a log shape. Cut each log into 8 pieces and roll each piece into a ball. Cover the balls with a damp towel while you proceed with the next step.

7. Lightly flour your work surface and roll each ball of dough into a circle 3½ inches in diameter. Keep the circles of dough covered with a damp towel. (You can let them sit for 4 to 5 hours.)

8. Put a small bowl of water in front of you. Divide the filling into 16 portions. With your finger lightly dampen the edge of a circle and spoon a portion of filling onto the center of the circle. Pick up the turnover and keep it in one hand. With the other hand fold the turnover in half and pinch the edges together to completely encase the filling. Repeat with the remaining dough and filling. *May be prepared to this point up to 3 hours in advance.* Cover with foil or plastic and chill.

9. Heat the oil in a medium saucepan. When it is hot but not smoking fry 2 or 3 samosas at a time, turning them to make them evenly golden. Cook only about 30 seconds; they should be light in color. Keep them warm in a 350°F oven as you proceed with the remaining samosas. Serve and enjoy.

Red Lentil Dal

Dal is a thick sauce-like mixture of puréed lentils or split peas and spices. It is usually served on rice and is the protein component of an Indian vegetarian meal. I think that red lentils make the most delicious dal. When cooked, they turn a rich golden color, and have a buttery, nutlike flavor.

SERVES 4 TO 6   ▶ **ELEGANT MENU 4**

1¼ cups red lentils
3 cups water
½ teaspoon salt
2 tablespoons Ghee (page 300) or oil
½ teaspoon black mustard seeds*
½ teaspoon turmeric
¼ teaspoon cayenne pepper
½ teaspoon ground cumin
½ teaspoon ground coriander
1 teaspoon minced fresh ginger
Thin lemon slices for garnish

* Black mustard seeds can be purchased in Indian food shops and some health food stores. They have a milder and nuttier flavor than yellow mustard seeds. Omit them if you cannot get them.

1. Rinse the lentils in a sieve under cold running water. Pick out any stones or foreign substances. Put the lentils in a medium-size saucepan along with the water and salt. Cook, uncovered, over medium-low heat for about 25 minutes, or until the lentils are almost completely smooth.

2. Heat the ghee or oil in a separate small skillet over medium heat and add the mustard seeds. After the seeds have stopped popping and spattering add all the spices and stir. Cook 1 minute. Very carefully add this mixture to the dal. Stir, then simmer the dal 2 minutes more. (If you used oil to cook the spices, then stir in 1 tablespoon of butter.) *May be prepared to this point up to 24 hours in advance. Cover and chill. Reheat over low heat.* Scrape the dal into a warm serving dish and garnish with lemon slices.

Puris (Deep-Fried Puffed Bread)

Once cooked, these flaky breads must be served immediately, which means that you'll be at the stove while everyone else is seated at the table. It actually isn't too troublesome because Puris take only a few minutes to cook, and if you are well organized you can do it with great aplomb. The method of making the dough for Puris is the same as that for tortillas, Samosas (page 186), and Mandarin Pancakes (page 114), though Puris are cooked differently. Once you discover how easy it is to handle the dough, you'll want to try all of these breads.

MAKES TWELVE 5-INCH BREADS; SERVES 6　　　　　　　　　　▶ ELEGANT MENU 4

2 cups whole wheat flour
½ teaspoon salt
3 tablespoons Ghee (page 300) or oil
¾ cup warm water minus 1 tablespoon
Oil for frying

1. Blend the flour and salt in a medium bowl. Add the ghee or oil and rub it into the flour with the tips of your fingers until it resembles a coarse, flaky meal.

2. Make a well in the center and pour in the water, then stir with a spoon until blended. Turn the dough onto a lightly floured board or work surface and knead for 7 minutes. Place the dough back in the bowl and cover with a slightly damp towel. Let rest for 30 minutes, or wrap in plastic and chill overnight. Bring to room temperature before rolling.

3. Divide the dough in half, roll each half into a cylinder, then cut each cylinder into 6 even-size pieces. Roll a piece of the dough into a ball between your hands, then flatten it into a disk. With a rolling pin roll the disk on a lightly floured surface into a 5-inch circle, turning the dough as necessary to keep the circle evenly round. Lightly flour the work surface as necessary. Repeat with the remaining dough and unevenly stack the puris as you go along, then cover with a slightly damp towel.

4. Pour enough oil into a medium skillet to reach a depth of 2 inches, and heat over medium heat until hot but not smoking. To test if the oil is hot enough drop a tiny piece of dough into it; it should sizzle immediately and rise to the surface. Slide 1 puri into the oil and press it down with a slotted spatula to keep it below the surface. It will immediately begin to puff up. Cook for 30 seconds, then turn over and cook another 30 seconds, or until lightly golden. Drain on paper towels and serve immediately, or you can keep them in a 250°F oven for the few minutes it takes you to finish the batch.

NOTE: Do not be surprised if all of the puris don't puff up perfectly. Sometimes that happens, but they are still delicious. If many of them don't puff up then perhaps they are not evenly round, or perhaps they have been rolled larger than 5 inches. In either case, form the uncooked dough into balls again and reroll into circles.

Orange Raita

Raitas are the "salad" component of an Indian meal. Their cool, refreshing character serves to contrast with the spiciness of many dishes.

▶ ELEGANT MENU 4

SERVES 4 TO 6

1 large navel orange
1½ cups plain yogurt
½ teaspoon ground cumin
¼ teaspoon salt

1. Wash the orange and dry very well. Grate half of the orange peel on the fine side of a grater. Put *half* of the grated rind into a medium bowl. Set aside the remaining grated rind for garnish.

2. Cut away the remaining peel and pith from the orange with a small, sharp knife and discard. Over a bowl, holding the orange in one hand, with the knife cut away each segment of fruit from the membrane on either side; the sections will fall out easily. Cut each segment in half.

3. Put half of the slices in the bowl and mash lightly to release their juice. Add the remaining orange pieces and mix.

4. Stir in the yogurt, ground cumin, and salt. Pour into a serving dish and garnish with the reserved orange rind. Cover and chill for at least 1 hour and up to 2 hours before serving.

Banana Raita

Combining mashed and sliced banana in this memorable raita gives it an appealing silken texture.

SERVES 4 TO 6

2 large ripe bananas
½ teaspoon ground coriander
Dash cayenne pepper
¼ teaspoon salt
1 cup plain yogurt

1. Peel 1 of the bananas and put it into a medium bowl. Mash it thoroughly with a fork until it is a purée. Stir in the spices and salt; then stir in the yogurt until well blended.

2. Peel the other banana and slice in half lengthwise. Slice each half into ¼-inch-thick slices and add to the yogurt mixture. Toss to blend.

3. Spoon the raita into a serving dish and garnish with a sprinkling of cayenne pepper. Cover and chill at least 1 hour before serving.

Raisin Chutney

Chutneys are a type of Indian condiment or relish. They are concentrated in flavor and spicy, and so just a small spoonful on your plate is all that's needed to add piquancy to your meal. This is my favorite chutney. It has an intense flavor—both sweet and spicy. It can be made well in advance and would make a wonderful gift for a chutney lover.

SERVES 4 TO 6   ▶ ELEGANT MENU 4

> 1 cup raisins
> 2 teaspoons minced fresh ginger
> ¼ cup water
> Dash cayenne pepper
> ½ teaspoon salt
> Juice of ½ lemon

1. Place all the ingredients in the container of a blender or food processor and blend until you have a coarse paste. You will probably have to turn off the machine and scrape down the sides a few times.

2. Scrape into a container with a tight cover. This will keep for up to 2 weeks in the refrigerator.

Orange Lassi

Lassi is the popular milkshake drink of India, made with buttermilk or yogurt and thinned with ice. It is served either sweetened, salted, or plain. Here is an interesting sweetened version that is made with orange juice and is served with crushed ice, Indian style.

SERVES 4   ▶ **BREAKFAST AND BRUNCH MENU 4**

Juice of 2 large oranges (about ½ cup)
2 cups buttermilk **G** or plain low-fat yogurt
2 tablespoons honey

In batches place all of the ingredients in the blender with some ice and blend until the ice is crushed. Pour into tall glasses and serve immediately.

TOFU IS AVAILABLE IN DIFFERENT FORMS—SOFT, SILKEN, firm, and extra firm—but I always seem to gravitate to a firm variety because I prefer its texture. Once tofu is fried it becomes chewy and delicious, and can become the basis for all kinds of dishes that customarily use chicken as the main ingredient. This soy food is ideal for vegetarians and vegans because it is a low-fat source of protein and is so versatile. Its

Tofu and Tempeh

mild flavor is an asset, for when tofu is cooked in spicy sauces, it soaks up the flavorings and becomes transformed.

Tempeh, on the other hand, has a distinct flavor. This soy cake is fermented and retains the strong flavor of the chopped soybeans from which it is made. Because of this, tempeh is handled differently and benefits from assertive sauces that cling to it. Both of these soy foods deserve the popularity that they have gained because they add so much to the vegetarian repertoire—nutritionally and aesthetically. See the Glossary to read more about tofu and tempeh.

Stir-Fried Asparagus, Tofu, and Red Pepper

A quick, attractive dish that is a great way to celebrate spring's first asparagus (or you could substitute broccoli, if you like). Brilliant red and green colors make this stir-fry a visual treat while ginger defines its flavor.

SERVES 4 ▶ INFORMAL MENU 3

2 tablespoons tamari or other soy sauce
2 tablespoons water
¼ cup Chinese rice wine or dry sherry
2 teaspoons cornstarch
1 pound asparagus (preferably thin)
¼ cup peanut oil
1 pound firm tofu, cut into 1-inch cubes and patted very dry
2 teaspoons minced fresh ginger
1 tablespoon water
1 large red bell pepper, cored and cut into 1-inch squares
8-ounce can sliced water chestnuts, rinsed and well drained
1½ recipes Perfect Brown Rice (page 292), cooked
1 tablespoon Asian sesame oil Ⓖ
A few drops hot spicy oil Ⓖ or Tabasco

1. Have all of the ingredients prepared and laid out in front of you. In a small bowl or cup combine the soy sauce, water, rice wine, and cornstarch, and set aside.

2. Cut off only the very tough bottoms of the asparagus, and with a sharp paring knife peel the bottom half of each one. Cut the asparagus on the diagonal into 2-inch lengths.

3. Heat a wok or large skillet over high heat until hot. Add the peanut oil, and when it is hot but not smoking add the tofu. Stir-fry until golden all over, about 5 to 8 minutes. Remove from the pan to a platter and set aside.

4. Reduce the heat to medium-high and add the ginger. Cook for 15 seconds. Add the asparagus and toss, then add 1 tablespoon of water. Cover the pan and cook for 2 minutes, or until the asparagus is almost tender (this will depend on the thickness of the stalks).

5. Remove the cover and add the red pepper and water chestnuts. Stir-fry uncovered for 3 minutes.

6. Return the tofu to the pan and toss. Quickly stir the soy sauce mixture and add. Toss and cook 1 minute.

8. Turn off the heat and sprinkle on the sesame oil and hot spicy oil. Serve immediately over rice.

Szechuan Braised Tofu and Vegetables

This is one of my favorite Chinese dishes. The tofu and eggplant absorb the hot, spicy sauce superbly and create a rich, haunting flavor. It is very easy to prepare, made even more so by setting all of the ingredients out in front of you close to the stove at the time of cooking.

SERVES 4   ▶ **INFORMAL MENU 4**

Oil
1 pound firm tofu, cut into strips ½-inch by 2 inches and patted very dry
1 small eggplant (¾ pound), peeled and cut into strips ½ inch by 2 inches
3 cups (8 ounces) sliced mushrooms
2 cups (8 ounces) green beans cut into 2-inch lengths
¼ cup plus 3 tablespoons water
1 tablespoon chili paste with garlic
3 tablespoons tamari or other soy sauce
4½ tablespoons Chinese rice wine or dry sherry

1. Heat about 3 tablespoons of oil over medium-high heat in a wok or large skillet. When the oil is hot but not smoking, add half of the tofu and stir-fry until lightly golden. Remove to a platter and add a little more oil to the pan if it is dry. Repeat with the remaining tofu.

2. If there is no oil left in the pan add a little more. Raise the heat to high. When the oil is hot but not smoking add the eggplant. Stir-fry for 4 minutes. It will probably absorb the oil, but do not add any more; just keep tossing.

3. Add the mushrooms and green beans, and stir-fry for 3 minutes. At this point if the mixture is very dry you can add a tiny bit of oil.

4. Add ¼ cup of the water, cover the wok or skillet, and cook for 5 minutes, or until the water is absorbed and the beans and eggplant are tender.

5. Add the tofu and toss.

6. In a small bowl blend together the chili paste, soy sauce, rice wine, and 3 tablespoons of water. Pour over the tofu mixture and toss until well coated.

7. Stir-fry 3 minutes more, or until the sauce is slightly thickened. Serve immediately on rice.

Tofu Francese with Artichoke Hearts

I have found that this favorite northern Italian lemon and butter sauce works wonderfully with tofu. In this dish tofu is dipped in an egg batter then sautéed with artichoke hearts and served in a light lemon, butter, and white wine sauce. If you are going to serve Perfect Brown Rice Pilaf (page 292) as an accompaniment, then cook the pilaf in advance and keep it warm in the oven while you prepare this.

SERVES 4 ▶ ELEGANT MENU 9

1 pound firm tofu
⅓ cup unbleached white flour
1 egg, beaten
Oil for frying
4 tablespoons butter
14-ounce can artichoke hearts, drained and quartered
Juice of 1 lemon
½ cup dry white wine
Freshly ground pepper to taste
4 thin slices lemon for garnish
4 parsley sprigs for garnish

1. Set all of the ingredients before you to ensure relaxed cooking. Slice the tofu into rectangular slices about 2½ inches long by 2 inches wide by ¼ inch thick—no thicker. Pat thoroughly dry with paper or cotton towels. Put the flour in one small bowl and the beaten egg in another. One by one dip the tofu slices into the flour to coat them completely, and lay them on a platter in front of you.

2. Pour enough oil into a large skillet to reach ¼-inch depth and heat it over medium-high heat until it is hot but not smoking. One by one dip a few slices of tofu into the beaten egg, then place them carefully in the hot skillet. Fry on both sides until golden brown. Remove and set aside on a platter covered with paper towels. Repeat with the remaining tofu.

3. Pour any remaining oil out of the skillet. Melt the butter, then sauté the quartered artichokes 3 to 5 minutes, or until they are heated through. Add the lemon juice, wine, and pepper, and bring to a simmer. Add the tofu and spoon some sauce over it. Cook, basting occasionally, 3 to 5 minutes more, or until the sauce has thickened slightly and the tofu is hot. Garnish each serving with a lemon slice and parsley sprig and serve immediately.

Skillet Tofu and Vegetables in Brandy Cream Sauce

If you've never particularly liked tofu, try it lightly fried in oil and then seasoned well, as it is in this dish. You'll find that its crisp texture makes it very appetizing, and the tofu will have absorbed the flavors of the sauce.

SERVES 4 ▶ **ELEGANT MENU 5**

1 pound firm tofu
3 tablespoons oil
3 tablespoons butter
2 cloves garlic, minced
1 medium onion, finely diced
3 cups (8 ounces) sliced mushrooms
1½ teaspoons unbleached white flour
1 bay leaf
1 medium carrot, grated
1 teaspoon minced fresh tarragon, or ½ teaspoon dried tarragon, crumbled
¼ cup brandy or dry sherry
½ cup heavy or whipping cream
¼ teaspoon salt
Freshly ground pepper to taste
1 tablespoon minced fresh parsley

1. Cut the tofu into 1-inch cubes and pat very dry.

2. Heat the oil in a large skillet over high heat until it is hot but not smoking. Add the tofu and sauté, tossing often, until it is golden, about 10 minutes. Remove to a platter and set aside. Discard any remaining oil.

3. Reduce the heat to medium and melt the butter. Add the garlic, onion, and mushrooms, and sauté for 10 minutes, tossing often. Sprinkle on the flour, toss, and cook 1 more minute.

4. Reduce the heat to a simmer and add the reserved tofu and all of the remaining ingredients except the parsley. Stir to blend and simmer for 5 to 10 minutes, or until the sauce has thickened. Add the parsley just before serving and toss to mix. Tofu gets too firm when reheated so it is best to serve this immediately.

Tofu Fra Diavolo with Spinach Fettuccine

Chunks of tofu are cooked in a tomato sauce with hot peppers, then spooned onto a bed of spinach fettuccine. I like to serve this dish with crusty bread so that it can be used to mop up all the delicious juices. I find that no grated cheese is needed, but you can add it if you like.

SERVES 4 ▶ **INFORMAL MENU 11**

1 pound spinach fettuccine
2 tablespoons olive oil
1 pound firm tofu, cut into ¾-inch cubes and patted dry
4 cloves garlic, minced
2 medium onions, finely diced
½ teaspoon dried red pepper flakes
2½ cups tomato purée
½ teaspoon salt
Freshly ground pepper to taste
Minced parsley for garnish

1. Bring a large (6-quart) pot of water to a boil. Add the fettuccine and cook until al dente, about 10 minutes.

2. Meanwhile heat the olive oil in a large skillet over medium-high heat until it is hot but not smoking. Add the tofu and cook until golden, tossing continuously. Remove to a platter and set aside.

3. If all of the oil has disappeared, then add just a little to cover the bottom of the pan. Lower the heat to medium and add the garlic, onions, and red pepper flakes. Sauté, tossing often, until the onions are tender, about 5 minutes.

4. Return the tofu to the pan and toss. Add the tomato purée, salt, and pepper. Simmer the mixture for about 8 minutes, or until the sauce is hot and thickened.

5. When the fettuccine is cooked, drain it very well in a colander and divide it evenly among the serving plates. Spoon the tofu and sauce on top of each serving. Garnish with the minced parsley.

Braised Tofu and Vegetables with White Wine and Tarragon

Tarragon is a less familiar herb to many, and that is unfortunate. Its slight licorice flavor marries well with white wine and mushrooms in a sauce, and here it enlivens the mild character of tofu. Tofu gets much firmer when reheated so it is best to cook this dish just before serving. If you want to get a head start earlier in the day, you can prepare all of the ingredients beforehand, and set them in front of you at the time of cooking.

SERVES 4

¼ cup oil
1 pound firm tofu, cut into 1-inch cubes and patted very dry
2 medium onions, minced
2 cloves garlic, minced
3 cups (8 ounces) sliced mushrooms
1½ cups minced peeled tomatoes (from 28-ounce can), well drained
2 teaspoons minced fresh tarragon, or 1 teaspoon dried tarragon, crumbled

SAUCE
⅓ cup dry white wine
1 teaspoon tamari or other soy sauce
1½ teaspoons tomato paste
¼ cup Vegetable Stock (page 290)
Dash cayenne pepper
½ teaspoon salt
Liberal seasoning freshly ground pepper

1. In a large skillet heat the oil over medium-high heat until it is hot but not smoking. Add the tofu and stir-fry until it is golden. Remove from the pan and set aside.

2. If the skillet is dry pour in a little more oil. Add the onions and garlic and sauté for 2 minutes. Add the mushrooms and sauté, tossing frequently, for 10 more minutes, or until they are brown and tender.

3. Add the drained, chopped tomatoes and tarragon, and toss. Add the reserved tofu and toss again.

4. Mix together the sauce ingredients in a small bowl, and pour over the tofu mixture. Reduce the heat to a simmer and cook slowly, tossing occasionally, for 10 minutes, or until the sauce has thickened. Serve immediately.

Curried Rice, Tofu, and Vegetables

This is a dish I like to take to a potluck supper. It is bright colored, easy to prepare, and will hold its heat if you put it in a hot covered baking dish, wrap the dish in newspaper, and place it in a plastic bag. As with any stir-fried rice dish, you must use cold cooked rice to get fluffy results. If you need to cool the rice quickly, spread it on a platter and put it in the freezer until it gets cold.

SERVES 4 TO 6

4 tablespoons oil
1 pound firm tofu, cut into ¾-inch cubes and patted very dry
1 red bell pepper, cored and cut into ½-inch dice
4 cups (12 ounces) sliced mushrooms
1½ teaspoons turmeric
2 teaspoons ground cumin
1½ teaspoons ground coriander
¼ teaspoon cayenne pepper
¼ teaspoon salt
4 to 5 cups cold Perfect Brown Rice, made from 1½ cups brown rice and 2½ cups water
    (see page 292)
1½ cups frozen peas, thawed
2 tablespoons tamari or other soy sauce

1. Heat 2 tablespoons oil in a large, preferably non-stick, skillet over medium-high heat until it is hot but not smoking. Add the tofu and fry until it is golden, tossing often. Set aside on a platter and cover with foil to keep warm.

2. Add the remaining 2 tablespoons of oil to the skillet and when hot add the red pepper and mushrooms. Sauté for 10 minutes, or until the peppers are tender and the mushrooms are brown.

3. Add all of the spices and the salt, toss to blend well, and cook for 1 minute.

4. Reduce the heat to medium and add the cold rice, peas, and tofu. Toss until well mixed, then add the soy sauce and toss again. Cook, tossing often, for 5 to 10 minutes, or until the mixture is piping hot. Serve immediately.

> NOTE: If you want to prepare this dish in advance, don't add the peas until you are ready to reheat it; this will ensure that the peas retain their bright green color. You should be aware that the texture of tofu becomes firmer and drier upon reheating, and so there is an advantage to making this dish just before you are ready to serve it.

Soba and Tofu

Buckwheat and tofu are both very good sources of protein and iron, and both are very low in fat. This noodle dish is prepared Japanese-style—in a broth—like the popular dish ramen.

SERVES 3

8 ounces soba (buckwheat noodles)
¼ cup oil
1 pound firm tofu, cut into 1-inch cubes and patted very dry
3 cups (8 ounces) thinly sliced mushrooms
1½ teaspoons minced fresh ginger
2 cups Vegetable Stock (page 290)
¼ cup tamari or other soy sauce
3 small scallions, thinly sliced

1. Bring a large (6-quart) pot of water to a boil and drop in the soba. Cook until al dente—about 10 minutes. Drain well.

2. Meanwhile, heat the oil in a large skillet over high heat until hot but not smoking. Add the tofu and stir-fry until golden, about 10 minutes. Remove from the pan and set aside.

3. Reduce the heat to medium and add the mushrooms. Stir-fry until the mushrooms are brown and tender, about 7 minutes.

4. Return the tofu to the pan and add the ginger. Stir-fry 1 minute. Add the vegetable stock and tamari and boil 2 minutes.

5. Place some noodles in each soup bowl. Spoon equal portions of the tofu mixture and broth over each serving. Garnish with the sliced scallions.

Braised Tempeh Napoletano

Tempeh is a delicious fermented soybean product made with ground soybeans. Unlike tofu it has a flavor of its own, and its firm, dry texture makes it very easy to work with. In this dish, tempeh is simmered in an aromatic tomato sauce with vegetables and herbs. I think it goes particularly well with brown rice. Because tempeh freezes well, I always keep some on hand so I can make this on a moment's notice.

SERVES 4 ▶ QUICK MENU 1

¼ cup olive oil
6 cloves garlic, minced
1 medium onion, diced
2 small zucchini, halved lengthwise and thinly sliced
1 large green bell pepper, cut into ½-inch dice
8 ounces tempeh ⒢, cut into ½-inch cubes
1½ cups finely chopped peeled tomatoes with their juice (from 16-ounce can)
2 tablespoons dry vermouth or dry red or white wine
2 tablespoons chopped fresh basil, or ¼ teaspoon dried basil
¼ teaspoon dried marjoram
¼ teaspoon dried oregano
¼ teaspoon salt
Liberal seasoning freshly ground pepper

1. Heat the olive oil in a large skillet over medium-high heat, then add the garlic and onion, and sauté for 2 minutes, tossing frequently. Add the zucchini and toss for 2 more minutes. Add the green pepper and tempeh, and cook, tossing occasionally, for 5 more minutes.

2. Add the tomatoes, vermouth, and all of the remaining ingredients, and stir well. Reduce the heat to a simmer and cook slowly for about 10 minutes, or until the sauce is fragrant and thickened. Do not overcook the vegetables; they should still retain a slight crunchiness. Serve immediately, or cover and chill up to 24 hours, then reheat slowly until piping hot.

Stir-Fried Tempeh with Hot Pepper Sauce

Stir-Fried Tempeh with Hot Pepper Sauce

Many people are surprised to learn that chile peppers do not harm the lining of the stomach—in fact, they aid digestion. Studies were done on various winners of chile-pepper-eating contests in Mexico and no adverse effects were discovered—and the winners had eaten thousands of them! It is true that one must build up a tolerance for hot foods; then somewhere along the line that tolerance turns into a craving, and that once-unbearable fiery sensation becomes a delight. Neophytes claim that the flavor of food is overpowered when it is too hot, but a veteran lover of spiciness can appreciate flavor and fieriness simultaneously. This tempeh dish, like other hot dishes in this book, will not scald your palate. It is moderately hot, but you can adjust the spiciness to your liking by cutting down or adding to the amount of red pepper flakes.

SERVES 4 ▶ QUICK MENU 9

3 tablespoons Chinese rice wine or dry sherry
¼ cup tamari or other soy sauce
½ teaspoon salt
¼ cup ketchup
1 bunch broccoli
3 tablespoons peanut oil
1 tablespoon minced fresh ginger
2 cloves garlic, minced
½ teaspoon dried red pepper flakes
4 cups (12 ounces) sliced mushrooms
8 ounces tempeh **G**, cut into 1-inch cubes

1½ recipes Perfect Brown Rice (page 292), optional

1. Mix together the rice wine, soy sauce, salt, and ketchup in a cup or small bowl. Set out all of the remaining ingredients before you to ensure relaxed cooking.

2. Cut off the broccoli florets just beneath the flower. Peel the stalks and cut into 1-inch logs. Put the florets and stalks in a wok or large skillet with ½ cup of water and steam, covered, just until they turn bright green, about 1 minute. Remove from the pan and set aside on a plate. Pour out any remaining water in the pan and wipe it dry.

3. In the same pan heat the peanut oil over high heat until hot but not smoking. Add the ginger, garlic, and red pepper flakes, and cook, stirring constantly, for 1 minute. Add the mushrooms and stir-fry for 3 minutes. Add the tempeh and stir-fry for 2 minutes. Add the broccoli and stir-fry for 2 more minutes.

4. Give the soy sauce mixture another stir, then pour over the tempeh and vegetables. Toss to coat, and serve immediately over rice.

NOTE: You can begin cooking this dish 10 minutes before the rice is done, or you can cook the rice in advance and keep it hot in the oven (325°F).

Tempeh in Curried Yogurt Sauce

"Woe to the cook whose sauce has no sting." We don't have to fear Chaucer's warning here where tempeh is braised in a spicy, gingery yogurt sauce inspired by the cuisine of India. Try this served on rice. You could finish the meal with a cup of apple cider heated with a cinnamon stick and a few cloves, for a delightful treat.

SERVES 4 ▶ QUICK MENU 5

¼ cup oil
2 medium onions, finely diced
5 cloves garlic, minced
4 cups (about 12 ounces) quartered mushrooms
2 teaspoons minced fresh ginger
1 teaspoon turmeric
1 teaspoon ground cumin
1 teaspoon ground coriander
½ teaspoon ground cardamom
⅛ teaspoon cayenne pepper
8 ounces tempeh Ⓖ, cut into ¾-inch cubes
1 cup peas (fresh or frozen)
1½ cups diced canned peeled tomatoes with their juice
1 cup plain yogurt
½ teaspoon salt
1½ recipes Perfect Brown Rice (page 292), optional
Fresh coriander or parsley sprigs for garnish

1. In a large skillet heat the oil over medium heat. Add the onions, garlic, mushrooms, and ginger, and cook about 7 minutes, or until the onions are tender.

2. Add the spices, cook 1 minute, then add the tempeh (and fresh peas if you are using them), and cook 3 minutes more, stirring occasionally.

3. Add the tomatoes, yogurt, frozen peas (if using), and salt. Reduce the heat to a simmer and cook for 5 minutes, stirring regularly. *May be prepared to this point in advance, chilled, and reheated within 4 hours. If the sauce is too thick after reheating, add a few teaspoons of water.*

4. Serve over brown rice and garnish with fresh coriander or parsley sprigs.

HERE IS AN ASSORTMENT OF SIDE DISHES TO MEET EVERY
need. The grain-based pilafs will add heft to a meal, and so
should be reserved for lighter entrées; whereas the egg noodles are delicate and go well with rich, sauce-based entrées.
For the vegetable accompaniments, let the season guide
you as well as color and contrasting texture. For example,

Companion Dishes

Zucchini, Red Pepper, and Snow Pea Sauté, a light mixture
of crunchy vegetables, sits nicely on a plate with soft and
creamy Noodle Timbales with Pesto Cream Sauce. When it
comes to companion dishes, they should add something
harmonious to the menu rather than detract from it, so aim
for compatibility in all areas: flavor, color, texture, richness,
and season. And don't hesitate to make an informal supper
from a combination of these tasty side dishes; it can be fun
to mix and match grain or starch dishes with the vegetable-
based ones.

Fine Egg Noodles with Light Garlic Sauce

SERVES 4 ▶ QUICK MENU 1

½ pound fine egg noodles
3 tablespoons butter, cut into pieces
1 clove garlic, minced
½ cup minced fresh parsley
¼ cup grated Parmesan cheese
Salt to taste

1. Bring about 2 quarts of water to a boil in a medium saucepan. Add the noodles and cook for about 5 minutes, or until al dente. Drain thoroughly in a colander.

2. Immediately return the pot to the stove and melt the butter with the garlic. Cook for 3 minutes over medium heat. Add the drained noodles and parsley and toss. Add the cheese and salt to taste and toss again. Serve immediately. *May be prepared up to 8 hours in advance, covered, and refrigerated. To reheat, place in a buttered baking dish, cover, and cook in a preheated 350°F oven for 15 minutes, or until hot and steamy. Toss occasionally. If the noodles look a little dry, sprinkle on a few drops of water to moisten while cooking.*

Bulgur Pilaf

Tossing and cooking the bulgur with a beaten egg ensures light, fluffy results, and heightens the nutty taste of the bulgur. This pilaf is so tasty that I don't hesitate to serve it with just a steamed vegetable when I want a simple, extra-quick meal.

SERVES 4 ▶ QUICK MENU 6

1 cup bulgur **G**
1 egg, beaten
1 tablespoon butter
⅓ cup fine egg noodles (or 1-inch broken spaghetti strands)
1 medium carrot, grated
1 medium onion, minced
2 cups strong-flavored Vegetable Stock (page 290)*
½ teaspoon salt

If you are making your stock out of a commercial vegetable powder base, use more powder in this case to make the stock stronger.

1. In a medium saucepan combine the bulgur and beaten egg. Toss well. Place over medium heat and stir continuously until the bulgur becomes dry and the grains are separate.

2. Make a well in the center and add the butter. When melted, add the noodles, carrot, and onion, and sauté for 2 minutes, stirring constantly to avoid burning.

3. Add the stock and salt, cover, and bring to a boil. Reduce the heat to a simmer and cook for 20 minutes, or until all of the stock is absorbed and the bulgur begins to stick to the pan. Do *not* stir or the bulgur will become mushy.

4. When all of the liquid is absorbed, remove the pan from the heat and gently fluff the bulgur with a fork. Cover the pan again and let sit for 5 minutes. Serve immediately.

> **NOTE:** To reheat add 1 tablespoon water and heat over low heat. Fluff with a fork occasionally. Or turn into a buttered baking dish with 1 tablespoon water and reheat in a 350°F oven for about 20 minutes, or until hot. Toss after 10 minutes.

Bulgur Almond Pilaf

Substitute ⅓ cup slivered almonds for the noodles and cook in the same manner.

Kasha Pilaf

The distinct rustic flavor of kasha (buckwheat groats) makes it a good choice as a companion to milder, rather than robust, entrées.

SERVES 4

1 tablespoon butter
3 cups (8 ounces) quartered mushrooms
1 medium onion, minced
1¼ cups kasha **G** (medium granulation)
1 egg, beaten
2¼ cups hot Vegetable Stock (page 290)
¼ teaspoon salt

1. Melt the butter in a small skillet over medium heat. Add the mushrooms and onion, and cook until the mushrooms are brown and tender, about 10 minutes.

2. Mix the kasha and egg together in a medium saucepan, and stir briskly over low heat until all of the kasha is coated with the egg. Turn the heat to medium and "toast" the kasha by stirring constantly until the grains are dry and separate, about 3 minutes.

3. Add the mushrooms and onion and toss. Add the vegetable stock and salt, and cover the pan. Simmer for 10 minutes, or until *all* of the liquid is absorbed. Fluff with a fork before serving.

Barley Pilaf

Barley has a unique nubby texture and is very filling, so I prefer to serve it with a vegetable side dish rather than a hearty main course. Mushrooms have a natural affinity to barley and lend a distinct flavor, so be sure to include them.

SERVES 4

1 cup barley
2 tablespoons butter
2 cups (6 ounces) quartered mushrooms
1 large onion, minced
¼ teaspoon dried thyme
1⅔ cups Vegetable Stock (page 290)
2 teaspoons tamari or other soy sauce
½ teaspoon salt
Freshly ground pepper to taste

1. Rinse the barley in a strainer under cold running water, then put it in a medium saucepan and cover it with water. Bring to a boil and cook for 2 minutes, then turn off the heat and cover the pan. Let sit for 1 hour, then drain thoroughly.

2. Preheat the oven to 350°F. Melt the butter in a medium flameproof baking dish over medium heat. Add the mushrooms, onion, and thyme, and sauté for 10 minutes, or until the mushrooms begin to brown. Remove from the heat.

3. Add the drained barley, vegetable stock, soy sauce, salt, and pepper, and toss to mix. Cover the baking dish and bake undisturbed for 1 hour, or until all of the liquid is absorbed. Do not stir until just before serving. Serve immediately or keep warm in the oven until you are ready. *May be prepared up to 48 hours in advance and chilled. To reheat, add a few tablespoons of water or stock and place in a 350°F oven until hot, about 20 minutes.*

> NOTE: If you do not have a flameproof baking dish, sauté the mushrooms, onion, and thyme in a skillet, then spoon them into a buttered baking dish and add the barley, vegetable stock, soy sauce, salt, and pepper. You can make this pilaf on top of the stove in a saucepan, but it inevitably sticks to the bottom of the pan, so I recommend the oven method.

Roasted Potatoes with Rosemary

These aromatic potatoes are in rather large pieces, like old-fashioned potatoes that would accompany a roast. If you prefer smaller diced potatoes, just cut back the cooking time to roughly 30 minutes.

SERVES 6   ▶ **THANKSGIVING FEAST MENU**

6 medium boiling (waxy) potatoes, peeled and cut into sixths
3 tablespoons olive oil
4 teaspoons fresh rosemary, or 2 teaspoons dried rosemary, crumbled
Freshly ground pepper to taste

1. Preheat the oven to 400°F.

2. Arrange the potatoes in a large baking dish or pan in one layer.

3. Pour the olive oil over the potatoes to coat evenly. Sprinkle on the rosemary and freshly ground pepper. Bake for 45 minutes, or until the potatoes are tender and brown, turning them occasionally for even browning.

Sautéed Greens with Garlic

Once you try this treatment of cooking greens, you'll want to make them a staple in your meal planning.

SERVES 4 ▶ INFORMAL MENU 2

1½ pounds (weight with stems) greens (either spinach, kale, collards, mustard greens, or escarole), washed, spun dry, and stemmed
½ tablespoon butter
2 tablespoons olive oil
4 cloves garlic, minced
Freshly ground pepper to taste

1. Coarsely chop the greens, then put them in a large skillet with just the water that clings to them. (For kale and collards add a few more tablespoons water.) Cover the pan and cook over medium heat until they wilt, about 5 to 7 minutes. They should retain their bright green color. (The kale or collards may take a little longer; taste to make sure they are tender.) Do not overcook.

2. Drain in a colander and press out all of the liquid with the back of a large spoon.

3. In the same skillet over medium heat melt the butter with the olive oil. Add the garlic and cook 2 to 3 minutes, or until it begins to turn golden. Be careful not to burn it.

4. Add the drained greens and mix well. Sauté for 5 minutes, or until hot and fragrant. Season with freshly ground pepper. Serve immediately, or you can reheat later if necessary.

Green Beans Provençale

So often green beans are picked too mature and are, consequently, thick and tough. This method of cooking ensures tender results for green beans that are thin or thick, but it is preferable, of course, to choose the thinnest and youngest beans available.

SERVES 4

1 pound green beans
3 tablespoons olive oil
2 large onions, diced
1½ cups chopped peeled tomatoes with their juice (from 16-ounce can)
¼ teaspoon dried basil
¼ teaspoon salt
Liberal seasoning freshly ground pepper

1. Snap the ends off the green beans. Wash and drain them and cut into 1½-inch lengths.

2. Heat the oil in a medium saucepan over medium heat. Add the onions and cook, stirring often, for 10 minutes, or until tender.

3. Add the tomatoes, basil, salt, and pepper and bring to a boil.

4. Add the green beans and toss. If there is not enough liquid add a few tablespoons of leftover tomato juice. Cover and bring to a boil, then reduce the heat to a simmer and cook, stirring occasionally, for 20 to 30 minutes, or until the green beans are tender.

> NOTE: If you want to prepare this in advance, then slightly undercook the green beans. When you are ready to serve them, reheat and cook until tender.

Chilled Green Beans with Sesame Sauce

These green beans are an excellent choice for a summer picnic.

SERVES 4 ▶ ELEGANT MENU 2

1 pound green beans
3 tablespoons peanut oil
1 tablespoon tamari or other soy sauce
2 teaspoons Chinese rice vinegar or other vinegar
1 teaspoon Asian sesame oil Ⓖ
Freshly ground pepper to taste
1 tablespoon sesame seeds

1. Snap the ends off the green beans. Wash and drain them.

2. Fill a medium saucepan with water and bring to a boil. Blanch the green beans for 5 minutes, or just until tender yet still crisp. Test by tasting one.

3. Drain and immediately immerse them in cold water for a few minutes to stop further cooking. Drain again very well.

4. In a small jar with a tight-fitting lid combine the peanut oil, soy sauce, vinegar, sesame oil, and pepper. Shake well.

5. Put the green beans in a serving dish and pour over the sauce. Toss well.

6. Place the sesame seeds in a small saucepan. Cook over medium heat, stirring constantly, until fragrant and lightly toasted, about 5 minutes. (Be careful not to burn them. Once they become hot they smoke slightly and exude a noticeable aroma, and at this point they are done.)

7. Immediately pour onto the green beans and toss well again. Cover and chill for at least 1 hour and up to 24 hours before serving. Serve cool, not cold.

Braised Broccoli with Wine and Garlic

I especially like to serve this fragrant broccoli alongside a dish that will not compete with its flavors, such a Mushroom Quiche (page 127).

SERVES 4 ▶ **INFORMAL MENU 13**

1 bunch broccoli
3 tablespoons olive oil
6 cloves garlic, chopped
½ teaspoon dried basil
½ cup dry white wine

1. Cut the broccoli florets into bite-size pieces. Peel the stalks (if you wish) and cut them into bite-size pieces.

2. Heat the olive oil in a large skillet over medium heat. Add the garlic and cook 1 minute. Do not let it brown. Add the broccoli and basil, and sauté for 7 minutes, tossing occasionally.

3. Add the wine and toss; then cover the skillet and reduce the heat to a simmer. Cook 2 to 3 minutes, or until the broccoli is tender yet still crunchy. Spoon into a warm serving dish and pour over any remaining sauce. Serve immediately.

Lemon-Glazed Broccoli Stalks Julienne

Here is a wonderful way to use broccoli stalks, which you may have around if you have used only the florets. I like to peel them because they cook more evenly and become very tender. Of course, there is some vitamin loss from removing the skin, but much of that is redeemed by using the entire stalk.

SERVES 4

2 large broccoli stalks (or the stalks from 1 large bunch broccoli)
1½ tablespoons butter
1 tablespoon lemon juice
¼ teaspoon sugar

1. Peel the skin off the broccoli stalks by making a slit in one end and pulling the skin downward. Cut the stalks in half, then slice them lengthwise into ¼-inch-thick slices. Cut each slice into matchsticks (julienne).

2. Melt the butter in a large skillet over medium heat. Add the broccoli stalks and cook, tossing frequently, for 3 to 5 minutes, or until tender yet still crisp.

3. Add the lemon juice, toss, then sprinkle on the sugar. Toss again and cook for 15 seconds. Serve immediately.

Sesame Broccoli

Here is a simple, low-fat way to prepare broccoli, and although it has an Asian character I find that it goes well with most entrées. You could also mix in sliced carrots for a colorful combination.

SERVES 4

1 large bunch broccoli
1 tablespoon sesame seeds
2 teaspoons Asian sesame oil **G**
1 tablespoon tamari or other soy sauce

1. Cut the broccoli into bite-size florets. Peel the stalks and cut them into comparable-size pieces. Steam both the florets and the stalks in a vegetable steamer until crisp yet tender. The broccoli should retain its bright green color.

2. Meanwhile toast the sesame seeds in a small saucepan or skillet over medium heat until they begin to smoke lightly and become fragrant. Shake the pan often and be careful not to burn them. Immediately remove from the heat and put in a small bowl.

3. Drain the broccoli well. Return it to the pot (without the steamer) over the heat, then mix the sesame oil and soy sauce together and pour over the broccoli. Toss well. Add the sesame seeds and toss again. Serve immediately.

Zucchini, Red Pepper, and Snow Pea Sauté

The lemon-soy glaze that coats these vegetables adds zip without overpowering their mild flavors.

SERVES 4 ▶ **ELEGANT MENU 7**

2 small to medium zucchini
2 large red bell peppers
¼ pound fresh snow peas
1 tablespoon butter
1 tablespoon oil
1 teaspoon tamari or other soy sauce
Juice of ½ lemon

1. Wash the zucchini and pat dry. Cut the ends off and slice in half lengthwise. Cut each half lengthwise again and slice into ½-inch-thick slices.

2. Wash and dry the red peppers. Core them and remove all the seeds. Cut into strips 1 inch wide, then cut the strips into 1-inch squares. The point is to have the vegetables approximately the same shape.

3. String each snow pea by grasping its stem and pulling down until the string is released. Cut the snow peas into thirds, or about 1 inch wide.

4. Heat ½ tablespoon of the butter and all the oil in a large skillet over medium-high heat until hot. Add the zucchini and sauté for 2 minutes, stirring frequently.

5. Add the red peppers and cook 3 minutes, stirring frequently.

6. Add the snow peas and toss. Mix the soy sauce with the lemon juice and add to the vegetables. Cook for 1 to 2 minutes, or just until the snow peas are heated through and the liquid is absorbed. (Do not overcook the vegetables; they should be crunchy.)

7. Remove the pan from the heat. Cut the remaining ½ tablespoon of butter into bits and add. Stir until blended and serve immediately.

NOTE: This dish should be cooked just before serving, but the vegetables can be cut up the day before.

Sautéed Grated Beets and Beet Greens

My favorite way to eat beets—quick, beautiful, and so tasty.

SERVES 4

1 bunch beets with their greens (about 4 medium beets)
2 tablespoons butter
1 teaspoon sugar
Extra butter

1. Cut the greens off the beets and set aside. Peel the beets with a vegetable peeler, then grate them on the coarse side of a grater, or shred them in a food processor.

2. Carefully wash the beet leaves and dry them. De-rib them in the following way: Fold each leaf in half (right sides together) and pull upward on the stem and rib until it peels off. Shred the beet greens by gathering them in bunches and cutting them into strips.

3. Melt the butter in a large skillet over medium heat. Add the beet greens and sauté for 1 minute.

4. Add the grated beets and toss. Cook, tossing often, until the beets are tender, about 5 to 7 minutes. Sprinkle the sugar on the beets, toss again, and cook 1 minute more. Serve immediately, with a pat of butter on each serving.

Brussels Sprouts with Lemon-Soy Glaze

This recipe has won over many confirmed Brussels sprouts haters. I find that Brussels sprouts are infinitely more delicious and attractive if they are halved or quartered when cooked. They become more delicate and are more colorful because they expose a yellow-and-white interior. Try this method even if you want to serve them plain with butter.

SERVES 4   ▶ **ELEGANT MENU 5**

1 pound Brussels sprouts
2 tablespoons butter
Juice of ½ lemon (about 1½ tablespoons)
1 tablespoon tamari or other soy sauce

1. Trim off any yellow leaves from the Brussels sprouts, and cut each one in half (unless they are tiny), and cut the large ones into quarters. Steam them until tender, not mushy, about 10 minutes. They should still retain a bright green color. Remove from the steamer.

2. Melt the butter in a large skillet over medium heat, then add the Brussels sprouts and sauté for 3 minutes, tossing often. Push them to the periphery of the pan, then pour the lemon juice and soy sauce into the center. Let it boil rapidly until the liquid is reduced by half, then toss the Brussels sprouts in it and cook another minute. Serve immediately.

Honey-Glazed Sugar Snap Peas with Carrots

Sugar snap peas look just like fresh peas in their pods, but they are slightly smaller and more tender, so you can eat the whole thing—pod and all. They are sweet and tasty and are also delicious served raw—try them on your next crudités platter. If you cannot get them, then try this dish with snow peas; they also make a wonderful side vegetable. Snow peas take less time to cook than sugar snaps, so if you are using them, cook them for only 3 minutes along with the final cooking of the carrots.

SERVES 6 TO 8   ▶ **ELEGANT MENU 6**

1½ pounds sugar snap peas
4 medium carrots, peeled
3 tablespoons butter
1½ tablespoons honey

1. Rinse the sugar snap peas under cold water and pat very dry. String them by grasping the top stem end and pulling down toward the flat side of the pea. This will string both sides at once. Cut the carrots crosswise into thirds. Cut each third into quarters vertically so that they resemble the shape of the sugar snap peas.

2. Bring about 1 inch of water to a boil in a large skillet. Add the carrots and cook, covered, for 3 to 5 minutes, or until they are tender yet still a little crisp. Drain thoroughly and dry the pan.

3. In the same skillet melt the butter over medium heat. Sauté the sugar snap peas for 5 minutes, stirring frequently, then add the carrots and cook 3 more minutes, or until the peas are tender yet still crisp and bright green. Drizzle on the honey and stir to coat. Cook for 1 minute, stirring constantly. Serve immediately.

Turnip (Rutabaga) Gratin

Rutabagas are the large yellow-fleshed root vegetables that are usually waxed, and are oftentimes called "yellow turnips." Actually, turnips are small and white-fleshed, and they have purple tops. I prefer rutabagas for their stronger, spicier flavor. Here is my favorite way of preparing them, which makes the most luscious side vegetable dish I know of. They are grated and sautéed, then baked with heavy cream and topped with a crisp crust.

SERVES 4   ▶ **ELEGANT MENU 9**

1 medium rutabaga (about 2 pounds)
1 large carrot
3 tablespoons butter
Salt to taste
Freshly ground pepper to taste
1 cup heavy cream
¼ cup Bread Crumbs (page 294)

1. Peel the rutabaga with a vegetable peeler or a paring knife and cut it into chunks for grating by hand or shredding in a food processor. You should have 7 to 8 cups grated. Peel and grate the carrot.

2. Melt 2 tablespoons of the butter in a large skillet over medium-high heat. Add the rutabaga and carrot and sauté for exactly 10 minutes, stirring regularly. Do not brown.

3. Preheat the oven to 375°F. Scrape the mixture into a lightly buttered medium shallow baking dish and season with the salt and pepper. *May be prepared to this point up to 24 hours in advance, covered, and refrigerated. Bring to room temperature before proceeding with the next step.*

4. Pour on the heavy cream, coating as much of the mixture as possible. Sprinkle on the bread crumbs and dot with the remaining tablespoon of butter. Bake for 20 to 25 minutes, or until the cream is thickened and mostly, not completely, absorbed. Serve immediately.

Chestnut Purée

Rich, intensely flavored, and naturally sweet, this aristocratic dish is not as time-consuming as it appears to be. You can prepare the chestnuts in advance and freeze them if you like. My method of removing the chestnut meat is by far the easiest I've found. If you want larger chunks (for another recipe) then cook the chestnuts for half the time. This is wonderful as a Thanksgiving side dish, and a little goes a long way.

SERVES 6　　　　　　　　　　　　　　　　　　　　▶ **THANKSGIVING FEAST MENU**

....

1½ pounds fresh chestnuts
¾ cup heavy or whipping cream
¾ cup milk
Dash salt
Pinch sugar
1 tablespoon butter

1. Fill a medium saucepan halfway with water and bring to a boil. Add the chestnuts and boil, covered, for 20 minutes.

2. Remove the pan from the heat and spoon out 3 or 4 chestnuts. With a large, sharp knife one at a time slice each chestnut in half and squeeze out the flesh into the container of a blender or food processor. If the flesh doesn't come out easily use the handle of a spoon and scoop it out. Repeat with the remaining chestnuts, removing only 3 or 4 at a time from the hot water. (If the flesh of any chestnut is dark or spoiled, then discard it.) *May be prepared to this point in advance, covered, and refrigerated for up to 2 days or frozen for up to 1 week.*

3. Add the cream, milk, salt, and sugar to the blender or processor along with the chestnut meats, and purée until almost smooth. Scrape down the sides as necessary.

4. Return the purée to the saucepan or a small skillet, and heat over medium-low heat until piping hot. If too thick add a little more milk. Add the tablespoon of butter and stir until melted. Serve immediately.

Braised Red Cabbage with Apples

You can't beat the color of this piquant side dish—a great choice to liven up the plate and palate. Choose this side dish for a fall or winter menu, such as for Thanksgiving or alongside Barley Pilaf (page 215).

SERVES 6 ▶ **THANKSGIVING FEAST MENU**

¼ cup olive oil
2 medium onions, halved vertically and thinly sliced
2 medium apples, peeled, cored, and thinly sliced
1 small to medium red cabbage (1½ pounds), cored, quartered, and shredded (8 cups shredded)
½ teaspoon salt
⅓ cup red wine vinegar
½ cup dry red wine
Minced fresh parsley for garnish

1. Heat the olive oil in a large (6-quart) stockpot over medium heat. Add the onions and apples, toss, and cook for 5 minutes.

2. Add the shredded cabbage, salt, vinegar, and wine, and toss well. Reduce the heat to a simmer, cover the pan, and cook the cabbage slowly, tossing occasionally, for 45 to 60 minutes, or until tender and flavorful but not mushy. (If too much liquid remains when the cabbage is done, then remove the cover and raise the heat. Cook until most of the liquid is evaporated.) Spoon into a serving bowl and garnish with parsley.

Sautéed Cabbage with Fennel Seed

Fennel seed adds a mild licorice undertone to this simple, peasant-style accompaniment. Try this alongside Kasha Pilaf (page 214) for a good match.

SERVES 4 ▶ QUICK MENU 10

1 tablespoon butter
1 tablespoon oil
½ teaspoon fennel seed
6 cups (about 1¼ pounds) finely chopped cabbage

Melt the butter with the oil in a large skillet over medium heat. Add the fennel seed and cook for 1 minute. Add the cabbage and sauté for 5 minutes, tossing frequently. Cover the pan, reduce the heat a little, and cook 10 minutes more, or until tender, stirring occasionally. Serve immediately.

DESSERTS CAN BE A CONTROVERSIAL TOPIC FOR THOSE of us who are dedicated to eating healthfully. I am of the school that sees dessert as a worthwhile pleasure, and one that is best approached with moderation. I don't need to eat

Desserts

dessert every night, but when I do want to indulge, it must be special. These desserts qualify. There are five categories of desserts offered in this chapter: Cakes; Pies and Tarts; Puddings; Fruit Desserts; and Cookies and Bars. Like a mother with many children, I love them all.

CAKES

Baking is an art that requires precision. When you select one of the cakes from this section, take the time to measure precisely, use the right-size pan, and approach this task with love. Because texture is so integral to a well-made cake, you need to ensure that you are providing the right conditions for the crumb to develop properly. These cakes range from homey favorites like Blueberry Streusel Cake and Gingerbread to elegant tortes like Mocha Walnut Torte. Except for the Hot Fudge Pudding Cake, they all freeze well, so don't hesitate to save a portion for a later date.

Blueberry Streusel Cake

A moist blueberry-filled cake that has a crisp, flavorful topping. It is delicious plain, but is spectacular when topped with lightly sweetened whipped cream. Although when I cook I usually choose foods that are in season, this blueberry cake can be a welcome reminder of summer when it is served in the late fall or winter, so I sometimes make it with frozen blueberries.

SERVES 12 ▶ QUICK MENU 1

....

2 cups unbleached white flour
2 teaspoons baking powder
½ teaspoon salt
2 cups (1 pint) fresh blueberries, rinsed and patted dry, or unthawed frozen berries
6 tablespoons butter, softened
1 cup sugar
1 teaspoon vanilla extract
½ teaspoon almond extract
2 eggs
1 cup milk

STREUSEL
⅓ cup unbleached white flour
⅓ cup sugar
½ teaspoon cinnamon
4 tablespoons chilled butter, cut into bits
Lightly sweetened whipped cream

1. Preheat the oven to 375°F. Generously butter and flour a 12 x 7 x 2-inch baking pan and set aside. (If you are using a glass dish, then set the oven at 350°F.) Try to time the baking so that the cake can come out of the oven about 30 minutes before you begin eating.

2. Combine the flour, baking powder, and salt in a large bowl and mix well. Add the blueberries and gently toss to coat.

3. Cream the butter with the sugar, vanilla, and almond extract in a medium bowl until well blended. Add the eggs and mix. Carefully add the milk and beat just until blended.

4. Add this wet mixture to the flour mixture and stir *by hand* just until blended. Pour into the prepared cake pan.

5. To make the streusel: Mix the flour, sugar, and cinnamon in a medium bowl. Cut the butter in with a pastry cutter or two knives until the mixture is evenly blended but still crumbly. Sprinkle evenly onto the cake batter.

6. Bake for 40 to 45 minutes, or until the top is evenly golden and a knife inserted in the center comes out clean. Cool on a wire rack for 10 minutes before removing from the pan. Invert onto a plate or platter and then flip again right side up onto another plate or platter. Serve warm or at room temperature plain or with lightly sweetened whipped cream.

Hot Fudge Pudding Cake

Hot Fudge Pudding Cake

This is a most unusual "cake" in which part of the batter rises to the top to form the cake layer, and a thick, creamy pudding develops on the bottom to serve as a sauce. Serve it warm, and for an outrageously good combination try it with vanilla ice cream.

SERVES 6   ▶ QUICK MENU 4

1¼ cups unbleached white flour
1¾ cups firmly packed light brown sugar
½ cup unsweetened cocoa powder
2 teaspoons baking powder
¼ teaspoon salt
⅔ cup milk
½ teaspoon almond extract
2 tablespoons melted butter
2 cups hot water

1. Preheat the oven to 350°F. Set out an 8 x 8-inch baking pan. (If the pan is glass then set the oven at 325°F.)

2. In a medium bowl mix together the flour, ¾ cup of the brown sugar, ¼ cup of the cocoa, the baking powder, and salt. Add the milk, almond extract, and melted butter, and mix again until blended. Do not overbeat. Spoon into the baking pan and spread evenly.

3. Combine the remaining ¼ cup of cocoa and 1 cup of brown sugar until well blended. Sprinkle evenly over the top of the batter.

4. Pour on the hot water but do *not* stir.

5. Bake for 35 minutes. Serve warm with some of the sauce from the bottom of the pan spooned on each serving.

Glazed Pear Cake

Here is a buttery upside-down pear cake that can be made with apples instead of pears—in which case you'd have apple pandowdy—but I find that pears make the most delectable version. Dark brown sugar creates a vivid glaze, so be sure to use that if you can.

SERVES 6 TO 8

4 tablespoons butter
⅓ cup firmly packed dark brown sugar
4 medium ripe but slightly firm pears (preferably Bosc), peeled, cored, and thinly sliced

CAKE
4 tablespoons butter, softened
⅔ cup sugar
1 teaspoon vanilla extract
1 egg
2 cups unbleached white flour
½ teaspoon cinnamon
3 teaspoons baking powder
½ teaspoon salt
1 cup milk

Sweetened whipped cream (optional)

1. Preheat the oven to 375°F. Melt 4 tablespoons of butter in a small saucepan over low heat, then brush some of it on the *sides* of a 9 x 9-inch cake pan. Mix the brown sugar with the butter in the saucepan and stir until melted. Pour into the cake pan and spread evenly.

2. Arrange the pear slices in neat rows on top of the glaze. If you have any leftover slices, chop them and evenly distribute them over the first layer.

3. With an electric beater cream 4 tablespoons butter, the sugar, and vanilla in a large bowl until blended. Add the egg and beat again until creamy.

4. In a separate bowl mix the flour, cinnamon, baking powder, and salt together thoroughly. Alternately add this dry mixture and the milk to the butter mixture and beat after each addition until well blended.

5. Pour the batter over the pears and spread evenly. Bake for 30 to 35 minutes, or until a knife inserted in the center of the cake comes out clean.

6. Cool on a wire rack for 10 minutes, then loosen the edges by inserting a knife all around. Lay a platter over the cake and invert. Serve warm or at room temperature, as is or with sweetened whipped cream.

NOTE: Leftover cake can be reheated in a slow oven (300°F) for 15 minutes or so, or until warm.

Carrot Cake with Cream Cheese Icing

So many people have their own versions of carrot cake. This is the best I've tasted; it is very moist and has the right touch of spice.

SERVES 16

2 cups unbleached white flour
2 teaspoons baking soda
2 teaspoons cinnamon
1 teaspoon salt
2 cups sugar
1¼ cups oil
3 eggs
3 cups grated carrot (about 7 medium carrots)
8-ounce can crushed pineapple, undrained
1 cup finely chopped walnuts or pecans

ICING
½ cup (1 stick) butter, softened
1 teaspoon vanilla extract
8 ounces cream cheese, at room temperature
2½ cups powdered sugar
1 cup ground walnuts or pecans for garnish (optional)

1. Preheat the oven to 350°F. Oil and flour a 9½-inch tube pan and set aside.

2. In a medium bowl combine the flour, baking soda, cinnamon, and salt.

3. In a large bowl beat together the sugar, oil, and eggs until well blended. Add the carrot, pineapple, and walnuts.

4. Beat the dry ingredients into the wet ingredients until well blended. Pour into the prepared pan and bake for 70 minutes, or until a knife inserted in the cake comes out clean.

5. Cool the cake on a wire rack for 10 minutes, then remove the cake from the pan by inverting it onto a plate. Invert it again onto another plate and cool completely.

6. To make the icing: With an electric beater cream together the butter, vanilla, and cream cheese until well blended. Slowly add the powdered sugar and beat until smooth.

7. Carefully place strips of wax paper partially underneath the bottom rim of the cake to keep the plate clean while icing the cake. Spread the icing all over the cake. Decorate the sides with ground nuts, if desired, by pressing them all around the cake. Remove the wax paper strips.

Gingerbread

This is a spicy version, which is interlaced with minced fresh gingerroot. Although it is still delicious served the day after, I prefer to serve it freshly made and still warm from the oven (or at room temperature) because it has a softer texture. If you prefer it this way also, time your baking so that the gingerbread has finished cooking about 1 hour before serving.

SERVES 9   ▶ **INFORMAL MENU 1**

½ cup (1 stick) butter
¾ cup molasses
½ cup honey
1 cup water
½ cup firmly packed light brown sugar
1 egg
1¾ cups unbleached white flour
2 teaspoons baking soda
½ teaspoon baking powder
1 tablespoon ground ginger
2 teaspoons cinnamon
½ teaspoon salt
2 teaspoons minced fresh ginger
Lightly sweetened whipped cream or powdered sugar (optional)

1. Preheat the oven to 350°F. Butter a round 10-inch springform pan or an 8 x 8-inch square pan. (If you are using glass set the oven at 325°F.)

2. In a medium saucepan combine the butter, molasses, honey, and water. Heat just until the butter melts and the mixture is blended. Stir occasionally. Remove from the heat.

3. In a small bowl beat the brown sugar and egg together until blended.

4. In a large bowl combine the remaining dry ingredients and fresh ginger and mix well.

5. Alternately add the molasses mixture and the egg mixture to the dry ingredients. Beat after each addition until well blended, but do not overbeat.

6. Pour into the prepared pan. Bake for 30 to 40 minutes, or until a knife inserted in the center comes out *almost* clean. (It continues to cook while cooling.) Cool on a wire rack.

7. Serve warm with lightly sweetened whipped cream, or dust with powdered sugar.

Mocha Walnut Torte

This very quick torte is unusually light and smooth, with the ground walnuts being barely discernible. It is covered with my favorite icing—a heavenly chocolate ganache—and the entire torte can be assembled up to 3 days before serving with no noticeable loss in texture or appearance.

SERVES 6 TO 8   ▶ **ELEGANT MENUS 5 AND 10**

5 eggs
1 cup sugar
1 cup walnuts
¼ cup unbleached white flour
2½ teaspoons baking powder

ICING

1½ cups heavy or whipping cream
4 ounces semisweet chocolate, chopped
2 tablespoons sugar
1 tablespoon instant coffee
Chocolate curls for decoration (see Note) (I use a Baker's German's sweet chocolate bar)

1. Preheat the oven to 350°F. Butter two 8-inch round cake pans and line the bottoms with wax paper, then butter the wax paper.

2. Blend the eggs and sugar very well in a blender or food processor. Add the walnuts and blend until they are very fine. Mix the flour with the baking powder, add to the batter, and blend until smooth.

3. Pour into the prepared pans and bake for 17 to 19 minutes, or until golden on top and springy to the touch. Cool on a wire rack for 5 minutes, then invert the pans and peel away the wax paper. Cool the cakes completely, about 1 hour.

4. Meanwhile make the icing. Combine the cream, chocolate, sugar, and coffee in a medium-size saucepan, and whisking steadily, bring to a boil over medium heat. Remove from the heat as soon as the mixture begins to boil and continue to whisk until the chocolate is melted. Pour into a large bowl (metal is best for quick cooling) and chill, uncovered, until ice cold, or cover and chill up to 24 hours. Occasionally stir the mixture for even cooling and to prevent hard chocolate from developing along the sides. It is a good idea to chill your beaters at this time also.

5. Whip the frosting with the chilled beaters until very stiff. To ice the torte: Spread 4 strips of wax paper around the edges of your cake plate or platter. Place the first layer top side down and adjust the wax paper so it will protect the plate from icing. Spread some icing over the top of this layer. Place the second layer on top so the bottom side is up, then spread the remaining icing over the entire torte and smooth as evenly as you can. Garnish with the chocolate curls, then remove the wax paper strips. Insert a few toothpicks into the top of the torte to prevent the icing from getting messy, then cover with plastic wrap and chill until ready to serve.

NOTE: To make chocolate curls place a semisweet or bittersweet chocolate bar over a flame or hot electric burner for a few seconds, or just long enough to slightly warm the surface. Do not let the flame get near it. With a vegetable peeler peel off a few curls onto the top of the torte. Repeat until the torte is nicely decorated.

Raspberry Almond Torte

Tortes are cakes made with ground nuts or bread crumbs and little or no flour, and they are usually only about 2 inches high. But there are many exceptions to this definition, and tortes look very different from one another. Unlike the Mocha Walnut Torte (page 242), which is very light and delicate, this torte has a delightful and distinct nutty texture, and is filled with a layer of raspberry preserves, then covered with whipped cream. Serve it with a demitasse of piping hot espresso for a spectacular combination.

SERVES 6 TO 8 ▶ ELEGANT MENU 7

5 eggs, separated
1 teaspoon vanilla extract
1 cup sugar
1 teaspoon baking powder
1 cup bread crumbs, preferably white bread
2 cups (9 ounces) ground almonds*
⅛ teaspoon salt

ICING

1 cup heavy or whipping cream, well chilled
2 tablespoons sugar
¼ teaspoon almond extract

⅔ cup raspberry preserves
1 tablespoon lemon juice
Chocolate curls for decoration (I use a bar of Baker's German's sweet chocolate)

Grind the almonds—a handful at a time—in a blender or food processor, and spoon into a measuring cup. Do not pack.

1. Preheat the oven to 325°F. Butter two 8-inch round cake pans and line the bottoms with wax paper, then butter the wax paper.

2. With an electric beater beat together the egg yolks, vanilla, and sugar in a large bowl until very pale and thick.

3. Mix the baking powder with the bread crumbs and add to the egg mixture along with the almonds. Beat until blended; it will be very thick and crumbly. After beating use a knife to break up the clumps into small pieces.

4. Clean the beaters thoroughly. In a separate large bowl beat the egg whites until they begin to foam. Add the salt, then beat until they are stiff but not dry. (They will beat better if they are warm or at room temperature.)

5. Stir one-third of the egg whites into the almond mixture to lighten the batter, then fold in the remaining egg whites with a rubber spatula until evenly blended. The batter will look somewhat clumpy.

6. Scrape into the prepared pans and smooth the tops. Bake for 25 minutes, or until lightly golden and springy to the touch. The cakes should also have begun to shrink from the sides of the pans. Cool on wire racks for 10 minutes, then invert and peel away the wax paper. Cool thoroughly, about 1 hour.

7. Meanwhile, whip the cream with the sugar and almond extract until very stiff. To assemble the torte place one layer top side down on a plate. Mix the raspberry preserves with the lemon juice and spread on evenly to within ½ inch of the edge. Top with the other layer top side down. Spread all over with the whipped cream and smooth it on evenly. Garnish with the chocolate curls.

> NOTE: To make chocolate curls place a semisweet or bittersweet chocolate bar over a flame or hot electric burner for a few seconds, or just long enough to slightly warm the surface. Do not let the flame get near it. With a vegetable peeler shave off curls onto the top of the torte until the cake is nicely decorated.

Peach Almond Torte

During the height of the peach season I love to make this sweet, buttery torte and serve it with espresso as part of a special meal. It is quick to make, and is best served warm or at room temperature. Although it is still delicious on the second day, it tends to get very moist from the juice of the peaches, so plan to make it on the day you will serve it.

SERVES 8 ▶ **SUMMER MENU 1**

½ cup (1 stick) butter, softened
1 cup sugar
½ cup ground almonds
½ cup unbleached white flour
1 teaspoon baking powder
2 eggs
½ teaspoon almond extract
4 ripe peaches, peeled and sliced ½ inch thick

TOPPING
1 tablespoon butter, cut into bits
1 tablespoon sugar
2 tablespoons unbleached white flour
½ teaspoon cinnamon

1. Preheat the oven to 350°F. Butter the bottom of a 9-inch springform pan.

2. In a large bowl cream the butter and sugar together until blended. Add the almonds, flour, baking powder, eggs, and almond extract, and beat until smooth and fluffy.

3. Scrape the batter into the springform pan and smooth over the top. Arrange the peach slices on top in one layer (they don't have to be neat).

4. In a small bowl make the topping: Toss together the butter, sugar, flour, and cinnamon. Cut the butter into the mixture until it is the texture of coarse crumbs. Sprinkle evenly over the peaches.

5. Bake for 50 to 60 minutes, or until golden brown all over. Cool on a wire rack for 10 minutes, then remove the sides of the pan. Serve warm or at room temperature.

PIES AND TARTS

Let's face it, when it comes to a memorable pie, crust is a key factor in the pie's success. Review the precise pie crust recipes (Pâte Brisée, Pâte Sucrée, and Almond Nut Crust) in The Basics chapter because once you master making pastry, you'll want to keep making these wonderful pies and tarts. And when you are pressed for time yet want a tart to celebrate the glory of summer fruit? Choose to make a Summer Fruit Tart that has a delicious no-fuss graham cracker crust to encase the tasty filling.

Rhubarb Tart

Here's a great way to celebrate spring and the arrival of rhubarb. The applesauce adds body to the filling without overpowering the luscious flavor of the rhubarb.

SERVES 12   ▶ INFORMAL MENU 3

1 recipe Pâte Sucrée (page 305)
5 cups rhubarb cut into ½-inch dice (1¼ to 1½ pounds)
½ cup unsweetened applesauce
⅓ cup unbleached white flour
1 cup honey
½ teaspoon ground cardamom
Sweetened whipped cream (optional)

1. Make the Pâte Sucrée following the directions only through step 5; do not prebake. (You will not need the extra egg white.) Chill for at least 20 minutes and up to 2 days. Cover well with foil or plastic wrap if you are going to chill for longer than 20 minutes.

2. To make the filling: Combine all of the remaining ingredients in a large bowl, and toss to blend well.

3. Preheat the oven to 400°F. Pour the filling into the prepared crust and bake for 5 minutes. Reduce the heat to 375°F and bake an additional 35 to 40 minutes, or until the crust is golden. Cool to room temperature before serving. Serve plain or with whipped cream.

Summer Fruit Tart

A quick tart which demands that the oven be on for only about 15 minutes—a welcome relief during hot summer weather. You can use almost any assortment of fresh fruit for the topping—strawberries, cantaloupe, kiwis, white grapes, etc.—but my favorite is a mixture of peaches, plums, and blueberries, offering a beautiful presentation of shades of yellow, red, and blue.

SERVES 8 ▶ **SUMMER MENU 4**

CRUST
- 14 graham cracker halves
- ¼ cup melted butter
- 2 tablespoons sugar
- Dash cinnamon

FILLING
- 8 ounces cream cheese, softened
- ¼ cup honey
- 1 teaspoon vanilla extract

TOPPING
- 2 ripe peaches, peeled and sliced ½ inch thick
- 3 ripe plums, peeled and sliced ½ inch thick
- ⅔ cup blueberries

GLAZE
- 2 tablespoons raspberry or red currant jelly
- ½ teaspoon water

1. To make the crust: Preheat the oven to 350°F. Place the graham crackers in a plastic bag and seal, removing any additional air. Roll over the bag with a rolling pin until fine crumbs are formed. Put them in a medium bowl and add the butter, sugar, and cinnamon. Toss well. Put this mixture in a 9-inch pie plate and press in place evenly. (It is helpful to use another pie plate to press down on the crumbs.) Bake for 10 minutes, or until evenly golden. Cool thoroughly on a wire rack.

2. To make the filling: In a medium bowl beat together by hand the cream cheese, honey, and vanilla until smooth. Spread onto the bottom of the thoroughly cooled pie shell.

3. Make a decorative topping with the fruit: for example, alternate slices of peaches and plums around the edge of the tart. Make a star out of plum slices in the center. Use the blueberries to make a border around the outer edge of the tart and fill in the spaces near the star.

4. Make the glaze by heating the jelly and water, stirring constantly, until the jelly is smooth. Carefully brush all the glaze onto the tart. Chill the tart for at least 2 hours, or until the filling and glaze are firm.

Pear Tart with Almond Nut Crust

I especially like this tart because it is not too rich, and the fruitiness of the filling is very pronounced. Any ripe pears will do, but I find that Boscs are particularly sweet and juicy.

SERVES 8   ▶ **ELEGANT MENU 8**

1 recipe Almond Nut Crust (page 307)
7 ripe but slightly firm pears, peeled, cored, and vertically sliced
2 tablespoons unbleached white flour
¼ cup honey

GLAZE
⅓ cup apricot preserves
1 teaspoon water

1. To prebake the crust: Preheat the oven to 400°F. Cover the crust with aluminum foil and press it into the sides. Line the crust with dried beans to weight it down and prevent shrinkage. Bake for 10 minutes. Remove from the oven and remove the foil and beans. (Save the beans for future use.) Reset the oven to 350°F.

2. Meanwhile in a large bowl toss the pear slices with the flour. Add the honey and toss again very well. Turn the pear filling into the crust and smooth over the top.

3. When the oven is at 350°F bake the tart for 25 minutes.

4. Meanwhile heat the preserves and water together until the mixture begins to boil. Pour into a strainer and press through into a small bowl.

5. Spread the glaze over the tart and return it to the oven to bake 10 more minutes. Cool thoroughly on a wire rack before serving.

Linzertorte

Here is a classic dessert that deserves its grand reputation. A buttery almond lattice crust reveals glistening raspberry preserves, and although it seems rather complicated to construct it really isn't that difficult. You can serve it plain, but it is especially good served with whipped cream or rich vanilla ice cream, and for the perfect finale, follow it with a demitasse of piping hot espresso.

SERVES 8 ▶ ELEGANT MENU 1

¾ cup (1½ sticks) butter, softened
¾ cup sugar
1 teaspoon grated lemon zest
2 egg yolks
1½ cups unbleached white flour
1 teaspoon cinnamon
½ teaspoon ground cloves
¼ teaspoon salt
1½ cups (about 6½ ounces) ground almonds
1¼ cups raspberry preserves
1 tablespoon lemon juice
1 egg white
Lightly sweetened whipped cream or vanilla ice cream (optional)

1. Cream the butter with the sugar in a large bowl until smooth, then add the lemon zest and egg yolks, and mix until well blended.

2. Combine the flour, cinnamon, cloves, salt, and almonds in a separate bowl, and stir until mixed. Pour into the butter mixture and mix just until combined and smooth; do not overwork the dough. Gather two-thirds of the dough into one ball and flatten it into a disk, then make a ball out of the remaining third of the dough and flatten that into a disk. Wrap individually in plastic and chill for 30 minutes. *May be prepared up to 2 days in advance, covered, and chilled, or prepared up to 2 weeks in advance and frozen. Thaw before proceeding with step 3.*

3. Remove the dough from the refrigerator; if it has chilled for longer than 30 minutes and is hard then let it sit at room temperature for 15 minutes, or until it is slightly firm. Butter a 9-inch springform pan, and with your fingers press the large ball of dough into the pan to cover the bottom and 1 inch up the sides.

4. Mix the preserves with the lemon juice and spread evenly over the bottom of the crust.

5. Roll out the remaining ball of dough between 2 pieces of wax paper until it is 8 or 9 inches in diameter, depending on the size of your pan. Slide the whole thing onto a plate and chill for 20 minutes, or freeze for 10 minutes.

6. Remove the top sheet of wax paper from the dough, then cut the dough into ½-inch-wide strips, cutting right through the wax paper. Take the center strip and lay it across the center of the torte with the wax paper side up, then peel off the wax paper. Place the second longest strip across the center in the opposite direction to make a cross, then peel off the wax paper. Press the ends of the strips into the sides of the crust as you go along. Place a strip on *each* side of *both* of these strips, and continue in this manner until the top is covered with the lattice.

7. Preheat the oven to 350°F. Carefully brush some of the egg white over the lattice. Bake for 40 minutes, or until the crust is evenly golden. Cool on a wire rack for 20 minutes before removing the sides of the pan. Serve at room temperature, with lightly sweetened whipped cream or vanilla ice cream if desired.

Raspberry Pie

Raspberry Pie

My sister Julianne created this memorable pie and it has proven to be one of my favorite desserts. It is beautiful to look at, has a distinct fresh raspberry flavor, and doesn't demand a lot of preparation time.

SERVES 8   ▶ **SUMMER MENU 2**

1 recipe Pâté Brisée (page 302) made with sugar
3 cups fresh raspberries
⅔ cup water
¾ cup plus 1 tablespoon sugar
2½ tablespoons cornstarch
2 tablespoons butter
⅔ cup heavy or whipping cream

1. Preheat the oven to 400°F. Line the chilled pie shell with aluminum foil and fill it with dried beans or rice. (You must do this to prevent shrinkage.) Bake for 10 minutes. Remove from the oven and remove the foil and beans. (Save for future crusts.) Prick the crust all over and return to the oven. Bake 3 to 5 additional minutes, or until the crust is evenly golden and completely cooked. If it begins to get too dark in some spots, then cover them with pieces of foil. Cool thoroughly on a wire rack.

2. To make the filling: In a medium saucepan combine 1 cup of the raspberries with the water, ¾ cup of the sugar, and cornstarch. Bring to a boil, stirring continuously, and cook until clear and thickened, about 3 minutes. Remove from the heat and stir in the butter. Cool to room temperature and carefully fold in the remaining raspberries. (You should reserve about 9 of the perfect ones for garnish.) Chill until the pie shell is thoroughly cooled.

3. To assemble the pie: Spread the raspberry filling evenly in the pie shell. Whip the cream and remaining tablespoon of sugar until very stiff. Decorate the top of the pie with the whipped cream and the reserved raspberries. (I like to put the whipped cream in a pastry bag with a star tube and decorate the pie in lattice fashion. Then I place the reserved raspberries where the lattice crisscrosses.) Chill for at least an hour before serving.

Maple Pecan Pie

Most pecan pies are cloying and leave one feeling a bit too satisfied at the end of a meal. I believe that you should leave the table with the feeling that you could enjoy one more bite, not that you had one too many. This recipe is not overly sweet, although a little does go a long way. I prefer it with unsweetened whipped cream for an interesting contrast in flavor.

SERVES 8   ▶ **INFORMAL MENU 5**

1 recipe Pâté Brisée (page 302) made with sugar
4 eggs
1¼ cups firmly packed light brown sugar
1 cup pure maple syrup Ⓖ
2 tablespoons melted butter
1½ cups whole pecans
Unsweetened whipped cream (optional)

1. Line a pie plate with the crust and chill for 30 minutes. Do not prebake it. Preheat the oven to 425°F.

2. Beat the eggs well with a wire whisk in a medium bowl, then beat in the brown sugar, maple syrup, and melted butter. Stir in the pecans.

3. Pour this mixture into the pie shell and bake at 425°F for 10 minutes, then reduce the heat to 325°F and bake an additional 35 to 40 minutes, or until a knife inserted in the center of the pie comes out clean. Serve warm or at room temperature, with unsweetened whipped cream, if desired.

Cranberry Fruit Tart

This stunning crimson tart will enliven the Thanksgiving table or any other fall feast.

SERVES 8 ▶ THANKSGIVING FEAST MENU

Pâté Sucrée (page 305)
4 cups (1 pound) fresh cranberries
¼ cup water
1 navel orange, rinsed well and dried
1 ripe but slightly firm pear, peeled, cored, and diced
¾ cup honey
¾ cup finely chopped walnuts, toasted
¼ teaspoon cinnamon
2 teaspoons cornstarch

TOPPING
1 cup heavy or whipping cream, well chilled
2 tablespoons honey

1. Prepare the pie crust and line a 10-inch quiche or tart pan with it. Bake blind as directed (20 minutes total), and allow to cool completely. (You will not need the extra egg white.)

2. Wash and pick over the cranberries to remove stems and any spoiled berries, then put them in a medium saucepan with the water. Cook over medium heat just until they begin to burst, about 5 minutes. Remove from the heat.

3. Meanwhile wash the orange and pat dry. Grate it on the fine side of a grater; try not to grate any of the white pith. Here is a good trick: Wind plastic wrap tightly around the grater and grate the orange rind against the plastic wrap. The grating edge will pierce through the wrap. When you've finished, you'll be able to peel off the plastic and with it, the gratings (instead of having to scrape them out of all the interstices). Don't worry—you will not get any plastic in the gratings. Peel the orange and discard the white pith. Separate the orange into slices, then cut each slice into thirds.

4. Add the orange zest, orange pieces, and all of the remaining ingredients (except the topping) to the cranberries and cook, stirring occasionally, for 3 more minutes, or until the juices thicken. Spoon into a bowl, cover, and chill until cold, about 3 hours or up to 24 hours.

5. Spoon the filling into the prepared pie shell and smooth over the top. Whip the cream with the honey until very stiff, then scrape it into a pastry bag with a star tip and pipe it on the tart in a lattice fashion. (Or spread it decoratively over the top.) Chill until ready to serve.

PUDDINGS

These are the ultimate comfort foods—easy to eat yet intensely flavored. They range in textures from the silkiness of Apricot Orange Mousse and Kheer to the more bready Indian Pudding and Summer Pudding. Yet each can do what puddings do best: provide a soft, sensuous conclusion to a complex meal.

Apricot Orange Mousse

This velvety mousse bursts with a tangy citrus flavor. This could be the perfect ending to a spicy meal.

SERVES 6 ▶ QUICK MENU 2

1½ cups (10 ounces) dried apricots
1 cup water
½ cup honey
¼ cup orange juice (from 1 large orange—reserve 3 thin slices for garnish)
1 tablespoon Cointreau, Grand Marnier, or Triple Sec
½ cup heavy or whipping cream, well chilled
2 egg whites, at room temperature
3 thin orange slices for garnish

1. Put the apricots, water, and honey into a medium saucepan. Partially cover, bring to a boil, then reduce to a simmer and cook for 10 minutes, or until the apricots are soft.

2. Pour the apricots and their liquid into a blender or food processor, add the orange juice, and purée until smooth. Spoon into a bowl and stir in the liqueur. Cover and refrigerate until chilled.

3. Meanwhile in a medium bowl whip the cream until stiff. (For best results chill the bowl and beaters beforehand.)

4. Wash and dry the beaters well. In a separate large bowl whip the egg whites until stiff but not dry. (The bowl, beaters, and egg whites should be warm for best results.)

5. When the apricot purée is chilled check the consistency; it should be like thick oatmeal. If necessary thin with a little liqueur, orange juice, or milk.

6. Spoon the chilled apricot purée into the egg whites and gently fold in. Add the whipped cream and fold in until well blended. Spoon into custard cups or attractive goblets and garnish with half of an orange slice twisted. Chill at least 1 hour before serving and up to 48 hours.

Kheer (Rice, Almond, and Cardamom Pudding)

This creamy pudding, fragrant with cardamom, adds a nice balance to a spicy Indian meal. It is rich; therefore, small portions will be very satisfying. Although it is simple to prepare it does demand a lot of stirring; so read a book, or prepare other parts of your meal while you are tending to this task.

SERVES 6 ▶ INFORMAL MENU 14

5 cups milk
¼ cup white rice (preferably converted rice)
⅓ cup honey
¼ cup chopped almonds, toasted
⅓ cup raisins
¼ teaspoon ground cardamom
½ teaspoon rosewater (optional)*
Chopped almonds for garnish

Rosewater can be purchased at specialty food shops and some pharmacies.

1. Bring the milk to a boil in a heavy-bottomed medium saucepan. Stir frequently to prevent a skin from forming. Reduce the heat to medium and cook the milk at a lively simmer for 15 minutes, stirring often.

2. Add the rice and continue to cook over medium heat for 30 more minutes, or until the rice is very soft. You must continue to stir frequently to prevent the mixture from overflowing or sticking to the bottom. If any skin forms, remove and discard it.

3. Add the honey, almonds, raisins, and cardamom. Cook 5 more minutes, or until the pudding is thick enough to lightly coat a spoon. (It gets very thick when chilled.)

4. Remove from the heat and stir in the rosewater. Pour the mixture into a large bowl or shallow pan (for quick cooling), cover with foil or plastic wrap, and chill at least 1 hour and up to 24 hours. Stir occasionally to prevent a skin from forming.

5. Serve in goblets or custard cups and garnish with some chopped almonds.

NOTE: Converted rice is considerably more nutritious than regular white rice because the rice is partially cooked (before the bran and germ are removed) in such a way that the nutrients are forced into the core of each kernel, then the bran and germ are removed so that the rice is white.

Indian Pudding

The unique mingling of cornmeal, molasses, and ginger makes this classic American dessert one of my favorites. It's quick to put together, nutritious, and so delicious, and it's best served warm; therefore, time it so that it comes out of the oven about 1 hour before you plan to serve it.

SERVES 6 ▶ QUICK MENU 5

4 cups milk
¾ cup cornmeal
4 tablespoons butter, cut into bits
1 egg, lightly beaten
½ cup firmly packed light or dark brown sugar
½ cup molasses
½ teaspoon salt
1 teaspoon ground ginger
1 teaspoon cinnamon
Heavy cream or vanilla ice cream (optional)

1. Preheat the oven to 325°F. Butter a 1½-quart baking dish.

2. In a medium saucepan bring the milk to a boil. Lower the heat and very slowly add the cornmeal, whisking it with a wire whisk all the while. Whisk until the mixture is smooth and has thickened, about 5 minutes. Remove from the heat and add the butter. Let cool for 10 minutes.

3. Beat in all the remaining ingredients until well blended. Pour into the prepared dish. Place this dish in a larger baking dish and fill the outer dish with enough hot water to reach halfway up the sides of the inner dish.

4. Bake for 1 hour and 45 minutes, or until a knife inserted in the center comes out *almost* clean. Let cool on a wire rack and serve warm as is, or with heavy cream poured on each serving, or try it with vanilla ice cream for an excellent combination.

> NOTE: To reheat leftover pudding cut it into a few pieces and pour on a little milk to moisten. Place in a preheated 350°F oven and turn off the oven. Heat for 15 minutes or so, or until it is warm throughout.

Summer Pudding

This English pudding requires only 3 minutes' cooking time—an important consideration on a hot summer day—but it must be chilled for 24 hours before serving so plan ahead. I prefer to make it with thinly sliced whole wheat bread for the added flavor and nutrients it provides, but white bread works well also. Present this on the prettiest platter you have, for its deep blue hue looks stunning when surrounded by vivid red strawberries.

SERVES 6 ▶ **SUMMER MENU 8**

3 cups (1½ pints) blueberries
1½ tablespoons sherry (preferably cream sherry)
½ cup honey
Dash nutmeg
8 thin slices whole wheat bread, crusts removed
6 strawberries for garnish (with hulls left on)
Lightly sweetened whipped cream (optional)

1. Combine the blueberries, sherry, honey, and nutmeg in a medium saucepan, and bring to a boil. Cook for 2 to 3 minutes, or until the berries split and the juices are released. Remove from the heat and let cool.

2. Line a 1-quart round mold or round bowl with the bread by laying a slice on the bottom and surrounding it with diagonally cut slices placed around the sides. There should be no spaces showing.

3. Pour the cooled blueberry mixture into the mold and cover the top of it with bread slices. Do not overlap any of the bread. Trim off any excess.

4. Place a small plate on the pudding so that it rests right on the top, covering it completely. Place a 2- to 3-pound weight on the plate to hold it firmly down. Chill the pudding with the weight for 24 hours.

5. When ready to serve remove the weight and plate, then loosen the edges of the pudding by sliding a knife or rubber spatula around it. Place a serving plate over the mold and invert the pudding onto it. Spoon any accumulated juices back over the pudding. Surround the pudding with the strawberries and serve at room temperature sliced into wedges. This is also delicious served with lightly sweetened whipped cream.

FRUIT DESSERTS

It's hard to beat a dessert that has been built around perfectly ripe fruit of the season. The naturally complex sweetness and fragrance of many fruits make them ideal ingredients with which to end a meal. Whether in something light and refreshing like Fresh Peaches with Honey Rum Sauce in a more substantial dish like a rich, homey Apple Crisp, fruit adds a lusciousness to desserts that is hard to resist.

Apple Crisp

This classic American dessert is a favorite of mine, but it must be well spiced and have a rich, crunchy topping, as it does here. I have found that almost any variety of apple will do (except Red Delicious—they're too mealy); if the apple is crisp and fresh and delicious as an eating apple, then it will be good for baking.

SERVES 6 ▶ INFORMAL MENU 12

....

8 medium apples, peeled, cored, and thinly sliced
¼ cup water
2 tablespoons firmly packed light brown sugar
½ teaspoon cinnamon

TOPPING
½ cup whole wheat pastry flour (or ¼ cup unbleached white flour and ¼ cup whole wheat flour)
½ cup firmly packed light brown sugar
1 teaspoon cinnamon
¼ teaspoon salt
6 tablespoons butter
Lightly sweetened whipped cream or vanilla ice cream (optional)

1. Preheat the oven to 350°F. Arrange the apple slices in an 8 × 8-inch baking pan or other shallow ovenproof dish of comparable size. Pour the water over them, then sprinkle on the brown sugar and cinnamon and toss gently.

2. To make the topping: Combine the flour, sugar, cinnamon, and salt in a small mixing bowl, and mix well.

3. Cut the butter into the mixture with a pastry cutter or your fingertips until it resembles coarse meal. Sprinkle evenly over the apples.

4. Bake for 30 to 40 minutes, or until the apples are tender and the topping is lightly browned. The topping will get crisp as it cools. Cool on a wire rack and serve warm or at room temperature. It is perfectly delicious served plain, and also exceptionally good topped with whipped cream or vanilla ice cream.

Rhubarb Cobbler

When I was a little girl, my friends and I would break off stalks of rhubarb and dip the raw ends into the sugar bowl, then bite off the sugary tip and squeal with delight over the overpowering tartness of the rhubarb. It was like biting into a lemon. That intense acidity mellows when rhubarb is cooked with a sweetener, but the characteristic tang remains, and it is what fans love about rhubarb. This cobbler brings out the best in rhubarb. Warm biscuit dough covers a rich-flavored, soupy filling, and is then topped with lightly sweetened whipped cream.

SERVES 6   ▶ INFORMAL MENU 16

FILLING

    6 cups (about 1¾ pounds) diced rhubarb (½-inch dice)
    1 cup honey
    2 teaspoons cornstarch
    Grated rind of 1 orange
    ¼ teaspoon cinnamon
    ¼ teaspoon ground cloves
    3 tablespoons butter

BISCUIT DOUGH

    1¾ cups unbleached white flour
    2 teaspoons sugar
    1 tablespoon baking powder
    ¼ teaspoon cinnamon
    4 tablespoons chilled butter
    ⅔ cup milk

    1 beaten egg

    Lightly sweetened whipped cream

1. Preheat the oven to 375°F.

2. In a medium saucepan combine all of the ingredients for the filling. Simmer until the rhubarb is tender but not mushy, about 10 minutes. Pour into an 8 × 8-inch cake pan.

3. To make the biscuit topping: In a large bowl combine the flour, sugar, baking powder, and cinnamon. Mix well. Cut the butter into bits and add. Cut it into the flour mixture with a pastry cutter or work it in with the tips of your fingers until it resembles coarse meal. Add the milk and stir just to mix. Gather the dough into a ball. If it is too dry add a bit more milk.

4. Knead the dough 3 or 4 times just to make it manageable. On a lightly floured surface roll it to fit the 8 × 8-inch pan. Cover the filling with the dough, and brush the top with some of the beaten egg.

5. Bake for 30 minutes. If the dough is browned before the 30 minutes is up then cover lightly with a piece of foil to prevent further browning. Let cool somewhat before serving. Serve warm with whipped cream.

> NOTE: To reheat, place into a 375°F oven for 10 minutes, or just until evenly warm.

Stuffed Peaches with Fresh Cherries and Almonds

This is an exquisite-looking dish that is easy to prepare. The dark red color of the cherries contrasts beautifully with the golden peaches. Sweet and juicy, when served they sit on a bed of almond-flavored whipped cream.

SERVES 4 ▶ QUICK MENU 6

5 ounces (about 1 cup) fresh dark cherries (Bing), pitted and quartered
⅓ cup finely chopped almonds (not ground)
2 teaspoons sugar
4 large ripe peaches (preferably freestone)
Juice of ½ lemon
⅔ cup chilled heavy or whipping cream
1½ tablespoons powdered sugar
½ teaspoon almond extract

1. Mix the cherries, almonds, and sugar in a small bowl.

2. Peel the peaches and carefully cut them in half vertically. Remove the stones and discard. If necessary scoop out a little of the center of each peach half to make it large enough to hold some filling.

3. Put the lemon juice in a small dish and one at a time toss each peach half in it. Use your hands to coat the peaches evenly with the lemon juice. (This will prevent discoloration.)

4. Fill each peach half with an equal portion of the cherry filling and press it in gently but firmly. Arrange the stuffed peaches in a shallow dish. *May be prepared to this point in advance, covered, and chilled for up to 24 hours. Remove 20 minutes before serving to take off the chill.*

5. Cream will whip better if you chill the beaters and bowl beforehand. Beat the cream in a medium bowl for a few minutes. When it begins to thicken add the powdered sugar and almond extract. Continue to beat until it has a nice whipped-cream consistency. (You can prepare the cream and chill it a few hours beforehand, but don't assemble the dish until you are ready to serve it.)

6. To serve, spread equal portions of whipped cream on 4 serving dishes. Place 2 stuffed peach halves flat side up on each bed of cream.

Pear and Apricot Crisp

Here is a nutritious dessert with a distinct fruit flavor that you can make 24 hours in advance. The apricots provide an interesting tartness, and the oatmeal and walnuts give it a deliciously crunchy topping.

SERVES 4 TO 6 ▶ QUICK MENU 10

6 ripe but slightly firm pears (preferably Bosc)
½ cup diced dried apricots
1 tablespoon unbleached white flour
⅓ cup honey

TOPPING

½ cup rolled oats (non-instant oatmeal)
¼ cup whole wheat pastry flour (or 2 tablespoons whole wheat flour and 2 tablespoons unbleached white flour)
½ teaspoon cinnamon
¼ cup firmly packed light brown sugar
3 tablespoons butter, cut into bits
¼ cup finely chopped walnuts

Lightly sweetened whipped cream (optional)

1. Preheat the oven to 400°F. Butter an 8 x 8-inch baking pan or other shallow pan of comparable size.

2. Peel and core the pears, then slice them into bite-size pieces and put them in a medium bowl with the apricots. Add the flour and toss to coat, then pour on the honey and toss again until blended. Scrape this mixture into the prepared pan and smooth over the top.

3. In the same bowl combine the oats, flour, cinnamon, and brown sugar, and mix well. Blend in the butter with the tips of your fingers until the mixture resembles coarse meal, then stir in the walnuts. Sprinkle this crumb mixture evenly over the pears.

4. Bake for 30 to 40 minutes, or until the fruit is tender and the top is golden. Serve warm or at room temperature. It is delicious as is or with lightly sweetened whipped cream.

Poached Pears in Red Wine with Raisins

This is a very pretty dessert. Dark red spicy wine colors the pears and makes them deep maroon on the outside while they remain white within. They are especially light and flavorful and are wonderful served after a rich meal.

SERVES 4
▶ QUICK MENU 11

4 ripe but slightly firm pears (preferably Bosc, Comice, or Anjou)
1½ cups dry red wine
2 tablespoons lemon juice
⅓ cup honey
Pinch ground cloves
1 cinnamon stick
½ cup raisins

1. Peel the pears and slice in half vertically. Remove the cores, then make a shallow incision in the necks to remove the strings.

2. In a large stainles steel or enamel skillet or 6-quart stockpot combine the wine, lemon juice, honey, cloves, cinnamon stick, and raisins. Bring to a boil.

3. Add the pears and spoon some liquid on them. Reduce the heat to a simmer and partially cover the pan. Cook the pears for 15 to 20 minutes, or until they are tender when carefully pierced with the tip of a knife. Do not overcook them. Turn the pears occasionally to baste them.

4. When the pears are done, remove them to a serving dish or individual decorative goblets, flat side up. Allow 2 halves per serving.

5. Boil the remaining liquid over high heat until reduced by one-third. Spoon some raisins into each core and pour the sauce over the pears. Serve warm, at room temperature, or chilled. *May be prepared up to 8 hours in advance.*

Poached Honey Pears Topped with Ginger Custard

This variation of the classic French dessert combines the sweet succulence of pears with rich, ginger-laced custard. It is not difficult to make, nor does it take much time, yet it bears a simple elegance.

SERVES 4 ► ELEGANT MENU 9

4 large pears, ripe but still slightly firm (preferably Bosc, Anjou, or Comice)
⅓ cup honey
¼ cup water

CUSTARD
1½ cups milk
4 egg yolks
¼ cup honey
2 tablespoons cornstarch
1½ tablespoons pear brandy, or 1 teaspoon vanilla extract
2 tablespoons minced crystallized ginger

1. Peel the pears and cut them in half vertically through the center. Carefully cut out the cores, then make a shallow incision in the necks to remove the strings.

2. In a large skillet mix the honey and water and bring to a boil over medium heat. Slip the pears in, flat side down, and cover the pan. Cook 5 minutes. Remove the cover, and cook uncovered for an additional 5 minutes, basting the pears frequently, or until they are tender when pierced with a skewer or cake tester. Do not overcook.

3. Remove the pears and place them in a shallow serving dish flat side up. Boil the syrup down until it is very thick and only 3 tablespoons remain. Pour onto the pears. Cover and chill until ready to serve.

4. To make the custard: In a medium saucepan over medium heat bring the milk almost to a boil.

5. Meanwhile in a medium bowl whisk the egg yolks and honey with a wire whisk until well blended. Add the cornstarch and whisk well again until perfectly smooth.

6. Slowly whisk in the hot milk, then pour the mixture into the saucepan. Over medium heat bring the mixture to a boil, whisking constantly, and boil 1 minute, or until it has thickened to the consistency of custard.

7. With a rubber spatula immediately scrape the custard into a bowl. Stir in the pear brandy or vanilla. Stir in 1 tablespoon of the ginger. Cover the custard with plastic wrap and press it directly on the custard to prevent a skin from forming. Chill until cold, about 1 hour. *May be prepared to this point up to 24 hours in advance, covered, and refrigerated until ready to serve.*

8. To serve the pears, arrange them in one large serving dish or in individual dishes. Spoon equal amounts of custard into the cavity of each pear. Garnish with the remaining tablespoon of minced crystallized ginger.

Baked Apples with Honey and Brandy

On a crisp fall or winter day, what could be more comforting than a spicy baked apple adorned with whipped cream?

SERVES 4   ▶ **BREAKFAST AND BRUNCH MENU 3**

4 large tart apples (such as Cortland or McIntosh)
½ cup honey
¼ cup brandy
2 tablespoons water
½ teaspoon cinnamon
Pinch nutmeg
Pinch allspice
⅓ cup chopped walnuts
1 tablespoon butter
Lightly sweetened whipped cream (optional)

1. Preheat the oven to 425°F. Butter a baking dish just large enough to fit the apples comfortably—an 8 x 8-inch pan works well.

2. Peel one-third of the top of each apple and keep the remaining skin intact. Core the apples. (If you do not have an apple corer the easiest way to do this is to cut two-thirds of the way down from the top of the apple around the core, going around the core a number of times until a smooth cut has been made, then repeating this from the bottom of the apple. Push the core out from the bottom through the top.)

3. Put the honey, brandy, water, cinnamon, nutmeg, allspice, and walnuts in a small saucepan, and heat just until the liquids have blended, about 1 minute. Remove from the heat, then one by one roll the apples in the mixture to coat well. Place them in the baking dish and pour the remaining liquid over them. Cut the butter into bits and place on top of the apples.

4. Bake, basting occasionally, for 30 minutes, or until an apple is tender when gently pierced with a sharp knife or cake tester. Do not overcook, or the apples will burst. Serve warm or at room temperature with the remaining syrup poured over them. They are especially good served with a spoonful of lightly sweetened whipped cream.

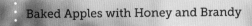
Baked Apples with Honey and Brandy

Maple-Glazed Baked Stuffed Apples with Crème Fraîche

A dessert that is relatively simple to prepare yet tastes so rich and satisfying. The apples are coated with maple syrup and filled with a mixture of walnuts, raisins, and spices that puffs up during baking. The sweetness of the apples and maple syrup is nicely contrasted by the tartness of the crème fraîche.

SERVES 4 ▶ ELEGANT MENU 2

4 large tart apples (such as Cortland or McIntosh)
½ cup pure maple syrup Ⓖ
⅓ cup finely chopped walnuts (not ground)
2 tablespoons raisins
½ teaspoon cinnamon
Pinch allspice
Pinch nutmeg
1 egg white
1 tablespoon butter
¼ cup water
1 recipe Crème Fraîche (page 299)

1. Butter a baking dish large enough to fit the 4 apples. Preheat the oven to 425°F.

2. Peel one-third of the skin off around the tops of the apples, leaving the remaining two-thirds of the peel intact. Core the apples. (If you do not have an apple corer the easiest way to do this is to cut two-thirds of the way down from the top of the apple around the core, going around the core a number of times until a smooth cut has been made, then repeating this from the bottom of the apple. Push the core out from the bottom through the top.)

3. Put the maple syrup in a small bowl. Roll each cored apple in the syrup, making sure to coat thoroughly both inside and out. Place the apples upright in the baking dish and reserve the syrup.

4. In a small bowl combine the walnuts, raisins, and spices. Add 1 tablespoon of the reserved maple syrup. Add the egg white and mix well. Spoon an equal amount of the mixture into each apple.

5. Pour the remaining maple syrup equally over each apple. Cut the butter into bits and place on top of each apple.

6. Cut 4 small pieces of aluminum foil—just large enough to cover the filling in each apple to prevent the raisins from burning—and lightly butter each one. Place 1 on top of each apple. (The filling will puff up during baking.)

7. Pour the water into the dish and move the dish around to blend the liquids. Bake the apples for 30 to 35 minutes, or until tender when gently pierced with a knife. Do not overcook them or the apples will burst. Baste occasionally with the syrup.

8. Serve warm or at room temperature, and pour any remaining syrup over the apples. Top each apple with some crème fraîche.

Fresh Fruit with Honey Zabaglione Sauce

Chilled zabaglione with whipped cream folded in makes a heavenly sauce for fresh fruit. Choose whatever fruit is in season—the best quality you can get—although I don't recommend apples because I find them too crunchy for this delicate sauce.

SERVES 6   ▶ INFORMAL MENU 13

4 egg yolks
4 tablespoons honey
¼ cup plus 1 tablespoon dry Marsala or Grand Marnier
⅔ cup heavy or whipping cream, well chilled
Fresh ripe fruit (berries, melon, plums, peaches, pears, bananas, oranges, mangos, kiwis, pineapple)

1. In the bottom part of a double boiler bring to a simmer enough water to barely touch the bottom of the pan that rests in it. Have ready a large bowl to scrape the custard into when done.

2. Meanwhile, off the heat put the egg yolks and 3 tablespoons of the honey in the top part of the double boiler and whip them with a wire whisk until they are pale and creamy. Add the Marsala or Grand Marnier and place this pan over the pan with the simmering water. Continue whisking the mixture until it begins to swell into a custard-like texture, about 7 minutes. Be very careful at this point not to overcook or you will end up with scrambled eggs. The mixture is ready when it can form soft mounds. With a rubber spatula immediately scrape the custard into the reserved bowl. Cool it slightly, then cover and refrigerate until well chilled, about 2 hours.

3. Meanwhile whip the cream with the remaining tablespoon of honey until it is very stiff. (The cream will whip better if you chill your beaters beforehand.) Fold into the chilled zabaglione until blended. *May be prepared to this point up to 4 hours in advance and chilled.*

4. Decoratively arrange some fruit (it should be at room temperature) on each serving plate and top with a generous spoonful of custard. Garnish each serving with a piece of attractive fruit.

> NOTE: If you do not have a double boiler, then you can make one by fitting a heat-proof bowl over the pan that contains the water.

Marinated Oranges in Grand Marnier Sauce

If top-quality sweet oranges are available, this fat-free, simple dessert is just the thing to serve as a light finale to a rich or heavy meal or as a sweet conclusion to a brunch.

SERVES 4   ▶ **INFORMAL MENU 15**

6 navel oranges
1 teaspoon honey
1 tablespoon water
¼ teaspoon cinnamon
Two 1-inch strips lemon peel
¼ cup Grand Marnier

1. Section the oranges in the following manner: cut the skin off with a sharp knife, then carefully cut each orange section out of the orange by cutting between the membranes right to the core. Let the orange sections and any juice fall into a medium bowl.

2. After all of the oranges have been sectioned, strain the accumulated juice into a small saucepan. Add the honey, water, cinnamon, and lemon peel to the saucepan. Boil over medium heat until reduced by half, about 3 minutes. It should look syrupy.

3. Remove the saucepan from the heat and take out the lemon peel. Add the Grand Marnier and stir to blend. Let the sauce cool until barely warm.

4. Pour over the oranges and toss to coat. Cover and chill for at least 1 hour and up to 24 hours. Bring to room temperature before serving.

5. Serve the orange sections on small serving plates in decorative patterns such as a circular sun design, or one behind the other in a vertical row. Pour equal amounts of the syrup over each serving. Alternatively, serve in decorative goblets.

Fresh Peaches with Honey Rum Sauce

This is simplicity itself—and the ideal dessert when peaches are at their height of freshness and you want a light, fat-free dessert.

SERVES 4 ▶ SUMMER MENU 3

2 tablespoons honey
2½ tablespoons rum (preferably dark)
6 ripe peaches

1. In a medium bowl mix the honey and rum together thoroughly.

2. Peel the peaches and slice in half. Remove the pits and cut each peach half into 4 slices and place in the bowl. Toss well, cover, and chill at least 1 hour before serving. Serve in decorative goblets or large wine glasses.

Brandied Fruit Compote

You could substitute different fruits in this delicious compote, such as oranges, pears, or figs; the idea is to have a mixture of dried and fresh fruit (all dried fruit is too heavy), and be sure to include the sliced banana. I love the combination of brandy and fruit flavors, and although it is not essential that you serve it with crème fraîche, I highly recommend it.

SERVES 4

▶ INFORMAL MENU 17

1 cup dried apricots cut into bite-size pieces
½ cup pitted prunes cut into quarters
½ cup golden raisins
1 medium apple, peeled, cored, and diced
Two 1-inch strips orange peel or lemon peel
1 cinnamon stick
1 cup apple cider or water
1 tablespoon honey
1 medium banana, cut into ½ inch slices
3 tablespoons brandy
Crème Fraîche (page 299) (optional)

1. Put everything in a medium saucepan except the banana, brandy, and crème fraîche, bring to a boil, then reduce the heat to a simmer and cook for 5 minutes.

2. Remove the orange peel and discard. Pour the compote into a bowl and add the sliced banana and brandy. Toss, then chill at least 1 hour. (If you are going to chill it longer, then cover the bowl.) *May be prepared up to 24 hours in advance. In this case don't add the banana until 1 hour before serving. When you are ready to serve, add a little more brandy if it has been completely absorbed.* Serve, as is or with a spoonful of crème fraîche, in decorative goblets or small dishes.

Chocolate-Dipped Strawberries

These are great served alone or alongside cookies, cakes, or other fruit desserts. They should be made the day you are going to serve them, for the berry "sweats" after a while and changes the texture of the chocolate. Using room-temperature strawberries ensures that the chocolate will adhere well.

► QUICK MENU 3

20 strawberries (½ pound), at room temperature
3 ounces semisweet chocolate

1. Wash the strawberries and dry very well with paper towels. Keep the hulls on. Place a large sheet of wax paper on a platter or cookie sheet and set aside.

2. In a double boiler over low heat melt the chocolate. Remove from the heat, keeping the chocolate over the double boiler pan. Dip the bottom two-thirds of each strawberry into the chocolate, leaving the top third bare. Place each strawberry on the wax paper and chill until set, about 1 hour.

NOTES: If you would prefer, you can melt the chocolate in the microwave. In a microwave-safe bowl, cook on high for 30-second intervals, stirring between each, until the chocolate is entirely melted. If the chocolate in the pan begins to harden before you are finished dipping, then return the double boiler to the heat and stir until soft again, or soften in the microwave for an additional 10 to 20 seconds.

Chocolate-Dipped Strawberries and Almond Butter Cookies (page 283)

Strawberries and Wine

This is a simple, low-calorie, and delicious dessert.

SERVES 4
▶ QUICK MENU 7

½ tablespoon honey
¼ cup dry red wine
2 pints (4 cups) strawberries

1. Combine the honey and wine in a medium bowl.

2. Wash the strawberries and pat dry. Remove their hulls, slice each strawberry in half—cut the very large ones into quarters—and toss in the bowl with the honey and wine. Cover and chill for at least 1 hour before serving. Serve in large wine glasses or decorative goblets.

COOKIES AND BARS

Some bakeries and food shops offer cookies that are delicious and special, but few can compare to great homemade cookies or brownies. There is a freshness that is immediately noticeable, and it makes the butter and sugar taste so much richer. For a special combination, pair cookies with a simple fruit dessert, such as Strawberries and Wine with Almond Butter Cookies, and you'll surprise and delight your guests and family.

Chocolate Chocolate-Chip Cookies

These are my idea of a great chocolate-chip cookie—crisp, buttery, and very chocolaty. You had better hide some of these if you don't want them all eaten in one sitting.

MAKES 4 TO 5 DOZEN

> 2 cups (12 ounces) semisweet chocolate chips
> 1 cup (2 sticks) butter, softened
> ½ cup white sugar
> ½ cup firmly packed light brown sugar
> 1 teaspoon vanilla extract
> 2¼ cups unbleached white flour
> ¼ teaspoon baking soda

1. Preheat the oven to 350°F. In a double boiler melt 1 cup of the chocolate chips. Set aside to cool slightly.

2. In a large bowl cream the butter with both sugars until smooth and fluffy. (Use an electric beater.) Beat in the melted chocolate and vanilla until well blended.

3. Beat in 1 cup of the flour and the baking soda until blended. Beat in the remaining flour; you might have to do it by hand at this point. Stir in the remaining chocolate chips until well mixed.

4. To get nicely shaped cookies drop by teaspoonfuls onto an ungreased cookie sheet about 2 inches apart from each other, and use the teaspoon to push the edges into a circle.

5. Bake for 15 to 17 minutes. Do not let burn. Let the cookies sit on the cookie sheet for a minute before removing. Cool on a wire rack. When thoroughly cooled store in a covered tin.

Cowboy Cookies

These are the prized cookies of my childhood. My mother, Rita, would make large batches of these crisp, buttery cookies, and it was a challenge for all of us to control ourselves and not overindulge. Even now when I visit her, this is the one dessert I look forward to. The brown sugar–oatmeal flavor is very pronounced, which makes these, in my estimation, the ultimate chocolate-chip cookies. (Incidentally, I never have been able to discover the origin of the name Cowboy Cookies.)

MAKES ABOUT 4 DOZEN

1½ cups unbleached white flour
¼ teaspoon baking soda
½ teaspoon baking powder
¼ teaspoon salt
1 cup (2 sticks) butter, softened
¾ cup sugar
¾ cup firmly packed light brown sugar
2 eggs
1 teaspoon vanilla extract
2 cups rolled oats (non-instant oatmeal)
1 cup chopped walnuts
2 cups (12 ounces) semisweet chocolate chips

1. Preheat the oven to 350°F. Butter a cookie sheet.

2. Combine the flours, baking soda, baking powder, and salt in a medium bowl.

3. Cream together the butter, sugars, eggs, and vanilla in a large bowl until fluffy. Add the flour mixture and mix well.

4. Beat in the oats, nuts, and chocolate chips. (You might have to do this step by hand.) The dough will be crumbly.

5. Drop by teaspoonfuls 2 inches apart on the prepared cookie sheet. Bake for 12 to 15 minutes, or until golden brown. Be careful not to burn them. Thoroughly cool on a wire rack before storing in a tin.

> NOTE: This recipe can be easily doubled, and these cookies freeze very well. Just be sure to keep them well stored in an airtight tin.

Almond Butter Cookies

Crisp, light, buttery, and richly flavored, these cookies could perhaps be equaled but not surpassed. I think they make a wonderful dessert, especially when served on a decorative platter with a side dish of fresh fruit or Chocolate-Dipped Strawberries (page 278).

MAKES 4 DOZEN

....

1 cup (2 sticks) unsalted butter, softened
½ cup sugar
¼ cup firmly packed light brown sugar
1 teaspoon vanilla extract
1 cup (about 4 ounces) coarsely ground almonds
2¼ cups unbleached white flour
¼ teaspoon salt

1. Cream the butter with the two sugars in a large bowl until fluffy. Add the vanilla and almonds and beat until well blended. Gradually beat in the flour and salt just until combined. Do not overbeat the dough.

2. Lightly flour a large sheet of wax paper. Turn the dough onto the wax paper and shape into a log 2 inches in diameter. Roll to cover completely with the wax paper; then refrigerate for at least 1 hour and up to 1 week.

3. When ready to use, cut the log into slices ¼ inch thick. (For an easy method mark off ¼-inch spaces with a ruler on the whole log and then slice.)

4. Preheat the oven to 350°F. Place on an ungreased cookie sheet about 1 inch apart and bake for 12 to 15 minutes, or until lightly golden on the edges. These cookies do not spread during baking. Cool on a wire rack before serving. Store in a covered tin up to 2 weeks.

> NOTE: You can freeze the dough and use it whenever you wish, although it does lose some flavor when frozen. Slice it frozen, or slightly thawed, and cook as directed.

Ginger Cookies

Cookies to me are a great dessert as long as they are rich and flavorful. These ginger cookies are crisp and buttery with a good dose of spiciness. They are quick to make, and you can prepare the dough up to 1 week in advance, or make it a few months in advance and freeze it, although there is a little flavor lost when frozen. Sometimes I serve them alongside a dish of rich vanilla ice cream, but that is by no means essential.

MAKES ABOUT 4 DOZEN ▶ SUMMER MENU 5

1 cup (2 sticks) butter, softened
½ cup firmly packed light brown sugar
½ cup white sugar
2 cups unbleached white flour
1½ tablespoons ground ginger
¼ teaspoon cinnamon
¼ teaspoon ground cloves
¼ teaspoon salt
Sugar to sprinkle on top

1. Cream the butter and sugars in a large bowl with an electric beater until well blended and fluffy. In a smaller bowl mix the remaining ingredients until well blended.

2. Gradually add the flour mixture to the butter mixture and beat until blended, but do not overbeat the dough. Gather it into a ball; it will be crumbly. (You can gather it into 2 balls and in the following step, shape each into a log, then freeze 1 for future use.)

3. Lightly flour a sheet of wax paper about 12 inches long. Put the dough on it and shape it into a log 2 inches in diameter. Roll up the log so that it is covered with wax paper. Chill it for 1 hour or up to 1 week, or freeze until ready to use. (If you keep it longer than a day or if you freeze it, wrap it in a plastic bag.) If frozen, thaw slightly before slicing.

4. Preheat the oven to 350°F. Slice the log into ¼-inch-thick slices—no thicker. An easy way to do this is to use a ruler as a guide and mark off ¼-inch spaces across the log. Place them on the cookie sheet 1 inch apart.

5. Bake 8 to 10 minutes, or until evenly golden. Be careful not to burn them. When done, immediately sprinkle some sugar on each cookie, then cool completely on a wire rack. Store in a covered tin.

Coconut Macaroons

Because these macaroons are made with unsweetened coconut rather than the commercial sweetened variety, they have a more pleasing coconut flavor.

MAKES 24 COOKIES

3 egg whites, at room temperature
Pinch cream of tartar
1 teaspoon vanilla extract
½ cup honey
2 cups unsweetened dried coconut

1. Preheat the oven to 275°F. Line a cookie sheet with aluminum foil and butter the surface of the foil.

2. Put the egg whites in a large bowl with the cream of tartar, and beat them until they hold stiff peaks. Add the vanilla and continue beating. Slowly pour in the honey, and continue beating until the meringue is very stiff, about 5 minutes.

3. Fold in the coconut with a rubber spatula until it is thoroughly blended. Drop the batter by teaspoonfuls onto the cookie sheet, using the back of the spoon to help shape the cookies into attractive mounds.

4. Bake for 30 to 35 minutes, or until golden. (If you would like the macaroons to be darker, slide them under the broiler for 30 seconds.) Allow to cool completely on a rack before serving.

NOTE: When storing these macaroons, put sheets of wax paper between the layers to prevent them from sticking together. Store in a covered tin.

Chocolate Oatmeal Bars

These fabulous bars have a rich brown sugar and oatmeal flavor and are covered with melted chocolate and chopped walnuts. They'd make a wonderful holiday gift wrapped individually in plastic wrap and neatly arranged in a decorative tin.

MAKES 24 BARS   ▶ QUICK MENU 9

1 cup (2 sticks) butter, softened
¾ cup firmly packed light brown sugar
1 egg yolk
1 teaspoon vanilla extract
1 cup rolled oats (non-instant oatmeal)
1 cup whole wheat pastry flour (or ½ cup whole wheat flour and ½ cup unbleached white flour)
1 cup finely chopped walnuts (not ground)
1½ cups (9 ounces) semisweet chocolate chips

1. Preheat the oven to 350°F. Butter and flour a 12 x 2 x 7-inch pan or dish. (If it is glass, then preheat the oven to 325°F.)

2. In a large bowl beat together the butter, sugar, egg yolk, and vanilla until smooth and creamy.

3. Add the oats, flour, and half of the walnuts. Beat just until blended; do not overwork the dough. (You may have to do this step by hand.)

4. With a rubber spatula or your fingers spread this mixture into the prepared pan and smooth the top. Bake for 25 minutes, or until it is a rich golden color.

5. Remove the pan from the oven and sprinkle on the chocolate chips. Return to the oven for 3 minutes, or until they are soft. With a spatula spread the chocolate evenly over the surface. Sprinkle on the remaining nuts and press them lightly into the surface.

6. Cool on a wire rack for 30 minutes, then chill for 1 hour, or until the chocolate is firm but not hard. Cut into 24 bars and serve when the chocolate is hard. To store, wrap them in pairs in foil, or store in a tightly covered tin.

Chocolate-Chip Fudge Brownies

The size of the pan will determine the texture of brownies. The smaller the pan the more cakelike the results. I prefer chewier brownies so I use a 9 x 13-inch pan. For best results make these the day before, and, by all means, *don't overcook them.*

MAKES 24 BROWNIES   ▶ INFORMAL MENU 2

....

4 ounces unsweetened chocolate
¾ cup (1½ sticks) butter
4 eggs
1½ cups sugar
1 teaspoon vanilla extract
1 cup unbleached white flour
1 cup (6 ounces) semisweet chocolate chips

1. Preheat the oven to 350°F. (If you are using a glass pan, then turn to 325°F.) Butter and flour a 9 x 13-inch pan and set aside.

2. In a medium saucepan melt the unsweetened chocolate with the butter over medium heat. Set aside to cool to room temperature. (This will help prevent a crust from forming on the baked brownies.)

3. In a large bowl beat the eggs, sugar, and vanilla until light colored and well blended. By *hand* stir in the chocolate mixture and blend. Add the flour and mix by hand until blended. Do not overbeat. (This must be done by hand or a funny crust will develop.)

4. Pour into the prepared pan. Sprinkle the chocolate chips evenly on the top, and carefully run a knife through the batter to immerse some of the chips.

5. Bake for 30 to 35 minutes, or until a knife inserted in the center comes out clean. Do not overcook. Cool on a rack completely (at least 3 hours) before cutting. Store in a covered tin or individually wrapped in foil or plastic wrap. To freeze, place individually wrapped brownies in a plastic bag and freeze up to 1 month.

EVERY COOK NEEDS A COLLECTION OF RELIABLE RECIPES for basic techniques that are used repeatedly in cooking. A flaky, tender pie crust; a garlicky vinaigrette with just the right balance of vinegar and oil; fluffy brown rice; and a fragrant,

The Basics

rich marinara sauce are just a few examples of staple recipes that you should be able to depend on.

Here are my favorite versions of "the basics." I've worked them out so they are delicious, foolproof, and easy to make.

Vegetable Stock

Here is a recipe for vegetable stock for those who want to or need to make it fresh. It would be dishonest of me to say that I make my own stock because I don't. Personally, I prefer to use vegetable powder or cubes from the health food store or boxed stock. They are extremely flavorful, have no preservatives or artificial ingredients, aren't overly salted, and allow you to spend your precious time elsewhere. When you make homemade vegetable stock you have to use a lot of vegetables to get a concentrated flavor, and you must cook them a long time. (However, if you have a garden, making vegetable stock can be a clever way to use oversized and imperfect vegetables that might otherwise go to waste.) If homemade stock greatly appeals to you, try this recipe; it is delicious and unfailingly easy.

MAKES 7 CUPS

8 cups water
¼ cup tamari or other soy sauce
3 carrots, washed, unpeeled, and diced
3 celery ribs (leaves included), diced
4 cups chopped cabbage
½ bunch fresh parsley (with stems), chopped
3 onions, diced, or 2 large leeks, thoroughly washed and sliced (green tops included)
6 cloves garlic, coarsely chopped
2 bay leaves
¼ teaspoon black pepper
Dash nutmeg

1. Put everything in a large stockpot and bring to a boil. Reduce to a simmer and cook for 1 hour, stirring occasionally.

2. Remove the bay leaves and discard. Strain the mixture through a fine mesh strainer.

3. Let the stock cool. Store in a tightly covered jar in the refrigerator, or pour into ice cube trays and freeze. When frozen, put the ice cubes in a plastic bag and use the cubes as needed. The stock will stay fresh in the refrigerator for 7 days. After 1 week bring the stock to a boil, then simmer for 10 minutes. The stock will keep fresh for 1 more week.

Perfect Brown Rice

Brown rice, if cooked properly, should be light and fluffy. Follow these rules to avoid gummy rice: use long-grain brown rice for extra lightness; use the proper size pan in proportion to the amount of rice cooked; add a little oil and salt to prevent foam from rising during cooking; never stir brown rice while it is cooking; and do not overcook the rice or the starch will escape from the grains and the rice will be gummy.

MAKES 2½ TO 3 CUPS COOKED RICE

1 cup long-grain brown rice
2 cups water or Vegetable Stock (page 290)
½ teaspoon salt
1 tablespoon oil

1. Put the rice in a strainer and rinse under cold running water. Turn it into a 1½-quart saucepan along with the remaining ingredients.

2. Cover the pan and bring to a boil. Reduce the heat to a simmer and cook undisturbed for about 45 minutes, or until all of the liquid is absorbed. There are a few ways to make sure it is all absorbed: Look to see that there is no bubbling liquid; use a knife tip to carefully make a small separation in the rice to see that the liquid is absorbed; and finally listen to hear if the rice has begun to stick to the pan (a sizzling sound)—if it hasn't, then there is still more liquid to be absorbed. You should taste the rice to make sure it is tender. If by chance it needs further cooking then add a little boiling water (do not stir), cover the pan, and simmer until it is all absorbed.

3. Serve immediately, or put into a covered baking dish and keep warm in the oven (350°F).

Perfect Brown Rice with Peas

Cook the rice in vegetable stock as directed. About 5 minutes before the rice is done sprinkle ½ teaspoon dried basil and 1 cup cooked fresh peas or thawed frozen peas on top of the rice. Do not mix. When all of the water is absorbed remove the pan from the heat. Gently toss the rice and peas and add 1 tablespoon of butter cut into bits. Cover the pan and let sit for 5 minutes. Serve.

Perfect Brown Rice Pilaf

Melt 2 tablespoons of butter in the saucepan. Add 1 large minced onion and sauté for 5 minutes. Add the uncooked brown rice and toss well. Cook 2 minutes. Add the vegetable stock, salt, and oil, and cook as directed in the basic recipe.

> NOTE: When making any stir-fried rice dish or cold rice salad dish that calls for cooked brown rice, use cold cooked rice to ensure lightness.

Bread Crumbs

I always have these on hand in the freezer. They are very quick to make and can be made with stale bread or fresh bread.

1. Save ends from bread (whole wheat preferred) and freeze them until you have enough to make bread crumbs, or use regular slices of bread. Toast the slices in the toaster (if you only have a few), or lay them on a cookie sheet and broil on both sides until golden brown. Be careful not to burn them.

2. Let the toast sit at room temperature until it is cool and dry. Turn the slices over occasionally so no moisture collects underneath from their heat.

3. Tear a few slices into small pieces and put in a blender or food processor. Blend until fine crumbs are formed. Pour into a plastic bag. Repeat with the remaining slices.

4. Freeze in the plastic bag and use them as needed. As you collect more crusts keep making bread crumbs and add to this bag, so that you always have some on hand.

> NOTE: **Two slices of bread will yield about 1 cup crumbs.**

Marinara Sauce

This is my favorite tomato sauce, very garlicky and flavorful. Dried herbs work fine here and add to its ease. Use it on Neapolitan Pizza (page 138), or simply serve on spaghetti or linguine for a quick meal.

MAKES ABOUT 3 CUPS

¼ cup olive oil
4 cloves garlic, minced
28-ounce can tomato purée
2 tablespoons red wine
2 teaspoons dried oregano
1 teaspoon dried basil
½ teaspoon dried thyme
½ teaspoon salt
Liberal seasoning freshly ground pepper

1. In a medium saucepan over medium-low heat, heat the olive oil and garlic. Cook for 3 minutes, or until the garlic is lightly golden. Stir often and be careful not to burn the garlic.

2. Add all of the remaining ingredients and bring to a boil. Simmer the sauce for 20 minutes. Stir occasionally.

Pesto

This Italian basil and garlic sauce is one of the greatest delicacies of all time. It is most often used as a sauce for pasta, but my favorite way to savor it is to spread it on lightly toasted French bread and eat it as an appetizer (page 28). Traditionally it is pounded in a mortar, but this blender method works just as well and it is a lot quicker. Many contemporary recipes call for the addition of pine nuts, but I find them superfluous and indistinguishable in pesto. The addition of butter, however, is pure magic.

MAKES 1⅓ CUPS   ▶ INFORMAL MENU 11

> 2 cups moderately well-packed fresh basil leaves (about 1 bunch basil), stems removed, rinsed, and patted dry
> ½ cup olive oil
> 4 cloves garlic
> ½ cup grated Parmesan cheese
> 2 tablespoons butter, softened

1. Put the basil, olive oil, and garlic in the container of a blender or food processor and purée until smooth. Turn off the machine and scrape down the sides as necessary.

2. Pour this mixture into a container and stir in the cheese. Stir in the soft butter and chill until ready to use. (Note: The secret of a smooth pesto is to stir in the cheese and butter by hand—not machine.)

3. If you are going to use the pesto on pasta, then thin the pesto with a few tablespoons of boiling pasta water just before saucing the pasta. Pesto will keep for 1 month if covered with ¼ inch of olive oil and stored in the refrigerator.

> NOTE: To prepare pesto for freezing don't add the cheese or butter. Freeze the basil, olive oil, and garlic purée in a tightly covered container for up to 6 months. Alternatively, freeze in ice cube trays then place the cubes in a Ziploc bag. When ready to use, thoroughly defrost, then stir in the cheese and butter.

Winter Pesto

In the midst of winter many people regret not having had the foresight to freeze batches of pesto when fresh basil was in season; others self-indulgently used up their supply much faster than they expected. In either case, here is a recipe that will satisfy pesto addicts anywhere, and can be made in any season.

MAKES 2 CUPS

3 cups tightly packed fresh spinach, stems removed, rinsed, and patted dry
1 tablespoon dried basil
4 cloves garlic, peeled and halved
¼ cup walnuts (optional)
½ cup olive oil
⅔ cup grated Parmesan cheese
2 tablespoons butter, softened
¼ teaspoon salt

1. Make sure the spinach is patted dry. Put the spinach, basil, garlic, walnuts, and olive oil into the container of the blender. Blend until smooth, turning off the motor and scraping down the sides as necessary.

2. Pour the pesto into a container with a tight-fitting lid, and stir in the cheese by hand until blended. Stir in the softened butter and salt by hand until blended.

3. If the pesto is to be used as a sauce for pasta, add a few tablespoons of the boiling pasta water to the pesto to thin it out before tossing it on the pasta.

NOTE: This pesto keeps well refrigerated for 2 weeks with a tablespoon of oil poured on the surface to prevent dryness. For freezing, omit the cheese and butter and freeze in an airtight container. Thoroughly defrost before using, and add the cheese and butter after it is defrosted.

Mayonnaise

Mayonnaise can be mastered with a little effort and a good dose of knowledge. There are two methods to making mayonnaise: either beating it by hand or making it in the blender or food processor. The hand-beaten method produces a smoother, glossier mayonnaise. Machine-made mayonnaise (made with a whole egg rather than with just an egg yolk) is quicker to make, has more volume, and will last longer because the ingredients are more finely bound together. I prefer to make it by machine because it is so quick.

MAKES 1 CUP

1 whole egg
½ teaspoon ground (dry) mustard
½ teaspoon salt
Dash cayenne pepper
1 cup oil (preferably ½ cup vegetable oil and ½ cup olive oil—olive oil adds flavor)
2 tablespoons lemon juice

1. Have all of the utensils and ingredients warm or at room temperature to ensure that the mayonnaise does not separate. Put the egg, mustard, salt, and cayenne pepper into the blender and blend for 30 seconds. Or, if you are using a food processor, combine them in the bowl of the processor and set the metal blade in place. Process for 60 seconds.

2. If using the blender remove the cover. While the machine (either the blender or the food processor) is still running add 1 teaspoon of the oil. Wait until it is incorporated, then add another teaspoon. Keep adding the oil at this slow pace until you have used ½ cup of the oil.

3. Add the lemon juice and blend. Add the remaining ½ cup of oil, continuing with a slow pace. You will probably have to stop the blender or processor and scrape down the sides occasionally as the mayonnaise thickens. Store in a covered container in the refrigerator for up to 6 days.

> NOTE: All is not lost if your mayonnaise separates. You can reconstitute it by adding one of the following to a clean bowl—an egg yolk, a tablespoon of very cold water, or a tablespoon of vinegar—and beating in a teaspoon of broken mayonnaise. Once it is blended add a little more mayonnaise, beat, then slowly beat in the remaining mayonnaise until it is well blended.

Crème Fraîche

This version of crème fraîche is similar to the kind you can purchase in France. The culture in the buttermilk thickens the cream and causes it to develop a tart flavor. It is so simple to prepare and is a wonderful addition to desserts, sauces, soups, or whatever.

MAKES 1 CUP

1 cup heavy or whipping cream
1 tablespoon buttermilk Ⓖ

1. Put the cream and buttermilk into a small jar with a screw top. Shake a few seconds to blend.

2. Let sit at room temperature for at least 8 hours if your room is warm and up to 24 hours if it is cool. Shake again to mix. It is ready when the cream is thick like sour cream. Chill until ready to serve.

> NOTE: If you are in a hurry for the crème fraîche and your room is cool, you can slightly warm your oven for a few seconds, then turn the oven off and keep the crème fraîche in there to thicken for 8 hours. Crème fraîche can be stored in an airtight container in the refrigerator up to 2 weeks. It will become increasingly tart with age.

Ghee

Ghee is a butter oil that is used in Indian cooking for its excellent keeping qualities. The milk solids and moisture, which promote rancidity in butter, are removed, thereby ensuring the ghee a longer life, and also allowing it to withstand higher temperatures than butter without burning. In addition, ghee has a distinctive nutlike flavor produced by slow cooking before straining; this distinguishes it from clarified butter.

MAKES ABOUT 1½ CUPS

1 pound unsalted butter

1. In a heavy medium saucepan heat the butter over medium heat until melted. Be careful not to let it burn.

2. Increase the heat to high and bring the butter to a boil, then immediately reduce the heat to the lowest possible point. Skim off the foam that has risen and discard. Repeat this process once more.

3. Keeping the heat at the lowest possible point, simmer the ghee, uncovered, for 45 minutes. The milk solids on the bottom will turn a golden brown.

4. Remove the pan from the heat and strain the ghee through two layers of dampened cheesecloth into a storage container with a tight-fitting lid. (Note: If there are any solids left in the ghee, strain it again to prevent it from later becoming rancid. The ghee must be perfectly clear.)

5. Store it in the refrigerator or at room temperature until ready to use. Ghee will solidify when chilled. It will keep safely at room temperature for 2 to 3 months. If chilled it will keep indefinitely.

Raspberry Vinegar

This vinegar has a fruity nuance which is delightful on salads, such as Mango and Avocado Salad with Raspberry Vinaigrette (page 54).

MAKES 2 CUPS

2 cups white wine vinegar or distilled white vinegar
1 cup raspberries

1. In a medium saucepan combine the vinegar and raspberries and bring to a boil. Turn off the heat and let sit until cool.

2. Strain through a fine-mesh strainer into a bowl. Strain again through double thicknesses of cheesecloth into a jar with a plastic screw top. Store in a cool, dark place. It will last indefinitely.

Pâté Brisée (Savory or Sweet Crust)

This is an all-purpose, flaky crust—great for savory pies and sweet dessert tarts. After much experimentation I have found that it is best to roll the dough right after mixing it; the traditional method of chilling the dough beforehand makes it unnecessarily hard to handle. Work quickly, though, to keep the butter cold.

MAKES ONE 9- TO 10-INCH CRUST

1¼ cups unbleached white flour
2 teaspoons sugar (for sweet), or ¼ teaspoon salt (for savory)
5 tablespoons chilled butter, cut into bits
2 tablespoons oil
3 to 4 tablespoons ice water

1. In a large bowl combine the flour and either the sugar or salt (depending upon whether you want a sweet or savory crust). Add the bits of butter and toss to coat with the flour.

2. With a pastry cutter or the tips of your fingers work the butter into the flour until it resembles coarse meal.

3. Sprinkle on the oil and toss, then sprinkle on 3 tablespoons of ice water and toss again. Gather the dough into a ball (if you need more water add 1 more tablespoon) and knead 3 or 4 times to help distribute the moisture. Gather into a ball again and flatten into a disc. (See Note on how to make the dough with a food processor.)

4. Lightly flour your work surface, your rolling pin, and the top of the dough. Roll it into a circle to fit your tart or pie plate. Make sure to keep turning the dough as you roll to keep it a perfect circle, and lightly flour underneath whenever it begins to stick. If it breaks at all pinch the edges together until mended.

5. Place the rolling pin on the center of the dough and fold one half of the pastry over it. Carry the pastry this way to your pie plate and unfold it over the plate. Press it in thoroughly and flute the edges. If you are using a tart pan then roll the rolling pin over the top of the pan to cut off any excess dough. Chill for at least 30 minutes, or cover and chill for up to 24 hours, or cover well and freeze. Proceed with your pie or tart recipe. If you need to prebake the crust, then follow step 6.

6. To prebake: Prick the pastry bottom all over and spread a sheet of foil over it. Press the foil into the sides, then fill with dried beans or aluminum pastry pellets to weight it down. Bake in a preheated 400°F oven for 10 minutes. Remove the foil and beans (save the beans for future crusts), and prick again. Bake an additional 5 minutes. Remove from the oven and proceed with your recipe.

> NOTE: To make the dough with a food processor combine the flour, sugar or salt, and butter in the bowl of a food processor. Set the metal blade in place and process for about 8 seconds, or just until coarse meal is formed. With the processor still running pour in the oil, then the ice water (try 3 tablespoons; if more is needed add a little more bit by bit), then stop the machine as soon as the dough begins to form a ball. There should be bits of butter visible in the dough; you don't want it to be perfectly smooth. Gather the dough into a ball, then flatten into a disk.

Pâté Brisée with Whole Wheat Flour

When I want to include more whole grains in my meal, I will often make a savory or dessert pie with this crust with wonderful results. This version produces a flaky crust with a nutty flavor.

MAKES ONE 9- TO 10-INCH CRUST

1⅓ cups whole wheat pastry flour (or ⅔ cup whole wheat flour and ⅔ cup unbleached white flour)
¼ teaspoon salt
5 tablespoons chilled butter
2 tablespoons oil
3 to 5 tablespoons ice water

1. Put the flour and salt into a large bowl, or mound it on a board or good work surface. Cut the butter into small pieces and add to the flour. Toss with the flour, then with a pastry cutter or the tips of your fingers work the butter into the flour until it resembles coarse meal. There should still be bits of butter visible, though.

2. Continue with steps 3 to 6 in the Pâté Brisée recipe on page 302.

Pâte Sucrée (Sweet Pie Crust)

The egg yolk in pâte sucrée gives the crust a cookie-like texture, making it ideal for fillings that are moist and delicate. A crust baked like this is completely cooked and is used when the filling for the pie does not have to be baked.

MAKES ONE 9- TO 10-INCH CRUST

> 1⅓ cups unbleached white flour
> ¼ cup sugar
> ½ cup (1 stick) chilled butter
> 1 egg, lightly beaten
> 1 egg yolk
> 1 teaspoon vanilla extract
> 1 egg white

1. Put the flour and sugar in a large bowl. Cut the butter into small bits, add, and toss with the flour.

2. Cut the butter into the flour with a pastry cutter or the tips of your fingers until it resembles coarse meal. Alternatively, pinch the flour and butter between your fingertips until it is evenly distributed and forms a coarse meal texture.

3. Beat the egg, egg yolk, and vanilla together until well mixed and combine with the flour mixture. Gather the dough into a ball and knead it 3 or 4 times to evenly moisten the dough. Gather into a ball again, then flatten into a disk. (See Note on how to make the dough in a food processor.)

4. Preheat the oven to 400°F. Lightly flour a work surface and the top of the dough. Roll out the pastry slightly larger than the pie pan into which it will fit. To keep the pastry round, turn it regularly while rolling, and lightly flour beneath it if necessary.

5. Drape the pastry over the rolling pin, carry it to the pie plate, and unfold it over the plate. Press it into the sides of the plate and flute the edges. If you are using a tart pan or quiche dish, then roll over the top of the pan with a rolling pin to trim the edges. Prick the crust a few times with a fork. Chill at least 30 minutes, or cover and chill for 24 hours, or cover well and freeze.

6. To bake blind (without a filling) line the pastry with aluminum foil, then fill it with dried beans or aluminum pastry pellets to cover the surface and keep it from shrinking too much. Bake for 10 minutes.

7. Remove the crust from the oven, and remove the foil and beans or pellets. (Save the beans for future use.) Lightly brush the crust with some of the egg white to coat it—this will seal the crust and prevent sogginess. Prick the crust again, then return it to the oven and bake for 10 to 12 minutes more, or until golden all over and crisp looking.

8. Cool on a wire rack until ready to use.

> NOTE: To make the dough in a food processor combine the flour, sugar, and butter in the bowl of a food processor. Beat the egg, egg yolk, and vanilla together and keep nearby. Set the metal blade in place and process for about 8 seconds, or just until coarse meal is formed. With the processor still running pour in the egg mixture, then stop the machine as soon as the dough begins to form a ball. There should be bits of butter visible in the dough; you don't want it perfectly smooth. Gather the dough into a ball, then flatten into a disk.

Almond Nut Crust

This nut-filled crust is fabulous with fruit fillings.

MAKES ONE 9-INCH CRUST

6 tablespoons butter, softened
½ cup sugar
1 egg yolk
½ teaspoon almond extract
⅔ cup unbleached white flour
⅔ cup (about 3 ounces) finely ground almonds

1. Lightly butter a tart pan and set aside. In a large bowl cream the butter and sugar with an electric beater until well blended. Add the egg yolk and almond extract and blend.

2. Add the flour and almonds and beat just until the mixture blends; do not overwork the dough.

3. Spoon the crumbled dough into the tart pan. Dust your fingers lightly with flour and press the dough firmly into the pan. Be sure to press it evenly into the sides. Chill for ½ hour. Proceed with your recipe.

Orange Almond Crust

Substitute the grated rind of 1 large orange for the almond extract.

CREATING HARMONIOUS MENUS REQUIRES THAT complementary flavors, colors, and textures come together to enhance all the components of the meal. Here are menus for all occasions, from quick suppers to elegant dinners,

Menus

along with seasonal menus and breakfast and brunch fare. Turn to these suggestions when you need guidance or when you want inspiration to create your own combinations. Just remember to strive for balance.

QUICK MENUS

Quickness and ease of preparation characterize the recipes in this section, but don't let that dissuade you from choosing one of these menus for a special occasion. The dishes are simple to prepare, yet are imaginative and interesting, and would be suitable for lunches, quick after-work dinners, as well as for pleasing guests.

▶ **MENU 1**
Braised Tempeh Napoletano (page 205)
Fine Egg Noodles with Light Garlic Sauce (page 212)
Blueberry Streusel Cake (page 234)

▶ **MENU 2**
Creamy Garlic Tofu Dip (page 72) with crudités
Penne with Eggplant Sauce (page 144)
Apricot Orange Mousse (page 256)

▶ **MENU 3**
Ricotta Basil Spread (page 24)
Polenta Puttanesca (page 158)
Chocolate-Dipped Strawberries (page 278)

▶ **MENU 4**
Cucumber and Grated Carrot Salad in Creamy Dill Dressing (page 58)
Bean Tostadas (page 136)
Hot Fudge Pudding Cake (page 237)

▶ **MENU 5**
Tempeh in Curried Yogurt Sauce (page 209)
Perfect Brown Rice (page 292)
Indian Pudding (page 259)

▶ **MENU 6**
Zucchini, Tomato, and Basil Frittata (page 115)
Bulghur Pilaf (page 213)
Stuffed Peaches with Fresh Cherries and Almonds (page 264)

▶ **MENU 7**
Stuffed Red Pepper Strips with Ricotta Basil Spread (page 31)
Linguine with Swiss Chard and Garlic (page 145)
Strawberries and Wine (page 280)

▶ **MENU 8**
Braised Curried Eggplant (page 177)
Fruited Rice Curry (page 179)
Indian Pudding (page 259)

▶ **MENU 9**
Spicy Cucumber Salad (page 59)
Stir-Fried Tempeh with Hot Pepper Sauce (page 207)
Perfect Brown Rice (page 292)
Chocolate Oatmeal Bars (page 287)

▶ **MENU 10**
Kasha Topped with Mushrooms in Sour Cream Sauce (page 143)
Sautéed Cabbage with Fennel Seed (page 232)
Pear and Apricot Crisp (page 265)

▶ **MENU 11**
Stuffed Mushrooms with Feta and Dill (page 32)
Spaghettini with Garlic and Hot Pepper (page 147)
Poached Pears in Red Wine with Raisins (page 266)

INFORMAL MENUS

These are "in-between" menus that require a moderate amount of attention and forethought. They aren't as elaborate as the Elegant Menus, yet could be suitable for casual entertaining, and they aren't as fast as the Quick Menus, yet could oftentimes make a rather easy meal with a little planning. They are just what are needed when you want to prepare a multicourse meal that is distinctive yet not too demanding.

▶ **MENU 1**
Indonesian Salad with Spicy Peanut Dressing (page 48)
Indonesian Curried Vegetable Stew with Coconut Milk (page 107)
Gingerbread (page 241)

► **MENU 2**
Avocado and Bathed Bread Vinaigrette (page 56)
Baked Mexican-Style Beans with Sour Cream and Chiles (page 164)
Sautéed Greens with Garlic (page 217)
Chocolate-Chip Fudge Brownies (page 288)

► **MENU 3**
Fresh Pea Salad Rémoulade (page 53)
Stir-Fried Asparagus, Tofu, and Red Pepper (page 197)
Perfect Brown Rice (page 292)
Rhubarb Tart (page 247)

► **MENU 4**
Simple Salad with Lemon-Soy Dressing (page 69)
Szechuan Braised Tofu and Vegetables (page 198)
Perfect Brown Rice (page 292)
(Fresh pineapple)

► **MENU 5**
Spinach Salad with Creamy Dill Dressing (page 51)
Fragrant Vegetable Stew with Corn Dumplings (page 105)
Maple Pecan Pie (page 254)

► **MENU 6**
Baked Eggplant Stuffed with Curried Vegetables (page 184)
Perfect Brown Rice (page 292)
(Plain yogurt)
Strawberries and Wine (page 280)

► **MENU 7**
Mexican-Style Stuffed Summer Squash (page 170)
Sautéed Greens with Garlic (page 217)
Fresh Fruit with Yogurt Lime Sauce (page 15)

► **MENU 8**
Spinach Salad with Creamy Dill Dressing (page 51)
Vegetarian Chili (page 103)
(Cornbread)
Poached Pears in Red Wine with Raisins (page 266)

► **MENU 9**
Asparagus Vinaigrette (page 57)
Baked Eggplant, Chickpeas, and Tomatoes (page 165)
(Hot French bread)
Apricot Orange Mousse (page 256)

► **MENU 10**
Arugula and Boston Lettuce Salad (page 49)
Baked Macaroni and Cheese with Cauliflower and Jalapeño Peppers (page 169)
Poached Pears in Red Wine with Raisins (page 266)

► **MENU 11**
Pesto on Toasted French Bread (page 28)
Tofu Fra Diavolo with Spinach Fettuccine (page 201)
Pear and Apricot Crisp (page 265)

► **MENU 12**
Arugula and Boston Lettuce Salad (page 49)
Chalupas (page 137)
Apple Crisp (page 261)

► **MENU 13**
Fresh Mozzarella, Roasted Pepper, and Black Olive Salad (page 63)
Risotto of Brown Rice and Mushrooms (page 156)
Braised Broccoli with Wine and Garlic (page 220)
Fresh Fruit with Honey Zabaglione Sauce (page 274)

► **MENU 14**
Indian Eggplant Dip (page 27)
Cashew Nut Curry (page 178)
Curried Cauliflower and Peas (page 181)
Perfect Brown Rice (page 292)
(Plain yogurt)
Kheer (page 258)

► **MENU 15**
Creamy Garlic Tofu Dip (page 72) with crudités
Cuban Black Beans and Rice (page 154)
Marinated Oranges in Grand Marnier Sauce (page 275)

► **MENU 16**
Baked Stuffed Artichokes with Pine Nuts and Lemon Herb Sauce (page 37)
Cauliflower and Pasta Soup (page 96)
Rhubarb Cobbler (page 262)

► **MENU 17**
Arugula and Boston Lettuce Salad (page 49)
Spaghetti Squash with Broccoli Butter Sauce (page 149)
Brandied Fruit Compote (page 277)

ELEGANT MENUS

When the occasion calls for a special meal that will delight the senses and be adventurous for cook and guest alike, choose a menu from this section. Although planning a meal that includes a number of carefully prepared courses is undoubtedly a time-consuming endeavor, it need not tax you so that you're exhausted by the time the guests arrive. You should relax before dinner, and the only way to do this is to prepare a great part of the meal in advance. Take advantage of the suggestions noted in most of the recipes for planning ahead, and you will enjoy the fruits of your efforts—and the company of your guests—a lot more.

▶ **MENU 1**
Arugula and Boston Lettuce Salad (page 49)
Rolled Stuffed Lasagna with Kale in a Tomato Cream Sauce (page 151)
Linzertorte (page 250)

▶ **MENU 2**
Miso Soup (page 102)
Moo Shu Vegetables with Mandarin Pancakes (page 112)
Chilled Green Beans with Sesame Sauce (page 219)
Maple-Glazed Baked Stuffed Apples with Crème Fraîche (page 272)

▶ **MENU 3**
Mango and Avocado Salad with Raspberry Vinaigrette (page 54)
Spinach Custard Ring with Tomato Cream Sauce (page 118)
Bulgur Almond Pilaf (page 213)

▶ **MENU 4**
Puris (page 189)
Vegetable Kofta (page 182)
Red Lentil Dal (page 188)
Perfect Brown Rice (page 292)
Orange Raita (page 190)
Raisin Chutney (page 192)
Kheer (page 258)

▶ **MENU 5**
Three-Layered Vegetable Pâté with Herb Mayonnaise (page 42)
Skillet Tofu and Vegetables in Brandy Cream Sauce (page 200)
Brussels Sprouts with Lemon-Soy Glaze (page 225)
Fine Egg Noodles with Light Garlic Sauce (page 212)
Mocha Walnut Torte (page 242)

► MENU 6
Hummus (page 30)
Tabbouleh (page 80)
Spanakopita (page 130)
Honey-Glazed Sugar Snap Peas with Carrots (page 227)

► MENU 7
Arugula and Boston Lettuce Salad (page 49)
Noodle Timbales with Pesto Cream Sauce (page 120)
Zucchini, Red Pepper, and Snow Pea Sauté (page 223)
Raspberry Almond Torte (page 244)

► MENU 8
Guacamole (page 25)
Black Bean and Cream Cheese Enchiladas (page 162)
Sautéed Greens with Garlic (page 217)
Pear Tart with Almond Nut Crust (page 249)

► MENU 9
Deep-Fried Cheese-Filled Polenta Balls (page 35)
Tofu Francese with Artichoke Hearts (page 199)
Turnip (Rutabaga) Gratin (page 228)
Perfect Brown Rice (page 292)
Poached Honey Pears Topped with Ginger Custard (page 268)

► MENU 10
Moroccan Tomato and Roasted Pepper Salad (page 64)
Vegetarian B'stilla (page 133)
Mocha Walnut Torte (page 242)

► MENU 11
Stuffed Mushrooms with Blue Cheese (page 33)
Leek Timbales with White Wine Sauce (page 122)
Bulgur Pilaf (page 213)
Pear Tart with Almond Nut Crust (page 249)

Thanksgiving Feast to Serve 6

Yogurt Herb Cheese Spread (page 23)
Walnut Loaf with Burgundy Sauce (page 173)
Chestnut Purée (page 230)
Braised Red Cabbage with Apples (page 231)
Roasted Potatoes with Rosemary (page 216)
Cranberry Fruit Tart (page 255)

This menu has all the wonderful associations one has with the fall season—herbs, nuts, chestnuts, fall vegetables, and fruits. I have served this meal to many non-vegetarians on Thanksgiving Day, and everyone has admitted that they didn't miss the turkey. The chestnuts can be prepared well in advance and frozen, the pie crust can be prepared and cooked 2 days before, and the yogurt cheese, walnut loaf, and pie filling can be prepared the day before. What will remain on Thanksgiving Day will be cooking the loaf, making the gravy, puréeing and heating the chestnut purée, preparing the cabbage and potatoes, and assembling the pie. None of these tasks demands much time, so you won't be a slave to the kitchen, as is oftentimes the case on Thanksgiving.

SUMMER MENUS

During the hot summer months one should be mindful of the value and comfort of preparing dishes that are suited to hot weather cooking and eating. Unfortunately, it took me a long time to learn this lesson. Many a guest has built up a sweat as a result of my unbridled enthusiasm for cooking whatever struck my fancy at the time. If I had an urge to prepare a spicy curry dinner or a particular dish that required baking, then no one could stop me. (I know that spicy food is eaten in many hot climates and the sweating that results from it cools the body, but I think that most people in cooler climates, who aren't used to such practices, would prefer to remain dry while dining.)

But this is a tale of the past. I now look forward to preparing dishes that complement summer weather and require little use of the stove. Marinades, cold soups, rice and pasta salads, and fresh fruit desserts are all delectable and much more compatible with this precious season. With an assortment of fresh vegetables and fruits in abundance and the addition of fruity olive oil, mayonnaise, yogurt, vinegar, lemon juice, and herbs, one can create the most flavorful of dishes, and all with a minimum of cooking. The little amount of cooking that is required can take place in the cooler hours of the night or early morning, and most of the recipes will benefit from being made in advance.

► **MENU 1**
   Tzatziki (page 22)
   (Pita bread)
   Curried Rice Salad with Apples and Cashews (page 76)
   Peach Almond Torte (page 246)

► **MENU 2**
   Arugula and Boston Lettuce Salad (page 49)
   Pasta with Uncooked Tomato and Fresh Basil Sauce (page 148)
   Raspberry Pie (page 253)

► **MENU 3**
   Iced Plum Soup (page 88)
   Tempeh Salade Niçoise (page 86)
   Fresh Peaches with Honey Rum Sauce (page 276)

► **MENU 4**
   Gazpacho (page 89)
   Marinated Pasta and Vegetable Salad (page 84)
   Summer Fruit Tart (page 248)

► **MENU 5**
   Marinated Tofu, Cucumber, and Radish Salad (page 60)
   Cold Sesame Noodles with Broccoli and Cashews (page 77)
   Ginger Cookies (page 284)
   Chocolate-Dipped Strawberries (page 278)

BREAKFAST AND BRUNCH MENUS

The line that divides breakfast and brunch is amorphous, although most people have a general idea of what they consider breakfast food and what comprises a suitable brunch. For me, breakfast is usually a simpler affair, in which I serve in some combination cereal, muffins, scones, yogurt, fruit, pancakes, or perhaps eggs, and breakfast is eaten in the early morning. Brunch is a more festive meal, oftentimes beginning with a fruit-based alcoholic drink, and including a wider variety of foods, which are more elaborately presented, such as quiches, special egg dishes, pastries, baked goods, etc., and frequently ending with a dessert. Brunch, being a combination of breakfast and lunch, is served in the late morning.

Here are some menus that range from the simple to the elaborate, and most of them have suggestions for advance preparation—something that is very important to the breakfast cook, who usually has to handle many dishes requiring attention at the same time.

► **MENU 2**

Fresh Fruit with Yogurt Lime Sauce (page 15)

French Toast with Orange and Brandy (page 3)

► **MENU 3**

Egg and Pepper Croustades (page 5)

Sweet Potato Home Fries (page 8)

Oatmeal Scones (page 9)

Prune Butter (page 14)

Baked Apples with Honey and Brandy (page 270)

► **MENU 4**

Orange Lassi (page 193)

Samosas (page 186)

Bombay-Style Curried Eggs (page 117)

Perfect Brown Rice Pilaf (page 292)

Brandied Fruit Compote (page 277)

► **MENU 5**

(Fresh strawberries and sliced mango, if in season) or Orange and Grapefruit Sections with Kiwi (page 16)

Irish Soda Bread (page 12)

Mushroom Quiche (page 127)

Roasted Home-Fried Potatoes and Onions (page 7)

Glossary

ASIAN SESAME PASTE This is a dark Asian paste that is made from ground roasted sesame seeds, and it has a much stronger flavor than tahini (Middle Eastern sesame butter). If you cannot get sesame paste, then peanut butter is a better substitute than tahini. Because the oil separates from the paste, I find that it is best to put it in a large bowl and whisk it until it is emulsified, then measure what is needed and return the remainder to the jar. You can store it in the refrigerator indefinitely. It can be purchased in Asian food stores, and some specialty food shops, health food stores, and supermarkets.

ASIAN SESAME OIL is a dark, strong-flavored oil made from toasted sesame seeds. It can be found in Asian food stores and sometimes in specialty food shops and large supermarkets. It is not the same thing as cold-pressed sesame oil (purchased in health food stores), which is lighter in color and milder in flavor. Toasting the sesame seeds before pressing out the oil makes the taste of Asian sesame oil stronger, so only a small amount is needed to flavor a dish. It is added at the end of cooking to impart its distinct flavor, rather than used for stir-frying.

BEANS, in their dried form, are a very important food for vegetarians and non-vegetarians alike because they provide generous amounts of protein and iron, and a moderate amount of calcium, while being low in fat. Although I usually use canned beans to save time (and I have found that I eat a lot more beans as a result), sometimes it's desirable to cook a batch of dried beans to use for multiple recipes. All dried beans, except lentils and split peas, should be soaked before cooking to cut back considerably on their cooking time. Pick them over to remove stones, etc., and rinse them in a strainer, then put them in a bowl, cover with plenty of water, and soak them overnight. Or you can put them in a pot with water to cover plus 2 inches, and boil them for 2 minutes. Cover the pot and let soak for 1 hour. Whether you soak them overnight or use the quick-soak method, you should drain them well, then cover again with fresh water and cook until tender. Do not add baking soda, for although it tenderizes the beans it also kills B vitamins. One cup of dried beans yields approximately 2½ cups cooked beans. It is always a good idea to cook extra beans because they can enhance so many vegetable dishes, or can be added to salads for extra protein. I oftentimes toss them with some vinaigrette and herbs, and keep them chilled to eat as a snack or appetizer.

BROWN RICE is rice that has had only its hull removed. It contains fiber, B vitamins, minerals, and some protein. White rice has had the bran layer and germ removed and has been polished. It then has almost no nutritive value and so it must be enriched. Brown rice has a nuttier flavor and chewier texture than white rice, and takes about twice as long to cook. For fluffy results try Perfect Brown Rice (page 292).

BULGUR is made from crushed wheat berries that were cooked beforehand. This precooking imparts a nutty flavor and reduces the cooking time of the bulgur. Contrary to popular belief bulgur and cracked wheat are not identical. Cracked wheat is not precooked and therefore has a faintly raw taste to it. Bulgur comes in different colors depending on the type of wheat used. A reddish-brown color indicates hard American winter wheat; a golden color indicates Middle Eastern soft wheat. It is available in different gradations from fine to coarse. I prefer the coarse variety for its nubby texture. Bulgur is an excellent source of protein and a good source of iron.

BUTTER Most professional cooks prefer sweet (unsalted) butter for its fresh, delicate flavor. If you must be very careful about your cholesterol count, then you can substitute margarine for butter in all of these recipes. I find that a change in flavor is most noticeable in baking, especially cookies, cakes, and pie crusts, but they will still be delicious. Margarine is usually quite salty, so cut back on the amount of salt in each recipe it is used in, or buy the unsalted variety. Salted butter (usually marked "lightly salted") is generally not as fresh as sweet butter because salt masks the flavor of rancidity if it develops, and therefore stores can get away with prolonging its shelf life. Rancidity would be very noticeable in sweet butter.

BUTTERMILK is so named because originally it was the by-product of the butter-making process. Today buttermilk is made by adding a lactic acid bacteria culture to pasteurized skim milk to produce a milk that is thick and tart. It actually contains no butterfat and has the same caloric content as skim milk. (Be sure to read the label because some brands add whole milk or cream.) As with yogurt, the friendly bacteria that are introduced help destroy harmful bacteria in the intestines, and aid in the production of B vitamins. Buttermilk is an excellent low-fat source of calcium, and makes a wonderful snack food because it is filling yet low in calories.

CALCIUM Recently there has been a lot of attention given to the need for more calcium in most people's diet, especially that of women. Osteoporosis—weak bones that lead to debilitating fractures, has reached epidemic proportions in the U.S., and white women over the age of sixty are the largest target group. It develops slowly, beginning at an early age, so people of all ages should be mindful of their calcium intake. Experts in bone disease recommend 1,000 to 1,200 milligrams of calcium a day, the equivalent of a quart of milk. But there are other excellent sources of calcium that are also low in fat, such as low-fat yogurt, buttermilk, skim milk, collard greens, kale, and broccoli; and tofu is a moderately good source. Spinach, Swiss chard, beet greens, and sorrel are also rich in calcium, but they contain oxalic acid, which binds with calcium, making it inaccessible to the body.

CHILES come in various shapes, colors, and sizes, and there are estimated to be between 300 and 1,500 varieties, ranging from sweet to fiery hot. The mild chiles called for in some of the recipes in this book can be purchased in 4-ounce cans. They impart a distinct flavor to dishes without any of the hotness associated with chiles. Never touch hot chiles with your hands, because if you inadvertently touch your face or eyes afterward, you will experience an unbearable burning. If this happens, flush your skin with plenty of water. Handle hot chiles, whether fresh, canned, or pickled, with rubber gloves, or when cutting them, use two small knives as though you were dissecting them. The seeds are the hottest part of the chile and are removed by most people except extreme chile aficionados. Chiles—even the most fiery varieties—aid digestion and don't irritate the stomach, as many people suspect. Your tolerance for them will greatly increase if you eat them regularly, and the flavor of the chile will be more pronounced as your taste buds adjust.

COCONUT AND COCONUT MILK I use unsweetened dried coconut to make coconut milk and to add to various dishes. Supermarkets tend to sell only a highly sweetened variety. To make coconut milk put about 3 cups hot water and 2¼ cups unsweetened dried coconut in a blender and blend for 1 minute. Put it through a strainer over a bowl and press out all of the liquid in the pulp; you will get about 2½ cups coconut milk. Discard the pulp. Store it in a tightly covered jar in the refrigerator for up to 4 days. It will eventually separate, and the thick, creamy film that rises to the top will be coconut cream. (If you want to use the cream for something like piña coladas, then spoon it off the top.) When you are ready to use the coconut milk, shake the jar to blend. If you want to make coconut milk out of fresh coconut, pierce the eyes of a coconut with an ice pick or skewer and drain out and discard the coconut water (or save for another use). Preheat the oven to 400°F, and bake the coconut for 15 minutes. Wrap a towel around it, then bang it with a hammer until it cracks open. Remove the meat from the shell with the tip of a strong knife and peel away the brown membrane with a vegetable peeler.

Cut the flesh into small pieces, place in the blender with hot water, and proceed as you would with dried coconut. If you want grated coconut instead of coconut milk, grate the flesh in a food processor.

FLOUR I prefer to use *unbleached white flour* over bleached all-purpose flour because it is not treated with chemicals. Whole wheat flour is an excellent source of protein. It is milled from a mixture of hard wheat and soft wheat, and has slightly more gluten than all-purpose white flour. Gluten is the protein component of wheat, which imparts elasticity to dough when mixed with water. Breads require a lot of gluten to achieve a chewy consistency; pastries require little or no gluten for flaky, tender results. *Whole wheat flour* is made from the entire kernel of wheat (wheat berry). I prefer stone-ground whole wheat flour because otherwise the flour is ground with steel rollers, which produce heat and consequently kill B vitamins and vitamin E. Whole wheat flour is an excellent source of fiber and B vitamins, as well as protein, and should be stored in a cool, dry place (preferably in the refrigerator) to prevent rancidity. *Whole wheat pastry flour* is a whole-grain flour that is made from a soft spring wheat that contains little or no gluten; this makes it ideal for pastries and quick breads. Whole wheat pastry flour can be found in most health food stores, and should be stored in a cool, dry place, preferably the refrigerator. If you cannot get this flour, then you can substitute half whole wheat flour and half unbleached white flour for similar results.

GARLIC The popularity of garlic has waxed and waned throughout history, and it has been said to cure everything from leprosy to the common cold. Luckily it is fully appreciated now, for its potential as a flavor enhancer is unequaled. Garlic is known to lower high blood pressure; in fact, you can purchase garlic oil capsules for this purpose. It is certainly worth getting into the habit of always using fresh garlic in cooking because dried garlic is a poor substitute. To make peeling easier remove a garlic clove from a head of garlic and cut off the tip that was attached. Place the blade of a large knife on its side on the clove and give it a thump with your fist. Peel away the skin, then mince the garlic. Some garlic has purplish skin and some has white skin. What determines its potency is not its variety but the temperature during its growing season. Coldness tends to increase its assertiveness. But, once picked, garlic should be kept in a cool, dark, well-ventilated spot, not the refrigerator.

GINGER Choose firm, plump roots with shiny skins and avoid ginger that is wrinkled and light in weight for its size. The skin is edible, but I prefer to peel it off because I don't like its texture. Store leftover ginger—either whole or chopped—in a tightly covered jar containing enough vinegar, sherry, or vodka to completely cover it, and refrigerate it for up to 6 months. You can freeze ginger wrapped in foil or plastic, but I find that its texture gets too spongy and it becomes difficult to grate or mince. You can make a delicious and potent ginger tea by chopping or thinly slicing about 2 tablespoons ginger and simmering it in 1½ cups water for 20 minutes or so. Strain it, then sweeten it with some honey. It is the best remedy to relieve the congestion of a cold, or the aches and pains from flu. To mince peeled ginger, slice it very thin, then stack the slices and cut into very fine strips. Cut these strips crosswise into very fine pieces.

HONEY It might surprise you to discover that honey is not indigenous to the U.S.; honey bees were brought to this country by the colonists. Maple syrup is the sweetener that the American Indians used. From a nutritional standpoint the value of honey lies in the fact that it is unrefined and untreated. Sugar has been bleached, and is devoid of all nutrients. Honey, if it is uncooked and unfiltered, has some vitamins and minerals, but not much to boast of. If taken in large amounts honey will act in the body the same way sugar does, though it is absorbed into the bloodstream a little more slowly. Mild-flavored honeys include clover, alfalfa, orange blossom, thistle, and tupelo. If you want to substitute honey for sugar in baking, use ¾ cup honey for every cup of sugar, reduce the liquid in the recipe by a few tablespoons, and add a bit of baking soda (about ½ teaspoon) to counteract the acid in the honey. Some honey producers pasteurize their honey to increase its shelf life (which is ridiculous because honey is naturally bacteria-resistant), and also dilute it with other sweeteners such as corn syrup; so buy uncooked, unfiltered honey, if possible. If honey crystallizes in the jar, then stand the jar in a bowl of warm water until it liquefies again; crystallization is not a sign of spoilage.

HOT SPICY OR CHILI OIL This Chinese oil comes under many names; all of them indicate what it is, a fiery hot oil made with chili extract. It is reddish in color, and is used in many Szechuan and Hunan recipes. You could substitute Tabasco sauce, but it won't coat the food the way chili oil does. It can be purchased in Asian food stores and in many health food stores and supermarkets, and will last indefinitely. If you have acquired a taste for hot food, then you'll probably enjoy chili oil sprinkled on vegetables and added to sauces and to many Chinese dishes.

IRON Vegetarians as well as non-vegetarian women should be particularly careful to get enough iron. There are many non-meat sources that can provide an adequate amount, and one should strive to get his/her intake from a variety of sources. Dried beans (including tofu and tempeh), bulgur, bran, seeds, almonds, molasses, dried apricots, and dried prunes are all excellent sources of iron. Cooking in a cast-iron skillet also adds iron to one's diet. Greens such as spinach, Swiss chard, and beet greens are rich in iron but they also contain oxalic acid, which prevents the iron from being assimilated and causes it to pass through the system. Vitamin C helps the body absorb iron, so it is wise to eat foods that are plentiful in vitamin C—such as citrus fruit, bell peppers, and tomatoes—in combination with iron-rich foods. Remember, though, they must be eaten during the same meal. Women need about 18 milligrams of iron a day (about 10 milligrams after menopause); men need a little less. Iron is partially destroyed in cooking, and you should be aware that canned beans have slightly less iron than dried beans you prepare yourself.

KASHA is ground buckwheat kernels that are cooked like rice and bulgur. It is sold in packages in supermarkets, and either in packages or in bulk in health food stores, and is available in fine, medium, and coarse granulation (I prefer medium). It is an excellent source of protein and a good source of iron.

MAPLE SYRUP This is the sweetener, indigenous to North America, that was discovered by the American Indians. Maple syrup is simply sap from sugar maple trees that has been boiled down to nearly one-fortieth of its original volume. Although the finest grade (Grade A) carries a heftier price,

I prefer the medium grade (Grade B) for its darker color and stronger flavor. In this book I use the term "pure maple syrup" to distinguish it from "pancake syrup" or "maple-flavored syrup," both of which are diluted with cheaper sweeteners, such as corn syrup. Although maple syrup is natural, that is, untreated, it is about 65 percent sucrose, and therefore acts like sugar in the body when eaten in large amounts. Once opened, maple syrup should be refrigerated. For pancakes or French toast it should be heated and served warm.

MISO This highly nutritious Japanese concentrate is a naturally fermented soybean and grain purée that is replete with friendly bacteria and digestion-aiding enzymes. It comes in various colors (the darker the color the stronger the flavor) and strengths, and is aged anywhere from 1 month to 3 years. It is sometimes used as a spread either alone or mixed with other ingredients, such as tahini, but its primary use is to make a delicious-flavored stock. It must first be diluted with a small amount of water before being added to soups, etc., or else the miso will remain in clumps. Miso is filled with protein, minerals, and vitamins, and is a good source of vitamin B-12. Store it in the refrigerator and it will last indefinitely; the high concentration of salt acts as a preservative.

OIL In this book, when a recipe calls for "oil" any flavorless or mild-flavored oil will do, such as corn, safflower, or vegetable oil. When either peanut or olive oil will enhance a dish, then that oil is specified.

OLIVE OIL There is a startling degree of variation in the quality and flavor of the numerous olive oils on the market. The key to the difference lies in the number of pressings and filterings the oil is subject to. "Extra virgin" olive oil is a full-bodied "first pressing" oil that has a robust, fruity flavor and a dark-green color. It is pressed without heat and is the most expensive of olive oils. "Virgin" olive oil is also an oil from the first pressing, but the flavor is more subtle because of additional filtering, and the color ranges from light green to golden. Herein lies the confusion. Olive oil that is bottled in this country is not subject to the strict labeling regulations that foreign bottled olive oil is. If the oil is made from further pressings of the remaining flesh and pits (which sometimes produces an unpleasant aftertaste), it can still be labeled "virgin" in this country, whereas it would be mandatory to label it "100% olive oil" in other countries. Therefore, make sure your olive oil is bottled in the country in which it is made—France, Italy, or Greece—and is marked "extra virgin," "virgin," or "first pressing" if you want a fruity olive oil. If you want a mild-flavored oil, then other types will suffice. Taste before using them to make sure they aren't bitter. Store olive oil in a cool, dark place, but not in the refrigerator. Olive oil can become rancid if exposed to hot weather for too long a period.

PROTEIN One often hears about "protein complementarity" with regard to non-meat sources of protein. It is a good idea to simplify the theory that Frances Moore Lappe detailed in *Diet for a Small Planet* so that it can become more useful in daily living. Except for soybeans, plant-based protein does not have all of the eight essential amino acids necessary to make it a complete protein. If some of these amino acids are missing, even partially, the use of all of the other amino acids for protein synthesis in the body is reduced proportionately. So one must match foods in order to make them "complete." Whole grains are complemented by dairy products, whole grains complement legumes, and seeds complement legumes. Complementarity exists between other food groups but not as well. It is important to remember that the combining of foods must be done during the same meal in order for it to be effective.

SUNFLOWER SEEDS are an excellent source of protein, iron, calcium, and potassium. They can be purchased, already hulled, in health food stores. Their flavor is heightened, like that of most seeds and nuts, if they are toasted before being used in cooking or eaten as a snack. Avoid buying those little snack packets of toasted sunflower seeds because they are always greasy, overly salted, and overpriced.

TAHINI, a smooth Middle Eastern butter made from hulled sesame seeds, is an exceptionally good source of calcium and is rich in protein and iron. Like peanut butter it is rather high in calories, but it is very nutritious. In addition to using it in Middle Eastern dishes such as hummus, I like to sweeten it with honey and use it as a spread on toast or rice cakes. It is a good idea to put the entire contents of the can or jar in a large bowl and whisk until blended because the oil separates from the tahini. Measure the amount needed, then return the remainder to the container. Store it in the refrigerator after it is opened. Read about Asian sesame paste (page 321) to distinguish it from tahini.

TAMARI is a kind of soy sauce that is aged in wooden vats for at least 2 years to develop a full-bodied flavor and color. Commercial soy sauce is not aged, and it is artificially colored and treated with a preservative. When stored in the refrigerator tamari lasts indefinitely. In addition to using it in Asian dishes, I like to put it in some Western-style soups and sauces for an added dimension in flavor. Tamari can be purchased in health food stores. If you cannot get any, then commercial soy sauce can be substituted for it. Some soy sauce is labeled "shoyu" tamari or just "shoyu." This means that it is made from wheat as well as soybeans, but its flavor is almost identical to regular tamari.

TEMPEH is a mixture of ground soybeans and a rhizopus culture (mold), which has fermented and been formed into a cake. This Indonesian staple, like most soybean products, is packed with nutrients—complete protein, iron, and vitamin B_{12}—and is very low in fat. It is usually cut into cubes and either steamed, sautéed, or fried, and then can be seasoned in myriad ways. When it is fresh, there are, oftentimes, black spots on it; don't worry about it—that's natural to tempeh. When it is spoiled it could have an ammonia smell, be slimy, or have blue, green, pink, or yellow mold on it. Check the expiration date on the package when you buy it. Tempeh freezes very well, so it is a good idea always to have a package or two in the freezer. It can be purchased at health food stores.

TOFU, also called bean curd, is a type of soybean "cheese" that is made through a process which is similar to cottage cheese making. Soybeans are cooked and mashed, then their liquid (soy milk) is pressed out of them and mixed with a coagulant to separate the curds from the whey. The curds are then pressed into cakes to form tofu. It is an excellent source of complete protein and iron, and a good source of calcium. It is very low in fat and easy to digest. Store it in the refrigerator, in water, in a covered container, and change the water every other day (unless it is purchased in a sealed container). It will keep about a week this way. It is spoiled when it shows signs of sliminess and tastes and smells sour. If you purchase it in a store that keeps it in open containers, and therefore exposes it to bacteria, before using it you can boil the individual cakes for 1 minute to kill germs, then pat them dry with paper towels. The change in texture will be negligible. You can freeze tofu by draining it and wrapping it in foil or plastic. The texture will change as a result; it will be crumbly and chewy, and therefore not suitable for dishes in which it should be cubed.

TOMATOES Oftentimes in the winter months the only fresh tomatoes available are the hothouse varieties or the ones shipped from far distances. These flavorless atrocities are picked unripe and green for easy shipment, and are exposed to ethylene gas to cause them to turn red. The skin is like leather, and they will never turn truly red, no matter how ripe they get. When these are the only tomatoes at the market, I substitute canned tomatoes, the best brand I can get. (This is one product in which the generic brand is often unacceptable because they seem to use less ripe "pinkish" tomatoes.) They are picked at their peak, and are infinitely more flavorful, tender, and colorful than their "fresh" distant cousins—hothouse tomatoes. Never leave leftover canned tomatoes in their can because the lead that seals the can will seep into food once the lead is exposed to air. To peel and seed a fresh tomato drop the whole tomato into a pot of boiling water and leave for 10 to 60 seconds, depending on its ripeness. (Summer garden tomatoes need be blanched only a few seconds.) Remove with a slotted spoon, and place under cold running water until it is cool enough to handle. With a sharp knife mark a very shallow X on the top of the tomato, then peel off the skin and discard. Cut the core out of the tomato, then cut the tomato in half horizontally, and very gently squeeze each half over a bowl until the seeds fall out. Discard the seeds.

TOMATO PASTE Most recipes that use tomato paste call for a small amount, which means that if you purchased it in a small can, you will have quite a bit left over. Rather than letting it get moldy in the back of your refrigerator, try scraping it into a small jar with a tight-fitting lid and freezing it. When you need some, just spoon out what you need and return the remainder to the freezer. It will keep, frozen, for 4 to 6 months. An alternative is to buy it in a tube, which will last longer than an opened can but not as long as the freezer method.

VEGETABLES It is good to learn about the proper purchasing, storing, and cooking of vegetables because many nutrients are easily destroyed through careless handling. It is always better, of course, to choose vegetables that are in season. They should be firm, glossy, and free of bruises. Leafy green vegetables should be crisp—not wilted—free of yellow spots, and not excessively dirty. Never wash vegetables before storing them in the refrigerator, because too much moisture will encourage bacteria and decay. The best way to protect the freshness of vegetables is to keep all vegetables—except potatoes and onions—in plastic bags with a few holes punched in them so air can circulate. However, many people, understandably, want to cut back on their use of plastic, and prefer to use paper bags. The vegetables will not last nearly as long as in plastic bags (unfortunately), but it is better than just keeping them loose in the refrigerator. Whichever type of bag you choose, store the vegetables in the crisper drawers in your refrigerator, because that is the coldest area and contains the most moisture. There is an increasing loss of nutrients as days pass, so use your vegetables as soon as possible. The easiest way to wash greens is to dunk them in the bottom part of a salad spinner that is filled with cold water, and let their dirt fall to the bottom. Remove the greens, and place them in the basket. Discard the dirty water, then spin the greens dry. The general rule for vitamin retention when cooking vegetables is to cook them as quickly as possible in the least amount of water, and eat them immediately thereafter. Vitamins B and C are the most perishable because they are water soluble and are easily destroyed in water, especially boiling water. Vitamins A and D are fat soluble, and are relatively resistant to destruction. Steaming, stir-frying, and sautéing are the cooking methods that preserve the most nutrients.

YOGURT is made by adding two live cultures—*lactobacillus bulgaricus* and *streptococcus thermophilus*—to warm milk and letting the cultures grow to thicken the milk and make it acidic. The cultures are known as "friendly bacteria," and one of the greatest benefits of yogurt is that these bacteria help clean the colon by destroying harmful bacteria that are present. Yogurt is also an excellent source of protein and easily assimilated calcium. It helps the body manufacture B vitamins, aids digestion, and can be enjoyed by people with milk allergies, because the milk sugar is partially digested by the friendly bacteria. I prefer low-fat yogurt because it is just as delicious as whole-milk yogurt, yet is significantly lower in fat. The yogurt called for in these recipes is always plain yogurt, unsweetened and unflavored. Read the label on the yogurt container; it should list just milk and yogurt culture as the ingredients. If it includes anything else, such as gelatin or modified food starch, find another brand.

Metric Conversion Charts

NOTE: Ingredient weights are averages based on information from the USDA National Nutrient Database for Standard Reference and individual product manufacturers; gram amounts may vary based on brand.

FLOURS AND GRAINS

1 cup barley, uncooked	200 g
⅔ cup bran	39 g
1 cup bread crumbs	110 g
¼ cup bread crumbs	28 g
1 cup bulgur, uncooked	140 g
½ cup bulgur, uncooked	70 g
1 cup cornmeal	140 g
¼ cup cornmeal	35 g
1¼ cups kasha (medium granulation)	205 g
1 cup rolled oats	90 g
1 cup long-grain brown rice, uncooked	185 g
¼ cup white rice	45 g
¾ cup wild rice	120 g
1 cup unbleached white flour	125 g
⅓ cup unbleached white flour	42 g
¼ cup unbleached white flour	31 g
⅔ cup wheat germ	77 g
1 cup whole wheat flour	120 g
¼ cup whole wheat flour	30 g
1⅓ cups whole wheat pastry flour	120 g
½ cup whole wheat pastry flour	45 g

SUGAR

⅓ cup firmly packed brown sugar	75 g
¼ cup firmly packed brown sugar	56 g
2½ cups powdered sugar	300 g
¼ cup powdered sugar	30 g
1 cup sugar	200 g
⅓ cup sugar	67 g
½ cup sugar	100 g

SWEETENERS AND JAMS

1 cup honey	340 g
⅓ cup honey	113 g
¼ cup honey	85 g
1 cup pure maple syrup	220 g
¼ cup molasses	60 g
1¼ cups raspberry preserves	400 g
⅔ cup raspberry preserves	210 g
⅓ cup apricot preserves	105 g
½ cup unsweetened applesauce	244 g

BUTTER

1 cup butter	2 sticks	240 g
½ cup butter	1 stick	120 g
¼ cup butter	½ stick	60 g
¼ cup ghee		55 g
¼ cup olive or vegetable oil		55 g

CHEESE AND DAIRY

¼ cup crumbled blue cheese	135 g
1½ cups cottage cheese	325 g
1 cup small-curd cottage cheese	225 g
¾ cup finely crumbled feta cheese	85 g
½ cup grated smoked Gouda	57 g
1 cup cubed Monterey Jack or Muenster cheese	132 g
⅓ cup grated Parmesan cheese	33 g
¼ cup grated Parmesan cheese	25 g
1 cup part-skim ricotta cheese	248 g
1 cup heavy or whipping cream	238 g
⅓ cup heavy or whipping cream	119 g
¼ cup heavy or whipping cream	79 g
¼ cup cream cheese	58 g
1 cup sour cream	213 g
⅔ cup sour cream	142 g
1 cup plain low-fat yogurt	245 g
½ cup plain low-fat yogurt	123 g

FRUIT, FRESH OR DRIED

1 cup diced dried apricots	160 g
2 cups blueberries	220 g
½ pint blueberries	113 g
⅔ cup dried cranberries	92 g
1 cup raisins	145 g
⅓ cup raisins	48 g
1 pint raspberries	230 g
1 cup raspberries	123 g
1 quart strawberries	576 g
1 pint strawberries	288 g
½ pint strawberries	144 g

VEGETABLES AND FRESH HERBS

1 cup alfalfa sprouts	33 g
1 cup fresh bean sprouts	104 g
1 cup broccoli florets	88 g
1 cup chopped cooked broccoli florets	156 g
1 cup shredded cabbage	90 g
3 cups grated carrot	330 g
4 cups finely chopped cauliflower	400 g
1 cup corn, fresh or frozen (thawed)	154 g
½ cup corn, fresh or frozen (thawed)	77 g
¼ cup chopped fresh dill	5 g
1 cup diced green beans	110 g
1½ cups sliced mushrooms	105 g
1 cup sliced mushrooms	70 g
¾ cup finely chopped mushrooms	53 g
½ cup finely chopped red onion	80 g
¼ cup finely diced red onion	40 g
½ cup slivered red onion	58 g
¼ cup thinly sliced red onion	29 g
⅓ cup minced fresh parsley	20 g
¼ cup minced fresh parsley	15 g
1 cup freshly shelled raw peas	145 g
1½ cups frozen peas	201 g
1 cup frozen peas	134 g
⅔ cup frozen peas	89 g
3 cups fresh spinach leaves	90 g
½ cup finely chopped tomatoes	90 g

LEGUMES

1½ cups dried black beans	291 g
1 cup lentils, brown or red	192 g
¼ cup lentils, brown or red	48 g

SEEDS AND NUTS

1½ cups almonds	210 g
½ cup ground almonds	50 g
⅓ cup chopped almonds	28 g
¼ cup chopped almonds	21 g
1 cup raw cashews	140 g
⅓ cup coarsely chopped dry-roasted cashews	37 g
¼ cup unsalted roasted cashews	31 g
⅔ cup crunchy natural peanut butter	173 g
1 cup ground pecans	80 g
⅓ cup coarsely chopped pecans	33 g
¼ cup pine nuts	30 g
½ cup sesame seeds	63 g
¾ cup tahini	228 g
1 cup chopped walnuts	120 g
1 cup ground walnuts	95 g
½ cup walnuts	50 g
⅓ cup chopped walnuts	40 g

OTHER

⅓ cup Asian sesame paste	256 g
½ cup unsweetened cocoa powder	43 g
2 cups unsweetened dried coconut	160 g
¼ cup unsweetened dried coconut	20 g
¼ cup ketchup	68 g
1 cup macaroni	105 g
½ cup miso	138 g
1 cup fine egg noodles	38 g
⅓ cup fine egg noodles	13 g
¼ cup tomato paste	66 g
1 cup tomato purée	253 g
⅔ cup tomato purée	169 g
¼ cup tomato purée	63 g
½ cup finely chopped water chestnuts	114 g

LENGTHS

16 inches	41 cm
12 inches	30 cm
10 inches	25 cm
9 inches	23 cm
8 inches	20 cm
7 inches	17.8 cm
6 inches	15 cm
5 inches	12.7 cm
4 inches	10.2 cm
3½ inches	8.9 cm
3 inches	7.6 cm
2 inches	5 cm
1½ inches	3.8 cm
1 inch	2.5 cm
¾ inch	1.9 cm
½ inch	1.25 cm
¼ inch	5 mm
⅛ inch	3.2 mm

TEMPERATURES

500°F	260°C
450°F	230°C
425°F	220°C
400°F	200°C
375°F	190°C
350°F	175°C
325 °F	165°C
300°F	150°C
275°F	135°C
250°F	120°C
85°F	30°C

WEIGHTS

1 pound	16 ounces	450 g
¾ pound	12 ounces	340 g
⅝ pound	10 ounces	283 g
½ pound	8 ounces	225 g
¼ pound	4 ounces	115 g
1 ounce	30 g	
½ ounce	15 g	

VOLUMES

1 gallon	16 cups	128 fl oz	3.8 L	
1 quart	4 cups	32 fl oz		950 ml
1 pint	2 cups	16 fl oz	475 ml	
1 cup	8 fl oz	250 ml		
¾ cup	6 fl oz	185 ml		
⅔ cup	5⅓ fl oz	158 ml		
½ cup	4 fl oz	125 ml		
⅓ cup	2⅔ fl oz	80 ml		
¼ cup	1 fl oz	60 ml		
2 tablespoons	1 fl oz	30 ml		

Index

in Carrot Cake with Cream
Cheese Icing, 240
in Fruited Rice Curry, 179
Maple Pecan Pie, 254
See also almonds; cashews;
walnuts

oats
Chocolate Oatmeal Bars, *286,*
287
in Cowboy Cookies, 282
in Granola, 6
Oatmeal Scones, 9
in Pear and Apricot Crisp, 265
oil, about, 325
oil, hot spicy or chili, about, 324
olive oil, about, 325–26
olives, kalamata
Fresh Mozzarella, Roasted
Pepper, and Black Olive
Salad, *62,* 63
in Polenta Puttanesca, 158–59
on Tempeh Salade Niçoise, 86
Onion and Cheese Filo Triangles,
36
onions, about, 122
oranges
Cranberry Fruit Tart, 255
French Toast with Orange and
Brandy, 3
in Fruited Rice Curry, 179
Marinated Oranges in Grand
Marnier Sauce, 275
Orange and Grapefruit Sections
with Kiwi, 16
Orange Lassi, 193
Orange Raita, 190
in Rhubarb Cobbler, 262

pans, about, xviii–xix
Parmesan cheese
in Baked Chickpeas Provençale,
166, 167–68
in Cauliflower and Cashew
Croquettes, 20–21
in Crustless Broccoli and
Cottage Cheese Pie, 126
in Deep-Fried Cheese-Filled
Polenta Balls, *34,* 35
in Egg Noodles with Light Garlic
Sauce, 212
in Farfalle with Broccoli Rabe,
146
in Goat Cheese Polenta with
Braised Greens and Garlic, 157
on Linguine with Swiss Chard
and Garlic, 145
in Pesto, 296
in Polenta Puttanesca, 158–59

in Risotto of Brown Rice and
Mushrooms, 156
in Rolled Stuffed Lasagna with
Kale in a Tomato Cream
Sauce, *150,* 151–52
in Simple Salad with Lemon-Soy
Dressing, 69
on Spaghetti Squash with
Broccoli Butter Sauce, 149
in Spinach Custard Ring with
Tomato Cream Sauce, 118–19
in Three-Layered Vegetable
Pâté with Herb Mayonnaise,
42–44, 45
in Winter Pesto, 297
in Zucchini, Tomato, and Basil
Frittata, 115
pasta
Cauliflower and Pasta Soup, 96
Tofu Fra Diavolo with Spinach
Fettuccine, 201
See also main-course pasta
dishes; noodles
Pâté Brisée (Savory or Sweet
Crust), 302–3
for Maple Pecan Pie, 254
for Raspberry Pie, *252,* 253
Pâté Brisée with Whole Wheat
Flour, 304
for Buttermilk Herb and Onion
Tart, *128,* 129
for Mushroom Quiche, 127
Pâté de Legumes, 40–41
Pâté Sucrée (Sweet Pie Crust), 305–6
for Rhubarb Tart, 247
Pâté, Three-Layered Vegetable,
42–44, *45*
peaches
Fresh Peaches with Honey Rum
Sauce, 276
Peach Almond Torte, 246
Stuffed Peaches with Fresh
Cherries and Almonds, 264
in Summer Fruit Salad, 68
in Summer Fruit Tart, 248
Peanut Dressing, Spicy, 48
pears
in Cranberry Fruit Tart, 255
Glazed Pear Cake, 238, *239*
Pear and Apricot Crisp, 265
Pear Tart with Almond Nut
Crust, 249
Poached Honey Pears Topped
with Ginger Custard, 268–69
Poached Pears in Red Wine
with Raisins, 266, *267*
peas
in Braised Curried Eggplant,
176, 177

Curried Cauliflower and Peas,
180, 181
in Curried Rice, Tofu, and
Vegetables, 203
in Eggplant Stuffed with Curried
Vegetables, 184–85
Fresh Pea Salad Rémoulade,
53
Honey-Glazed Sugar Snap Peas
with Carrots, *226,* 227
in Samosas, 186–87
in Tempeh in Curried Yogurt
Sauce, 209
in Vegetable Kofta, 182–83
Peasant Cabbage Soup, 98
Penne with Eggplant Sauce, 144
peppers. *See* bell peppers; chile
peppers
Perfect Brown Rice, *291,* 292–93
in Cuban Black Beans and Rice,
154–55
in Curried Rice, Tofu, and
Vegetables, 203
for Fruited Rice Curry, 179
with Peas (var.), 293
Pilaf (var.), 293
for Stir-Fried Asparagus, Tofu,
and Red Pepper, *196,* 197
for Stir-Fried Tempeh with
Hot Pepper Sauce, *206,*
207–8
for Tempeh in Curried Yogurt
Sauce, 209
Pesto, 296
freezing, 296
in Noodle Timbales with Pesto
Cream Sauce, 120, *121*
on Toasted French Bread, 28,
29
in Tomatoes Stuffed with White
Beans, 82, *83*
pies and tarts, 247–55
Cranberry Fruit Tart, 255
Linzertorte, 250–51
Maple Pecan Pie, 254
Pear Tart with Almond Nut
Crust, 249
Raspberry Pie, *252,* 253
Rhubarb Tart, 247
Summer Fruit Tart, 248
See also crusts; main-course
savory pies and tarts
pilafs, 213, 214, 215, 293
Pizza, Neapolitan, 138–139
Plum Soup, Iced, 88
Poached Honey Pears Topped
with Ginger Custard, 268–69
Poached Pears in Red Wine with
Raisins, 266, *267*

Acknowledgments

I am especially grateful to Matthew Lore, president of The Experiment, for discovering the first incarnation of this book and suggesting its rebirth. Cara Bedick's editorial suggestions were clear, creative, and valuable and so to her, a big thank-you. I'd also like to thank Molly Cavanaugh and Nicholas Cizek for their patience in assembling a workable manuscript.

About the Author

JEANNE LEMLIN is the award-winning author of five cookbooks, including *Quick Vegetarian Pleasures*, and winner of a James Beard award. A vegetarian since age 15 and a pioneering vegetarian cookbook author, she has written for numerous national magazines, including *Yankee Magazine, Cooking Light*, and *Gourmet*. Lemlin has made numerous appearances on the Food Network. Currently a high school English teacher, she lives in Great Barrington, Massachusetts.